Advance Praise for

ONE SUNNY AFTERNOON

"When you read this book, you will understand how trauma, like snow drifts, builds up layer by thin layer. The highlight is the har-rowing description of what teenage life can descend into when, for whatever reasons, you have developed no boundaries. Eventually, unsavoury characters infiltrate your life and you have no agency to keep them out. Since you have no control, you become an alcoholic to deal with the tragedy of your life. Jetté Knox takes you step-by-step through bullying, cruelty, and rape. She never rings a false note on this terrifying journey from girlhood to adulthood."
—Catherine Gildiner, bestselling author of *Good Morning, Monster*

"Caught in the maelstrom of a past catastrophe, the anxious mind can crumble. And re-crumble. For Amanda Jetté Knox, negative thinking was an invitation back to the lonely child who was bul-lied and sexually abused. From that young girl who found solace in drugs and alcohol to the adult who was attacked by vicious trolls for sharing her story of a transgendered family, Jetté Knox shows us how a triumphant life is accessible despite enormous hurdles. Not only is PTSD navigable but with acceptance, vulnerability, and love; stored memories have the power to bring ultimate freedom."
—Susan Doherty, award-winning author of *The Ghost Garden*

"Trauma and shame and the PTSD that comes with them require frank and often uncomfortable discussions in order to get to the germ of the issues and move on in a healthy manner. Amanda Jetté Knox has had more of her share of all of it, and her journey back to sound mind, body, and relationships is a combination of harrowing and rewarding, inspiring and cautionary, and her brutally honest self-awareness is alternately welcome and witty. In the end, her life experiences and what she has gleaned from them will help anyone at any level of trauma and shame find their way back."

—David Pevsner, author of *Damn Shame*

ONE SUNNY AFTERNOON

ONE SUNNY AFTERNOON

A Memoir of Trauma and Healing

~

AMANDA JETTÉ KNOX

VIKING

VIKING

an imprint of Penguin Canada, a division of Penguin Random House Canada Limited

Canada · USA · UK · Ireland · Australia · New Zealand · India · South Africa · China

First published 2023

www.penguinrandomhouse.ca

LIBRARY AND ARCHIVES CANADA CATALOGUING IN PUBLICATION

Title: One sunny afternoon : a memoir of trauma and healing / Amanda Jetté Knox.
Names: Jetté Knox, Amanda, author.
Identifiers: Canadiana (print) 20230149405 | Canadiana (ebook) 2023014974X |
ISBN 9780735244634 (softcover) | ISBN 9780735244641 (EPUB)
Subjects: LCSH: Jetté Knox, Amanda. | LCSH: Jetté Knox, Amanda—Mental health. |
LCSH: Psychic trauma—Patients—Canada—Biography. | LCSH: Anxiety disorders—
Patients—Canada—Biography. | LCSH: Affective disorders—Patients—Canada—
Biography. | LCSH: Resilience (Personality trait) | LCGFT: Autobiographies.
Classification: LCC RC552.T7 J48 2023 | DDC 616.85/210092—dc23

Book and cover design by Kate Sinclair
Cover image © eberhard grossgasteiger from Pexels

Printed in Canada

10 9 8 7 6 5 4 3 2 1

Penguin
Random House
VIKING CANADA

For Emmy,
a bright light in my childhood and beyond

contents

preface

WELCOME TO SATURDAY AFTERNOON in a quiet emergency room in Ottawa, Ontario. It's late May 2020, in the middle of the first wave of the COVID-19 pandemic, and I'm sitting in a moulded plastic chair attached to another moulded plastic chair that no one can sit on because it's covered in tape for social distancing purposes.

My face is streaked with tears, wetting the blue mask the triage nurse had me put on a few minutes ago.

Coloured arrows line the floor so there is no mistaking where to go. I had to follow the blue ones to get to this seat. Plastic curtains taped to the floor and ceiling serve as dividers between "people with infectious symptoms" and "people here for other reasons who probably don't want to be sitting near people with infectious symptoms." I'm in the latter group, sharing that space with two other individuals who look as uncomfortable as I am, casting weary glances around the room at the slightest cough from the other side of the plastic.

I watch the day unfold through the large windows next to me. If you were outside of the hospital, as opposed to inside this waiting room, you might almost forget the pandemic for a few hours. It's the kind of day that takes your imagination onto the patio or into the backyard, welcoming in the warmth after a long Canadian winter, your mind filling with the promise of what's to come. Beautiful days are often like that, but weekends with good weather are a special kind of magic around here.

I picked a lousy day to almost die.

Yes, I almost died today. I almost wasn't here anymore to wear a wet mask and sit next to a chair with tape on it. I had a plan and the opportunity. But for some reason I haven't yet figured out, I decided to get in my car and drive to the hospital instead. When I got here, I asked the hospital staff to protect me from myself.

I still can't get over that this all went down on my favourite day of the week. Saturdays are for binging an entire season of a sitcom or tackling a home renovation. Not too long ago, I painted the front hall on a Saturday, listening to music on a Bluetooth speaker and annoying the kids with my middle-aged suburban version of Kesha. Saturday night is for staying up late and having fun. It's when my wife and I visit friends or go see a movie.

But this particular Saturday will shape my view of weekends for months to come. In fact, it's going to change everything—from how I see myself to how I make my way through the world. I can recognize, even as I sit in this uncomfortable chair two feet from the makeshift plastic germ barricade, that this will be the case.

But I am *alive*. And that, I will tell myself, over and over until I start to believe it, is a good thing.

It's a good thing. It's a good thing. It's a good thing.

Hello from my breakdown: the absolute lowest point of my adult life. Also, nearly the end of it.

I brought us here first because now the worst part of this story is out of the way. Well, sort of. We'll come back here later and in greater detail because it's a pivotal time. It was also, in many ways, the start of something wonderful.

That wasn't what it felt like in the moment, however. What it felt like was that I had almost killed myself because I believed I was completely worthless and the world didn't want me in it anymore. It would take a lot of work to stop believing that and begin to see this terrible headspace as a starting point to get somewhere better.

For us to be able to handle life in a healthy way, a bunch of moving parts inside us, including our mental and emotional wellbeing, need to work together, kind of like a car's engine. For some folks, their engine—or brain—runs smoother for longer; their inner mechanics are in better shape to navigate the challenges life throws at them. These people have a keener ear to detect the early rumblings of trouble under the hood—such as stress, overwhelm, fear or sadness—before the entire operating system breaks down. And because of that, they can veer off the road to attend to it, narrowly avoiding disaster.

And then, unfortunately, there's the rest of us. We're the ones who, for whatever reason, were gifted a glitchy mental engine from the start and didn't develop the skills to hear the early signs of trouble. We're the ones who stand on the side of the road with the hood up, desperately trying to figure out why everything is smoking.

Or is that steam? Who knows? Glitchy engines don't come with a manual.

Don't lose hope, fellow road warrior. This book is for us and written by one of us. That one of us is me, a forty-something person who, at the height of my career, with four great kids and a loving partner, almost lost everything because my mental health collapsed. I had no idea how sketchy my inner mechanics were, and I didn't realize that the patchwork fixes I had tried to implement over the years were only prolonging the inevitable: a life-threatening mental health crisis.

And when I did break down, I didn't have the tools to fix myself. I was stranded on an empty road. In order to get going again, I had to confront some mighty uncomfortable truths about myself and the life I had built up around me. I'd thought I finally had it all together, but this belief was a mirage that nearly cost me everything.

The emergency room visit and all that led up to it was the final breath of my previous life. So in a way, a part of me did die that Saturday. It was an ugly and painful death. A scorched and smouldering forest. A drenched landscape after a flood. The chasm in a field after an earthquake. (Feel free to insert other natural disaster metaphors here—they're fun.)

But then, as happens after most disasters, there was new growth. And that's what this book is really about. It's about coming back from that disaster I didn't think I could come back from—and doing so with a shiny new toolbox. Because yes, we can come out of this kind of emotional collapse stronger, healthier, happier and wiser. We can bring the best parts of ourselves into a new way of living that is better than what we had before.

While I hope this book finds readers who desperately need it, it's not just for people who are in the worst moment of their lives. Perhaps you're worried that you're on your way to that moment, even if you're not quite there yet. Falling apart might seem sudden, but it can be years in the making—years of repeating the same patterns and expecting different results. If you see yourself reflected in my words, please take note and get that emotional engine tune-up before the operating system starts shutting down completely. Prevention is always best.

But maybe you don't have a mental illness or haven't experienced trauma—you're one of those people with a purring engine. Maybe you're reading this to help someone else. Maybe you want to better understand a loved one's struggle because what they're going through is foreign to you. This book is also for you, so you can be a helpful part of someone's support system. As one of those someones who had other someones there when I needed them most, I thank you. Your compassion matters more than you know.

You may have no idea who I am, and if that's the case, allow me to give you some history. I wrote a book called *Love Lives Here: A Story of Thriving in a Transgender Family*, which is about how my family changed over the course of a very short period of time. I won't take up too much real estate here to describe it all. But since pieces of these changes and the memoir that chronicled them are particularly relevant to this story, I'll quickly summarize them here.

In 2014, our middle child came out as transgender at the age of eleven. My spouse and I were immediately supportive, if struggling to learn how best to provide that support. What little I knew about trans children, and trans people overall, came from media portrayals that depicted them as mentally unstable, traumatized, deceitful and possibly dangerous. Because of this, I had a lot of unlearning to do before I could take in the information that would help me be present for my child. The idea of raising someone who was trans was frightening. Transphobia was rampant in society, and comprehensive rights and protections seemed a long way away. The task felt daunting and more than a little overwhelming at times.

When *Love Lives Here* was published, our child identified as a trans girl, meaning someone who was assigned male at birth but identifies as a girl. More recently, they've let us know they're actually nonbinary, meaning their gender identity is not defined in terms of male or female. Just so there is no confusion for those who read my first book, it should be mentioned that we used she/her pronouns for our child in *Love Lives Here* and now we use they/them pronouns. In 2014, nonbinary identities were not as widely discussed as they are today. While our child knew for certain they weren't a boy, they could see no other option but to move from one binary identity to another, from boy to girl. Thankfully, society has made big strides since then to recognize a whole spectrum of gender. As a family, we continued to give our kid space to figure themselves out—all kids are figuring themselves out in various ways anyway—and that is how they arrived here.

The year after our child first came out, my spouse came out as a transgender woman. This, in many ways, was far more challenging for our family. After eighteen years of marriage, a conversation on a rainy evening in a Walmart parking lot took me completely by surprise. I had no idea there could be two trans people in a family of five. How was that possible? My biggest concern, outside of society's still-dismal treatment of the trans community and the hate I was sure she would receive, was whether our marriage could survive this after already weathering many other storms. Transition is a long road.

Fast-forward through some extremely difficult months: we made it! And we not only made it, but our relationship got stronger and happier. My wife, beneath the misery of the mask she was forced to wear for so long, is a wonderful partner. The love we have for each other is now stronger than ever. In August 2017, we even decided to renew our vows to celebrate our twentieth wedding anniversary and threw an excellent party.

Not long after, we began the adoption process to welcome a fourth child—a teenager who had been friends with our non-binary kid since middle school—into the family. We completed that process in January 2020, when she was seventeen, making us a family of six. A few months before the adoption is where readers arrive at the end of *Love Lives Here*.

Throughout this time, my family had been involved in advocacy and activism surrounding trans issues. As a parent passionate about ensuring our child had a future filled with acceptance and possibilities, I was particularly dedicated. I continued to write about our family's journey through these transitions on the blog

I had created in 2006, called *The Maven of Mayhem*. Over time, I morphed from a parenting blogger to a LGBTQ rights and mental health writer, tackling topics like living with a lifelong anxiety disorder and combating the misinformation surrounding medical care for trans youth. Sharing personal experiences was a way to connect with readers who were searching for the kind of information I wish I had come across more easily when I needed it most. This type of writing had never been my intention, but as it turned out, I wasn't bad at conveying important points about LGBTQ issues in accessible and relatable ways. What's more, the world was curious to know what it looked like to affirm a trans child and go through a transition with a partner. I just happened to be a writer who was present in these areas at the right time, adding my voice to the choir of many who were already doing this work in their own ways.

I love my job. But doing that job with the history I have nearly killed me.

I'm telling my story of mental illness, trauma and recovery in the hopes that others will see themselves in it and find hope. In some of my worst moments, it was hope that kept me going—the hope that maybe, just maybe, I could find a way out of the darkness. I want to give that hope to someone else who needs it. Personal stories allow us to exercise our empathy by walking in someone else's shoes. They can help us feel less alone when we see our emotional state and experiences reflected in another.

The other crucial thing personal stories are good for: removing the shame and stigma surrounding mental health issues.

Western society has taken some big strides in openly discussing mental illness and trauma disorders, but we still have a few hills to climb. Just ask someone if they would be as comfortable mentioning a lunchtime therapy session as they would a doctor's appointment. I'm guessing for many the answer would be no. Unfortunately, mental illness and accompanying disorders are still often seen as personal failures or weaknesses. We're not strong enough, or we don't look for the positive enough, or we don't get outside enough, or we just don't try hard enough, or we just like to play the victim because we enjoy the attention. This stigma does not help anyone get better.

Let's kick these dangerous misconceptions to the curb, shall we? Some of the strongest people I know have a mental illness or disorder, and they often exert massive amounts of energy just to get through their days. The exhaustion that comes with having to do everyday things when your mind is in crisis is indescribable to those who haven't experienced it. There is no failure here, only incredible perseverance. It's beyond time to change this tired narrative.

Some final important points before we close out this introduction.

First, I'm a professionally certified coach who specializes in shifting mindsets, navigating change, and building confidence. But I'm not a mental health professional, and you should discuss any mental illness or trauma disorder takeaways from these pages with one—or your doctor—before trying them. Because our brains and bodies are unique to us, what works for one person might not work for another, or could even have unintended consequences.

Please prioritize your own health and wellbeing by making sure you have appropriate guidance and support.

Second, this book contains a boatload of stuff that could be triggering, including suicide and suicidal ideation, abuse, childhood sexual assault, eating disorders, homophobia, transphobia, fatphobia (lots of things with "phobia" at the end, basically), addiction, bullying and harassment. Some of these are merely touched on, while others are discussed in detail. But I promise that nothing mentioned in the following pages is there for shock value. If I bring it up, it's because it's relevant to my healing and hopefully someone else's.

If, at any time, you feel overwhelmed by what you're reading, put the book down, take a break, talk to someone, do some breathing or go for a walk. And reach out for professional support if you're in crisis. There is a list of emergency resources at the back.

Finally, most of the names and identifying details in this story have been changed to protect the privacy of those individuals. I was especially careful when talking about people from my past, some of whom harmed me, but undoubtedly carried their own trauma while doing so.

With that, I will see you on the other side of these pages.

ONE

the adaptive captive

BRAINS. THEY BREAK SOMETIMES.

"Break" isn't the scientific term, of course, but that's what it feels like. When the brain isn't functioning in the way it should, it affects everything we do, from our perception of ourselves to how we see the world around us. Unfortunately, when a brain has been "broken" for a long time, we might stop noticing it's a problem; a warped perception becomes our new normal. Humans are highly adaptive creatures, which allows us to get used to our environment—including our internal one—relatively fast.

This is especially true of children. We form a foundation in childhood that is largely constructed out of safety, love and connection. This is what we build the rest of our lives upon. When some key ingredients are lacking in that foundation, however, the emotional life we build will not be stable. But with no sense

11

of what makes up a solid foundation, how would a child know the difference?

When I was a kid, I thought my brain was fine, thank you very much. Sure, there was some weird stuff going on inside my head, but I had no way of knowing it was unusual. Didn't everyone's brain lead them to dark places they couldn't find a way out of? Didn't everyone forget who they were sometimes and feel completely detached from the world around them? In the spirit of equality, the adults in my life had often pointed out the ways in which we were all the same. I figured this had to be true across the board, including inside our heads. And if that wasn't the case—if I was alone in feeling this way—did I really want others to know? What if that made me even weirder than I already felt?

In most respects, I was a pretty average kid. I grew up in the eighties—the decade of *Back to the Future* and a new artist called Madonna—and did all the average things kids seemed to do at the time, including watching Saturday morning cartoons, riding around the neighbourhood with rainbow streamers attached to my bike handles and sending in an official name change form for my Cabbage Patch Kid because Kelly seemed like a far better fit than Olivia.

When I was six, my parents moved us into the red-brick home they still live in today, nestled comfortably on a treed lot in a neighbourhood full of other wartime homes in Gatineau, Quebec. I was an only child at the time, but they went on to give me three siblings who kept the home energetic, chaotic and (mostly) fun. We ate home-cooked meals and I read *Popular Mechanics* in my dad's garage while he tinkered away on whatever he was trying to fix that day. We rarely travelled, but when we did, it was usually to visit family. My grandparents lived on a farm on Prince Edward Island, and I spent many weeks there during the summer months, pretending I was Anne of Green Gables and running through the wheat fields with the salty smell of the nearby Atlantic Ocean in every breath.

As a teen in the late eighties and early nineties, I lived in thick blue eyeliner and used an abundance of hairspray on bangs that even the cast of *Beverly Hills, 90210* would have envied. I frequented busy malls, watched iconic movies like *Ghostbusters* and *Return of the Jedi* and precariously fastened the bottom of my jeans with safety pins to make them tighter like my schoolmates'. Sometimes they popped open in the middle of class, stabbing me in the calf as I screamed silently at my desk, but we do what we must for Mistress Fashion.

If I close my eyes, I can vividly recall many great memories from my childhood. But there were other things that I was deal-ing with too. There were also events that I don't fully remember, or that have started resurfacing only more recently. They were formative in a not-so-good way.

My biological father exited my life when I was a baby, which would have left an even larger void had it not been for my stepdad— undeniably my dad in all the important ways—who arrived on the scene when I was a toddler and raised me as his own. I found out about my birth father's abandonment when I was seven, which left an emotional scar I still have today. My parents had no choice but to tell me by then. As soon as I could both read and reason, I started to question why I had a different last name than my mom and dad, not understanding I still carried the name of the man who was on my birth certificate. My parents carefully and delicately explained that my birth father was not a bad person—he just had some problems he couldn't work out while also being a father. This is what made him leave, they said. Not that he didn't love me.

It was the kindest and gentlest conversation, but as a child, I found it all but impossible not to internalize his departure as me somehow not being enough for him to stick around for. I carried that loss with me into adulthood, as many children with absentee parents do. There can be trauma even in what we do not remember. "Will this person who claims to love me leave me too?" is something I've asked myself countless times throughout the years.

Over time, I've learned that the specifics of what happened in my life tend to matter much less than the effect. For this and other reasons, I'm not going to do a deep dive into every single traumatic experience and will instead share only a few pivotal events. A full inventory is not helpful here and would probably turn this into a thousand-page book. What's most important today is not what caused my trauma, but what it did to me then, how it affected me well into adulthood and how I ultimately was able to heal from much of it.

Childhood trauma is heartbreakingly common. According to the US Department of Health and Human Services, more than two-thirds of children under the age of sixteen have experienced at least one traumatic event. These events can include abuse, neglect, a serious accident, a life-threatening illness, the loss of a loved one, war experiences, community violence and more. Why some children go on to develop post-traumatic stress disorder (PTSD), complex PTSD (CPTSD) or other trauma disorders as a result of those events while others do not isn't entirely clear. For whatever reason, I had the cards stacked against me in this department, I guess, and became one of those kids whose trauma compiled into a full-blown disorder that I went on to live with for several decades.

What we experience as children, good or bad, can be quickly assimilated into our lives and shapes who we will become. Some of these experiences, no matter how big or scary they might be, we end up keeping to ourselves. Maybe it's because we feel these experiences will be dismissed as the product of a vivid imagination, or because we simply don't know how to tell anyone. As children, we often lack the vocabulary to get our point across and therefore don't even try, or give up quickly in frustration if we do.

When I started having panic attacks at age five, I didn't know what they were, and I didn't have the words to tell anyone about them. The first one I remember happened about a year before we moved to the red-brick house. We were waiting for a house to come up for sale in my parents' desired neighbourhood and were staying in a rented bungalow in a nearby area. We lived there for only about a year, but I can still draw a map from memory. I loved the place.

The bungalow seemed huge to a kid my age. I would run from room to room with our terrier-beagle mix, Sam, at my heels. The two of us were inseparable. I was feisty and fearless back then, my blonde pigtails and green eyes often framing a smile. "You were a happy kid before you started school," my mom still tells me. And I was, except for the acute and wildly unpredictable anxiety I was too scared to share with her.

When I experienced my first panic attack, I was in a closet in our spare bedroom. (Ironically, being in the closet would become a big part of my overall character arc.) I don't remember why I was in the closet just then. I might have been playing hide-and-seek with Sam, or imagining I was in a spaceship—two of my favourite games. All I could see from my dark vantage point was a sliver of light coming from the spare bedroom beyond. The room was filled with still-packed boxes, ready to be moved again to somewhere more permanent, and an ironing board set up for weekday morning de-wrinkling sessions.

Without warning and seemingly without cause, the sliver of light beneath the door began to grow smaller and move farther away. In its place, the darkness around me grew into an infinite expanse. Imagine being in a cavernous pitch-black room, sitting up close to one of those old-school TVs on a cart they used to wheel into classrooms. Suddenly, the cart begins rolling away from you. There's no other light, just the image on the screen getting smaller and smaller, until it's nothing but a pinprick in the distance. That was what was happening to me, except the light was the crack in the door, getting farther and farther away. All around, the blackness enveloped me. I was alone in this strange place, away from everything and everyone I loved. And I was terrified.

I swore my heart was about to beat right out of my chest. My body felt cold and tingly. My breathing came shallow and fast. I wanted to call out for someone, but I couldn't form any words; my throat was hoarse and tight. Now, in this imaginary spaceship closet, I was going to float into nothingness as if I were really in space. I would never see my parents again. I would never see Sam again. I would never live in the house we were going to buy in our new neighbourhood. They would never know what had happened to me. Where did Amanda go? Hey! When did this closet become a portal to nothing?

Years later, I would learn this tunnel vision was a symptom of a panic attack. We often use the terms "panic attack" and "anxiety attack" interchangeably, but there are some key differences. An anxiety attack often happens alongside anxiety we have for a specific reason, such as "my dog was almost hit by a car just now" or "I got yelled at by my boss" or "I was thinking about something scary." It also tends to have a gradual onset. Panic attacks, on the other hand, aren't triggered by anything we can put our finger on. They seem to pop into existence, throw us into utter chaos and then dissipate. The adrenaline our body produces when in a state of panic isn't sustainable, so these events usually don't last more than a few minutes. But when you're between the start and the end of one, time does not exist. It's a unique dimension of sorts, where minutes can feel like gruelling hours of mental and physical upheaval.

Thankfully, like everything else, a panic attack does end. And when it did for five-year-old me, the pinprick of light slowly made its way back, filling my eyes. I was no longer in an expanse of darkness. The light from the crack in the bottom of the door was now at its proper size again, with the boxes and the ironing board just outside the closet. I pushed the door open and emerged, bewildered. I felt a sense of relief and utter exhaustion as the adrenaline and fear left my body.

Over time, I grew used to having panic attacks—or rather, as used to having them as you can become when you're young, can't reason yet and don't understand what's going on. They became my unexpected companions, showing up at random intervals to interrupt whatever I was doing. I began making room for them in my life, accepting that they would happen and creating plans for what I would do when one came knocking.

If I'm on my bike and the road starts getting far away, I thought to myself, *I'll stop and move to the side to wait it out.*

If I'm in class and everything gets smaller, I'll focus on the teacher so that I can still see her in the dark, even if she's tiny.

The darkness would find me no matter where I was or what I was doing. It would envelop me within seconds, reducing any view I had to a faraway pinprick of light. It was so frightening and fantastical that I didn't dare tell anyone. Where would I even begin?

Looking back on this as a parent, I find it heartbreaking that I went it alone in the anxiety department at such a young age. But as a child, held captive by what was likely a full-on panic disorder, I adapted. I learned to live with it, not knowing what it was and wondering if other people experienced the same thing.

They must, right?

But what if they didn't? What if I was the only one this was happening to? In that case, there was something wrong with me, and if I told anyone about it, that would be embarrassing. Other people might make fun of me, and they were already doing enough of that without my help. I was targeted by bullies as early as my preschool years, when a group of three kids would follow me around during outdoor time and make fun of me for playing alone. (Joke's on you, team: I wasn't alone because you were there with me the whole time.) Sam, Angèle and Maxime made fun of my appearance, from my clothes to my long braided hair. They made up songs about how stupid I was and how I didn't speak French well in this all-French school. I dreaded weekdays because it meant my parents went to work and I had to spend my time with kids who were mean to me.

I seemed to have the words "Very different—can be used as verbal and/or physical punching bag when bored" written somewhere conspicuous, because wherever I went, I was a target for bullying. At school, at summer camp, at birthday parties or at the park, if someone needed a few laughs at another's expense, I was it. This was my life until grade nine—an unrelenting barrage of attacks on everything from my treasured sticker book to the way I walked down the halls. As an adult, I now know that bullying is about having power and control over another. It didn't matter what I did to fit in back then—my tormentors would simply find something new to use against me. I rarely stood up for myself and I never fought back. I just put up with it, either laughing along like I was in on the joke or walking away, hoping they would get bored and move on to another target. Instead, it just made me easier prey.

So yes, it probably was best to keep my mouth shut about all this weird tunnel stuff—and anything else that might make me stand out more than I already did. The last thing I wanted was to be different in a new way. With this decision, the stage for Not Telling Anyone What's Wrong with Me was set. I had learned to try to hide everything that might attract more attention. And if I'm good at anything at all, it's consistency.

Unfortunately, my brain would end up playing an even worse trick on me. I would have to keep that to myself too.

It was 1983, the year magician David Copperfield shocked his audience by making the Statue of Liberty disappear. I was seven years old, and I nearly disappeared too.

We lived in the red-brick house now, a cozy four-bedroom that once again seemed much bigger to my young self than it was. I was in my parents' room, sitting on their bed and playing with some ceramic animal figurines from my mother's childhood that she kept in a drawer. They were mostly white and brown, with small accents of pastel colours here and there: pink inside the rabbit's ears, green for the kitten's eyes. My mom let me take them out as long as I was careful, so I would play with them on her bed to avoid breakage. That day, as usual, I was making up stories about their lives: Rabbit was trying to figure out how to tell Rooster she didn't want to be friends with him anymore (he was being a bit of a bully lately), while Rooster was coping with being madly in love with Kitten (which made him irritable with Rabbit, you see).

I started to feel strange. Light-headed. Nauseated. The room looked a little fuzzy. The familiar feeling of anxiety rose in my chest. I assumed another tunnel vision episode was about to happen and braced myself for it.

Instead, I suddenly didn't know who or where I was. I looked around in fear, then down at hands I assumed were mine, holding two little figurines I hadn't seen before. I was sitting on a bed I didn't know. Was it mine? Did it belong to someone else? Where was I? *Who* was I? Everything was alien. I was taking the whole room in for the first time, as if I were Alice in Wonderland after falling down the rabbit hole.

There is nothing in the world that can prepare you for forgetting who you are. It's like suddenly dropping into a life that isn't your own, knowing you should recognize it but simply can't. I knew I hadn't just woken up in someone else's body, even if that was what it felt like; that only happened on TV. This had to be my own life that I had somehow forgotten everything about. I don't believe this episode, or any future ones, lasted for more than a few minutes at most, but it was a bewildering few minutes. It felt like the episodes with the shrinking light, but with a great deal of added confusion. I searched for anything—anything at all—that might connect me to this room, these hands, these little figurines. I couldn't find it. I was immobilized, too scared to move off the bed.

Slowly, I came back to myself, like I was walking out of a thick fog. Elements of the world around me became clearer, bit by bit. A familiarity washed over me. After desperately trying to find my bearings in a storm of sudden amnesia, I was returned to the world. The sick feeling that came on at the beginning was the last symptom to leave.

"Oh, *that's* who I am," I whispered with profound relief. "I'm Amanda. I'm seven. I'm in grade two. I'm going to be a big sister soon. These are my hands. These are my mom's special toys from when she was little. This is my parents' bedroom." I whispered these facts to myself to commit them to memory, hoping never to forget a single one again.

But I would forget. I had no control over when these experiences would occur. The sick feeling would overcome me at random moments. Usually, I was alone. But sometimes, people would be around when it happened or would come by in the middle of an episode. One time, my mother walked into my room, and I tried to act as normally as I could while navigating a conversation with a complete stranger and also being a complete stranger to myself. I mostly just listened and nodded as if what she had to say made sense, and I tried not to look as lost as I felt. I didn't tell her what was happening; if I didn't know her, how could I trust her with a situation this serious? Midway through our chat, my memory returned, and I breathed a sigh of relief at recognizing the face in front of me.

Years later, a psychologist I was working with for anxiety would say she was surprised these episodes were not combined with or did not evolve into dissociative identity disorder, previously known as multiple personality disorder, in which a mind forms two or more separate identities to cope with a reality peppered with unpredictability and at times overwhelming fear. Dissociative disorders are closely linked to childhood trauma.

"For whatever reason, your mind didn't go in that direction," the psychologist explained. "I guess you must have found other ways to cope."

I was in my late thirties at the time and had never considered this possibility before. It was the first time I had shared details of these events with a mental health professional. Up until then, I was certain this was a normal reaction to anxiety for children, and as such, I had never brought it up.

Whatever path my mind had decided to take when I was younger, I would have made the best of it because children have an incredible capacity to adapt, to normalize what is happening and run with it.[1] These experiences will be carried into their adult lives, which is precisely what happened to me. I adapted.

But adaptability is not living—it's surviving. How is it living when you're coping with something that wounds you further every time your internal alarm bells are set off? How is it living when your brain numbs your emotions to keep you safe?

There was a lot going on with me by the time I entered sixth grade. I was not only hiding a high level of anxiety and its accompanying symptoms from the world, but also trying to make sense of my budding sexuality. At eleven, I was beginning to develop crushes, except they were on the wrong people: a sporty girl in my class, Suzanne Somers on *Three's Company*, all three of Charlie's Angels and, of course, the incredible Lynda Carter as Wonder Woman. According to everyone I talked to, everything I learned at church and in Catholic school and every example the media showed me, I was a girl, and I was supposed to like boys.

These expectations came in many different forms. "Do you have a boyfriend yet?" an adult might teasingly ask. "Any cute boys in your class?" All romantic plot lines in movies, television shows and books were between a boy and a girl or a man and a woman. In the Bible, all of humanity sprung from the love between Adam and Eve. While I wasn't regularly told that homo-sexuality was a sin, the society I grew up in strongly suggested it. Marriage was between a man and a woman. Having babies was why people had sex. Deviating from these ideas was wrong and could send you to hell. The path was laid out for me from a young age: I would meet a boy, fall in love, get married, have children and grow old with him.

But I didn't like boys at all—not in that way, anyway. I just wanted to be friends with them. I kept thinking I simply hadn't grown up enough to be attracted to them yet. Maybe I needed more time to mature. Maybe I was just confused about my feelings for some girls. Thinking they were pretty didn't mean anything, right? But no matter how many weeks or months went by, and no matter how many friends went on and on about their schoolyard or Hollywood crushes, I still had no desire to even kiss a boy. I briefly "dated" one in fifth grade, which entailed sometimes holding hands at recess. His grand romantic gesture was making me a wooden cross in his dad's workshop to wear around my neck. (Did I mention we went to a Catholic school?)

One day, I admitted to my long-time friend Mara that I thought one of our female classmates was pretty. I must have said it in a way that indicated something more than "she has great hair" because Mara gave me a look that had me knee-deep in shame in no time. I don't recall her saying much in response, but when we had a big falling-out a few months later, she weapon-ized this conversation against me.

Not long after our split, other kids started calling me a lesbian. This was one of the harshest insults you could lob at a girl in the schoolyard. It was synonymous with "perverted" and "dangerous"—even if those exact words weren't used.

Maybe it was the Catholicism we were steeped in from a young age, but in the schoolyard, it was believed that lesbians were perverts because they deviated from the sexual norm in a sinful way and sought out far more innocent girls to seduce them. Being considered a lesbian meant being a social pariah; no one would go near you.

School had always been a lonely place for me, but it felt especially isolating now. Nobody wants to talk to the lesbian lest they be accused of being one themselves.

One morning, I walked into the yard and saw Mara and the group of girls she had defected to. They were all lined up wearing long skirts. I found that strange, since they were generally the pants-wearing type. As I approached, they cast devious glances at each other and emitted the odd giggle. In the typical morning chaos, piles of students were filing off the school buses all around us.

"Hey, Amanda!" the girls shouted in unison as I walked by. "Look at this!"

Suddenly, all five lifted up their skirts. I gasped in horror over what they were about to reveal to the entire schoolyard, before realizing, with relief, that they were all wearing gym shorts underneath.

"Are you disappointed?" Mara called.

"Were you expecting more?" her new friend asked.

"Of course she was," exclaimed another. "Did you see her face? She was so excited!"

They burst into laughter. "Lesbian!" they called as I walked away, shocked and embarrassed. "You're disgusting, lesbian!"

Other kids joined in the laughter. Some whistled. One bumped into me, hard, almost knocking me to the ground. I heard a teacher say something stern to the group as I strode quickly forward with my head down. I didn't look up, and I didn't look back.

School hadn't even started for the day, and I already wanted to run home. I wanted to run far and fast away from feeling so different, so disgusting, so *perverted*. For years, I had watched from the outside as others appeared to fit in, to be normal. Why couldn't I do that too? Why did I have to be the one people pointed fingers at? Why couldn't I just feel like them? Be like them? *Not* be me? I was the English kid in a French school. I was the kid with the crushes I could never talk about. I was the one who got singled out each time, either ignored or mocked, my heart broken at the end of nearly every day. I didn't fit in whatsoever. And even when I was alone, I sometimes couldn't remember who I was. No wonder. Why would I want to remember? Maybe my brain was just trying to run because the rest of me couldn't.

I had known for a long time that these feelings and attractions were a part of me, but I had to keep pushing them down for my own safety. I can't overstate how traumatic it is not to be yourself. Actively hiding and suppressing parts of who I was had devastating effects. It made me worried and insecure, always waiting for someone to notice I was playing a role instead of being myself—a self they would undoubtedly judge. But in the eighties, being out as a young queer kid was all but impossible. Many children who did come out were still subjected to conversion therapy, a dangerous practice that aims to suppress or change a person's sexuality or gender and is now illegal across Canada and in several other countries. The idea was that if children could learn to live as who the world expected them to be—rather than be gay, trans, bisexual or anything else not considered "normal"—they would have easier lives. This was seen as preferable to facing active discrimination throughout their lives or having to "live in sin." These "therapies" involved many different methods, including forcing children to pursue more stereotypical interests in line with the gender they were assigned at birth and associating same-sex attractions with negative imagery or sensations.

Trauma has layers. Being queer in the eighties had created a new one for me to affix to the ones already in place. I buried significant parts of who I was beneath that new layer, where they would remain for a long time.

As puberty began to ramp up around age twelve, my tunnel vision terror trips stopped. I was no longer a little kid stuck in the darkness, taking a break from riding a bike in order to ride out the panic. I stopped having moments when I forgot who I was.

Instead, I was a fiery, angry, wounded teenager. Trauma had taken on a new form.

lashing out

ONCE, WHEN I WAS ABOUT TEN and sick with the flu, my grandmother made me a hot toddy to help me sleep. It's a mixture of whisky, hot water and honey—something her own parents had given her as a child when she was under the weather. I took a sip as I stood in the kitchen, the sweetness hitting my tongue just before the burn of the alcohol hit the back of my throat. I winced at the taste but continued to drink it when my grandmother promised it would help me sleep. I still remember the feeling of warmth that washed over me as I lay in bed a few minutes later, drifting blissfully off into dreamland. It felt like magic. The alcohol dulled the sickly discomfort in my body while also quieting the noise in my mind.

My mind has always been noisy. It was a lot like a grade school music class: sometimes out of tune and usually off tempo. Most of my thoughts were loud, distracting and increasingly painful as

I got older. Every time I was bullied at school, I replayed those moments in my head compulsively for days or weeks after. Each malicious word hurled at me by others was repeated in my mind countless times. Every instance in which I was scolded for not doing a good enough job at something by an adult in my life—be it a teacher, a neighbour or my parents—was an instance I played back to myself. Every hit, physical or verbal, was recorded and replayed in some way. I was a failure. I was no good. I deserved the bad in my life. I did this to myself. Over and over and over, like a playlist with one sad song on repeat.

But when the alcohol hit me that first time, my brain pressed pause on that out-of-tune playlist. I stopped thinking negative things and instead felt . . . pleasant. I remember staring up at my bedroom ceiling, unbothered and serene. I didn't know a person could feel like this. Was this how others felt? Could I feel this way more often? I had to get more of this magnificent drink.

As it turned out, I could definitely get more, as long as I was careful. My parents had a liquor cabinet that held several dusty, largely untouched bottles. My mom rarely drank, and my dad mostly enjoyed beer. Liquor was for guests, who rarely asked for it, and with many bottles to choose from, it would be easy to take a little bit from one, then another whenever I wanted it. No one would even notice that the liquid was disappearing.

It started innocently enough. One night, after a particularly bad day of bullying at school, I tried to recreate my grandmother's hot toddy recipe. I made sure my parents weren't around before I snuck some whisky out of the cupboard and guesstimated the amount my grandmother had added to the hot water and honey.

It worked, to an extent. The warm feeling wasn't quite as warm, and while the memories of the day did quiet down, the quiet wasn't nearly as soothing as the first time. I tried again a couple of days later, adding a bit more liquor. Maybe I had gotten the proportions wrong. The numbing effect was stronger that time, but it still didn't recreate the original magic.

Sit in on a twelve-step meeting long enough, and you will hear stories about that "first drunk" or "first high." Many people with substance abuse disorders talk about chasing that magnificent feeling for a lifetime but never being able to relive it, no matter how much they try. In a funny way, it kind of reminds me of the first time I saw the Canadian Rockies. My eyes took in the sheer size of these magnificent mountains and the height of their peaks. I've since seen them three more times, and while they're still incredible, the awe I initially experienced has never been recreated. Chasing that first drunk is a lot like that, but without a great vacation attached to it. And you don't want to see the photos.

I hunted for that perfect feeling all throughout my tween and early teen years. My desire to relive that first moment, when all the world's problems slipped blissfully away, kept me seeking. By age thirteen, I began to spend my time with others, both inside and outside of school, who were on a similar quest. I had always had a few good friends who were there for me, even when it felt like no one else was. But looking at them now was like holding a mirror up to what I was becoming: an apathetic, miserable person who could no longer find hope—a far cry from who I had been not long before. So I pushed them away in favour of other students as angry with the world as I was. There was no judgment among those also looking to escape their unhappiness. But for me, at least, the escape was always short-lived. No matter how drunk or high I got, the problems in my life would come roaring back the minute sobriety found me again. I couldn't escape myself.

In grade 7, called secondary I in Quebec, I was set on fire in front of my classmates by two girls who had been harassing me throughout our elementary years. They gathered a large group of students, found me outside, sprayed my back with hairspray and threw matches at me as I ran. My sweater caught on fire. I stopped, dropped and rolled on the grass, which likely saved me from severe burns. But that day, which led me to transfer to a new school, really shook me up. After that incident, experiencing numbness became even more valuable. I needed to make the cruelty of the world go away.

Because I was a minor, though, substances were often hard to come by, and I usually had to seek out people older than me to acquire them. Meanwhile, I was beginning to realize that alcohol was a messy, expensive way to forget your problems, and I was worried my parents would eventually get suspicious about all the liquor I had been pouring out of bottles at the back of the cabinet. So when a new school friend, Giselle, wanted to introduce me to a hash dealer, promising me affordable prices and a good high, I jumped at the chance. We took a bus to his place one chilly December evening.

This was the night I met Nathan.

Nathan was nineteen and had an apartment in the heart of town with a couple of friends. Not interested in college, he made his living selling drugs. Nathan took a liking to fourteen-year-old me as soon as I walked in the door. His attraction was obvious, and he didn't try to hide it. He wouldn't leave my side, following me from room to room, sitting next to me and continually engaging me in conversation. Because I wasn't used to positive attention from guys, this made me uncomfortable, but it also left me a little flattered. At school, I was bullied daily about my appearance, with other kids telling me how ugly I was at every opportunity. Asking me out on dates had become a joke boys played so their friends could get a laugh. It was nice that Nathan seemed genuinely interested in me, especially because he was older and clearly the life of the party. In fact, if it weren't for Nathan, there wouldn't even have been a party. The group of eight people gathered in his apartment were all friends and clients of his. They all seemed to like him, and he seemed to like me. Maybe, I thought, it was because he was more mature than high school kids. No matter the reason, I soaked it in. His attention made me feel special.

Nathan was already a few drinks in when Giselle and I dropped by, and I found him a little handsy. He kept touching my shoulders, my back and my long curly hair while telling me how beautiful I was. When Caro, an older girl from my high school, showed up and started loudly telling everyone what a loser I was and how Nathan should make me leave, he quickly jumped to my defence. "We might be friends, Caro, but this is my guest, and you need to be respectful."

Wow, I thought in amazement. *No one has ever defended me like that.* I watched a scowl cross Caro's face, but she didn't dare say a word. In fact, she didn't speak another word to or about me for the rest of the evening—not where Nathan or I might hear her, anyway. I was quietly elated. Nobody stuck up for me at school, which was probably why Caro thought I would make a great verbal punching bag outside of school hours too. But not on Nathan's watch. He put his arm around me as he defended me. The life of the party had my back.

Unfortunately, while Nathan was protective in his own way, his idea of "respect" was sorely lacking. I learned this in the worst way later that evening when he invited me to his bedroom, where it was "quieter." We could talk there, he said. He wanted to get to know me, he said. I was young and naive, and also hoping he was going to cut me a private deal on my purchase, as my babysitting and paper delivery money wasn't going to buy as much hash as I had hoped. Instead, he asked me to sit on his bed, and then, with no hesitation, he leaned in for a kiss. It was a beer-infused, sloppy mouthful. I pulled back, trying not to show my disgust. I was his guest, after all, and he was being so nice to me.

"Hey," he said. "It's okay. Just relax. In case it isn't obvious, I really like you."

He leaned in again, putting his hand on my thigh, and instead of feeling sparks like I'd been told I would when my first romantic kiss happened, I felt deeply uncomfortable, which filled me with guilt. Why was I feeling this way? Wasn't this what I wanted? A guy was into me, which never happened. He had stood up for me, which also never happened. So I let the kiss happen. I felt guilty at the thought of saying no. I also worried that if I rejected his advances, he would reject me, and that one moment of safety I'd felt earlier would be gone. I wanted to feel safe and special for once. It was just a kiss anyway, right? What's the harm in one kiss?

Nathan's hands moved like lightning under my top. I pulled them back out again.

"Whoa! I don't want to do that," I said.

"Oh! I'm sorry," he replied. Then something seemed to occur to him. "Wait! Are you a virgin?"

"Uh, yes," I said shyly.

"How old are you?" he asked.

"I'm fourteen. Why?"

Any respectable nineteen-year-old would have quickly apologized for ever touching me in the first place, opened the bedroom door and sent me on my way. I was five years younger than him and a minor. Instead, Nathan replied, "It's okay. We can take it slow if you'd like." He began to climb on top of me, gently pushing me down onto the mattress.

I had never been in this situation before and didn't know what to do. I wanted to stop it, but sticking up for myself was hard to do. I preferred to make people happy; it was a lot easier than causing a scene. Letting Nathan have sex with me when I wasn't interested would have been an extreme form of making someone happy at my own expense, though, and I didn't want that. After a couple of minutes of letting him grope me, I said, as delicately as possible, "Hey, you're great, but I really don't want to do this right now. I just met you. Can we please stop?"

Looking the tiniest bit frustrated, Nathan rolled off me and stood up. "Okay. Fine." He sighed.

I felt tense, as if he would yell at me and kick me out at any minute. If that happened, I knew Caro would never let me live it down, and it would be all over the school in a matter of days. I had just made my life even worse than it already was.

As I mulled over my fate, Nathan seemed to compose himself, and a smile appeared on his face. "It's fine. I understand. Can you do something for me before you leave, though? Just one thing. You'll like it, I promise."

"Uh, sure. I guess," I replied.

He stood in front of me and asked me to close my eyes. A strange request, but I did it. *I hope he's not going to try to kiss me again*, I thought. Still, anything he had to offer was better than what he had been trying to do to me on that bed. He could lean in for a kiss, and then we could go back out into the living room to join the rest of the group—no harm done.

"Here, let me show you what to do," he said breathily. He grabbed my arm and moved it toward him, placing something warm and hard in my hand.

My eyes leapt open as I quickly pulled my hand away from a part of his body I had no interest in touching.

"Hey, I said it's okay. It's not bad, right?" he asked. "You liked that, didn't you? Nothing to be scared of, even if you've never done it before."

"W-what are you doing?!" I stammered. "I said I don't want to do that!"

He was standing, pants down, between me and his bedroom door, still looking pleased with himself, as if he were giving me a gift I didn't yet know I wanted. Mortified and disgusted, I knew I had to get out of there. Screw what Caro might think if I left in a hurry.

Before he could do more than start to pull his pants up, I walked around him, out the bedroom door and into the living room, trying to look as natural and composed as possible. I don't know if I was successful; I certainly didn't feel composed at all. I grabbed my jean jacket and told Giselle that I had to go catch the bus. Yes, right now. No, I didn't need to check the schedule first.

Nathan, sweatpants now pulled all the way up like a big boy, followed a few paces behind me. "I can walk you to the bus stop," he said with a hint of neediness in his voice.

"No, that's fine. I know where it is," I replied, not looking back. I needed to leave this place *now*. I had to get home *now*. I said goodbye to everyone and walked out the duplex's front door into the snowy evening.

Nathan called to me from the doorway. "Amanda! Can I see you again?" When I didn't answer, he called out again, sounding even more desperate. "Please?"

I stopped a few feet from the building, thinking furiously. What was the best thing to say to get me as far away from him as possible?

"Okay," I called back, not meaning it.

The phone rang the next day. On the other end of the line was a very apologetic Nathan. I would have avoided the call if I had known it was him, but I had no clue he'd asked Giselle for my number after I left the night before. I was so embarrassed about what had happened in his apartment, I hadn't told her or anyone else about it. Giselle probably thought she was doing me a favour by giving him my number.

He wanted to see me again, he said. His voice was sweet and insistent. "I can make it up to you," he pleaded. "I promise that won't happen again. It was so stupid of me. I shouldn't have had that much to drink."

I listened to him explain away his actions, my resolve slowly softening. Finally, I let my guard down and told him he could take me out on a date. It was almost Christmas, after all, and nobody likes to be sad during the holidays. Having someone to spend time with, especially someone who could help me get high and forget my troubles, was welcome.

We went out on one date and then another. He was charming and funny, and he seemed to really like me. He built up my trust along with my ego, making me feel like I was the most important person in the world to him. After a while, I started believing that my first impression of him was all wrong. People make bad decisions all the time when they're drunk, right?

One night while we were chatting on the phone, Nathan asked if I cared about him. I said yes. He asked if I felt ready to lose my virginity and said he would love to help me experience that.

"I think I will be soon," I replied. I knew this was something most people eventually do. Sex with him wasn't what I really wanted. But maybe, I thought, I should just bite the bullet and get it over with. Maybe I was making too big a deal of it.

"Tell you what," he said. "Your parents are going out on New Year's Eve, right? What if I come over after they leave, and we see what happens? No pressure. If you don't want to, that's fine. We'll just watch the ball drop or something."

"Okay," I agreed. "I like that plan." No pressure. We could just see what happens. Perfect.

On New Year's Eve, my parents did go out together—a rarity for them with four children at home. My younger siblings were fast asleep. I was anxiously watching out the front window. Nathan had called me a few minutes earlier from a pay phone to say he was grabbing a cab up to my place from the bar.

The bar? I hadn't realized he was going there first. He had been drinking. I could tell because he sounded a lot like he had the night we met. Alarm bells started to go off in my mind, but I did my best to ignore them. I wanted to have a nice night with him. I wanted to trust him. I wanted to believe that he genuinely cared about me, and that he wouldn't be the gross, sloppy monster he had been that first night.

Not long after, Nathan got out of the cab and sauntered over to the front door. I let him in quietly, and he enveloped me in a big hug. We sat on the living room couch, where I tried to make small talk and he tried to do nothing but make out with me.

"Let's go watch TV in the basement," I suggested, "so we don't wake up my brothers and sister."

We went down to the family room and sat on that couch instead. I put on MuchMusic—the Canadian equivalent of MTV—and we started watching a countdown of the year's top music videos.

Or at least, I started watching it. Nathan could not keep his hands off me.

"Let's just watch this for a bit, okay?" I asked.

"Come on," he whispered into my ear. "It'll be nice, I promise." He climbed on top of me and started hiking up my shirt.

"Nathan," I said, "come on. I just want to watch TV."

Nathan didn't stop. Every time I moved one hand away, his other would take over. He was like a drunken squid. His larger body pressed my smaller one into the sofa. The stench of beer and cigarettes on his breath made me want to gag. He became more forceful each time I tried to pry him off me.

"Please stop," I pleaded quietly, starting to get nervous. "Stop. I don't want to. I'm not ready."

"You're ready," he said. "Trust me. It's not a big deal. Just relax. It's going to feel so good. You'll love it." The mask had slipped off. He was no longer the nice guy.

Could I have been louder in my protests? Could I have fought harder? All I could think about were my siblings, asleep upstairs, and I worried what might happen if we woke them. Would they be terrified if they heard me screaming? What if they got out of bed? What might they see? What would he do to me, or to them? Who knew what he was capable of? In that moment, I had to choose between a terrible situation and what could become an even worse one. I chose the former.

I watched TV as my boyfriend did the unspeakable. I focused intently on the flashing screen, taking in video colour palettes and outfits and anything else that would distract me from what was happening. Weirdly, what was on television is what I remember most from the actual rape.

After an indeterminate amount of time, Nathan collapsed in a sweaty heap on top of me. "See? That felt good, right?"

I don't remember what I replied, but I remember being careful about what I said. I didn't want to upset him.

"Hey," he said cheerily, getting off the couch and pulling his pants back up. "I'm getting hungry. Want to order pizza? Did your parents leave you any money?"

Pizza. Paid for by me. Unbelievable.

But that's what we did. We ordered pizza, ate it and watched the ball drop. I felt numb about what had just happened, which was likely the only thing stopping me from falling apart. Nathan left in a cab shortly after midnight, kissing me before going and promising to see me again soon. I waved feebly as the cab drove off, the smile on my face dropping as soon as I closed the front door. I threw the empty pizza box on the back deck so my parents wouldn't see it and greeted them as happily as possible when they got home. Then I went to bed, eager to forget one of the worst nights of my life.

Nathan called a couple of times after that, but I refused to talk to him. Unfortunately, we would wind up seeing each other once more a few months later, and that encounter would mess me up in a whole new way.

I didn't tell many people what had happened with Nathan. The handful of friends I did confide in—the ones I was drinking with regularly—didn't see what he did as a problem. Despite our age gap, most viewed what had occurred between us as consensual. In reality, a fourteen-year-old in the province of Quebec could not legally consent to sex with someone five years older. There are leaps and bounds in maturity between fourteen and nineteen. The law recognized that, but not everyone around me did. Society also still largely viewed rape as something perpetrated by a stranger, not a boyfriend. Back then, if you invited a guy over to your house and ended up having sex, it was assumed you wanted to. Did I perhaps hint I wanted to sleep with him and give him the wrong idea? What was I wearing that night? Was it sexy? Why did I invite him over at all when my parents weren't home? Why did I take him down to the basement? Did I firmly say no, or was I more ambiguous? Why didn't I fight tooth and nail? Why did I have pizza with him afterward?

These were the questions I was asked by the few people I told, and my answers did not seem to garner me any sympathy. In their minds, I had led him on. They believed I had wanted to have sex with Nathan, plain and simple. If I regretted it now, that was my own doing. I should have thought about that before I invited him over, rather than make myself the victim now because I regretted my decision. One person, whose support would have been especially important to me at the time, went so far as to angrily call me a "little slut." Those words broke me. In some ways, the aftermath was worse than the rape itself. Nathan had hurt my body, but these reactions from the people I depended on to get through the experience hurt my soul. For years after, I would replay that New Year's Eve in my mind, wondering if I had said or done anything that somehow made it my fault.

Hurt stacked on top of hurt. What was worse than being raped was being raped and not having anyone believe me. It played into the doubt I already had, twisting my mind up. I started to withdraw from nearly everyone around me and lost interest in the things I used to enjoy, like drawing and playing guitar. I listened to metal and hard rock like Metallica, Mötley Crüe, and Guns N' Roses, which filled my ears with rebellion and spoke to the anger I was feeling inside. My grades started slipping along with my attendance. The makeup I wore got darker and more dramatic. It was a mix of "notice me" and "stay away."

Hurt turned to anger. I began to live the way others thought of me. People wanted to call me a slut? A liar? A pervert? A menace? A waste of life? I could be all those things. Challenge accepted. At fourteen, I began trading sex with guys in their twenties for alcohol, drugs and the attention I desperately craved. I met them through friends and at parties. If they had something on them to help me forget my problems, I was more than happy to give them my time. I let them tell me they cared about me, knowing full well they would never call me again after our initial encounter. I pretended not to care, numbing myself with substances whenever possible. As always, numbness was what I needed more than anything. It was my reprieve from the pain I felt every day.

One night, when the pent-up emotional pain became overwhelming, I used a razor and cut my wrists. It wasn't deep enough to put my life in danger; that wasn't the intention. I wanted to release the hurt I was carrying and find that numbness again. It worked. The sharp sting of the blade and the sight of my own blood unleashed a flood of tears. For the next few months, I would cut my legs or arms whenever I felt the need for that release, then shamefully cover the wounds with bandages and long clothing.

I lied compulsively and ran away from home on more than one occasion. I stole money from my parents and their friends and shoplifted from stores. I was the thorn in every teacher's side—when I showed up to class at all, that is. The few friends I still had, loyal and concerned up to that point, pulled away from me, either because their parents told them to or because they didn't want to get sucked into my self-destructive vortex.

I feared no consequence, least of all death. Every morning I woke up was painful. Every night I went to bed hoping not to wake up again. I hated the world and hated myself even more.

Sometimes, it takes a big thing to wake you up—a seismic catalyst for change, if you will. My catalyst happened at fourteen and involved cocaine, bad sex and a literal gun to my head. It's almost its own rock song.

"I'm just going out for a bit," I said to my mom one afternoon in the late spring of 1991. Since getting expelled from school a few weeks before, I had been on a tight leash at home. My parents, the school nurses, the guidance counsellors and the vice-principal had done everything they could to help me stay in school, but I was far beyond caring about my education. The world was not a kind place. Why keep trying to be a part of it? Why try at all? There was no point. As much support and as many warnings as I received from school administrators, I continued to skip most of my classes. Eventually, they had no choice but to ask me to leave.

My parents had no idea what to do about my out-of-control behaviour. They had pushed for me to go to rehab to deal with my substance issues and had scoured the area looking for any mental health resources. Unfortunately, there was little out there for young teens who were charging headlong into an early grave. Nobody seemed to think the problems faced by people my age could be serious. Substance abuse? At fourteen? Not likely.

"Where are you going?" my mom asked suspiciously.

"Just getting together with a friend at McDonald's," I lied, meeting her eyes as convincingly as I could. "I need to get out for a bit. I'll have a burger and bus home right after, okay?"

Dan was a twenty-year-old guy I had slept with once on the promise that we would start dating. He unceremoniously dumped me by phone a couple of days later, saying I wasn't his type, which was code for "I already had sex with you, and I'm moving on to my next conquest." But he had just called again out of the blue and said he wanted me to go drinking with him and some friends, which was code for "There are no new potential conquests available at the moment, and I'm hoping to sleep with you again." My substance problems were out of control at this point, and my options for alcohol were limited since my parents had discovered my liquor cabinet raiding. This was a way to numb myself for a couple of hours. I agreed to meet him at the park behind the local arena.

I should never have gone in the first place. Dan, like all the guys I was dating or sleeping with back then, did not exactly represent the best of humanity. But even that aside, seeing Nathan in the park with Dan when I arrived should have been enough for me to turn around, hop on a bus and head home. I didn't know they were friends, so his appearance was a complete shock. I hadn't seen Nathan since New Year's, and being in his presence again came with a wave of nausea and anxiety. Memories of being pinned down on the basement sofa played out in my mind like flash cards. My instincts told me to leave, to run as far and fast as I could from these two men, each of whom had already hurt me in his own way.

But then I saw the booze.

"Hey!" Dan called, holding up two bottles. "I have schnapps and orange juice! Want me to make you a fuzzy navel?"

I wanted a drink. So badly. I ignored my better judgment, took a deep breath and walked over.

"Hi, stranger," Nathan said, seemingly happy to see me. "It's been a while."

"Yeah," I said, not taking my eyes off the cup Dan was pouring me. "Parents. You know."

Nathan seemed to accept my flimsy excuse for not calling him back, and we carried on as if nothing had happened. Good. I had secured the ability to drink my feelings away for a couple of hours.

While I'd intended to be out only for the evening, that's not what happened. Nathan's new girlfriend joined us too, making our surprise reunion extra awkward and giving me an excuse to drink a little faster. Macie was a friendly and beautiful exotic dancer (Nathan made sure to proudly mention her profession several times). She was kind to me and seemed to have no problem with the history Nathan and I shared—his version of it, anyway. As the sun started going down and the breeze picked up, she asked if we wanted to go back to her place. By that time, I'd had far too much to drink already. The light buzz I had hoped for had turned into something much stronger.

"I just want to stop by and see someone for a minute," Macie said. "His place is right over here."

Macie's dealer conveniently lived right next to the arena we had been drinking behind. Dan and I held back as she and Nathan knocked at the door. But even from our vantage point several feet away, we saw the dealer's scowl as he took in the two of them together, his eyes trailing down to Nathan's arm wrapped tightly around Macie's waist like some kind of prize. Some brief words, money and a small package were exchanged before the dealer all but slammed the door in their faces.

"I can't believe I used to date that asshole," Macie sighed. We walked the four or five blocks to her place, street lights illuminating the sidewalk as we went. I leaned tipsily on Dan, who didn't seem to mind at all.

This was almost my last evening alive, and I didn't even know it.

I don't know what time I woke up the next day, but it was bright out, likely the middle of the morning, and three people were leaning over me wearing worried expressions like something out a movie. My head hurt and I was immensely thirsty. This was going to be a brutal hangover.

"Are you okay?" Macie asked. "We weren't sure if we should call an ambulance."

I sat up, wincing at the light shining through the windows, my vision blurry. I had been lying on Macie's thin living room carpet, which I remembered falling asleep on after Dan and I had sex—unprotected sex, I now recalled. *Shit.* The condom had broken, and he whispered something to me like: "Don't worry. If you get pregnant, I'll help you take care of the baby." He had fed me the most ludicrous line imaginable, and I, too intoxicated and wounded on the inside to care, nodded in agreement.

"Yeah, I'm fine," I said, rubbing my temple. "Why are you all looking at me like that?"

They were still watching me carefully, as if I might crumble into dust at any moment.

"You don't remember what happened last night? At all?" Dan asked incredulously. "With Matt and the gun?"

Who and the *what* now?

What I remembered from last night was as blurry as my vision. I recalled refusing a line of cocaine when it was offered to me, convinced that by doing so, I was avoiding becoming an addict. I remembered drinking far more than I had planned to. I remembered bits of the awful and potentially dangerous condom-less sex with Dan, which grossed me out now to think about. At some point, I blacked out and must have fallen asleep on the floor. I was just waking up.

But the apartment looked different than I had remembered. There were some obvious things out of place. Big things. A dining chair was lying on its side next to the table, and the couch where we'd sat the night before was pushed out from the wall by about a foot. Something had happened while I was passed out, and this group of panicked people were about to tell me what it was.

The story they told came in frantic bits and pieces as they collectively filled the gaps as they remembered them. Matt was the dealer whose house we had visited the night before. Apparently, Macie had broken up with him a few days earlier and was now seeing Nathan (who, I had desperately wanted to tell her, was probably not a huge step up in the boyfriend department). The previous night, while Nathan and Macie were asleep in the bedroom and Dan and I were passed out on the floor in the living room, Matt had entered the apartment with a gun. The front door was at ground level, and there were stairs leading up to the living area. When he walked into the dark apartment, he saw Dan and me on the floor, passed out, and likely assumed we were Macie and Nathan.

"I don't remember hearing him come in," Nathan explained. "But I woke up for some reason and decided I would go take a piss. And when I walked out of the bedroom," he recalled, his eyes wide in the retelling, "I saw him pointing a gun at your head."

Nathan called out, startling Matt, and waking up everyone but very inebriated me. Macie pleaded with Matt to think about what he was doing, and he lowered the weapon, likely when he realized he had been pointing it at the wrong person. There was a struggle, which is how the furniture got rearranged. Nathan and Dan overpowered Matt and pushed him down the flight of stairs into the apartment door. The full force of Matt's body hit the door, breaking the frame, and he staggered off into the night.

Nathan, Dan and Macie had been awake ever since, unable to properly close the door and worried that Matt would come back to finish what he'd started. Nobody knew what had happened to the gun, or even if there were any bullets in it. Maybe his plan was to wake up his ex-girlfriend and scare her. But Macie, knowing Matt, assumed it was loaded. She believed that if anyone could kill a person out of spite, it was him.

"We thought that maybe you got hurt in all of the chaos and we didn't notice," said Macie. "I guess you were just really drunk, huh?" She laughed, but the humour never reached her eyes. The three of them seemed badly shaken by what had happened.

This story couldn't possibly be real, I told myself. A jealous ex-boyfriend seeking revenge? A gun to my head? A fight breaking out while I slept through it on the floor? No way. They were messing with me, and I expected them to burst out laughing any second. But as I looked around, I realized I had all the proof I needed that this story was true. Not only had the apartment seen a fight, but the door frame was broken and the drywall by the front door was dented in, as if something heavy had fallen into it. But most importantly, the fear on their faces told the story. This had really happened. And if the gun was loaded as Macie suspected, I had almost died. If Nathan, the man who had taken so much from me six months earlier, had not come out of the bedroom when he did, I might never have woken up.

I needed to go home. I needed my mom. I was in way over my head. But how would I explain this to my parents? How would I tell them that I had put myself in a dangerous situation and almost didn't make it out? I didn't know how, and I couldn't bear to imagine what they would think of me when they found out. The shame was too great.

So I avoided facing up to it. I stayed at Macie's for the rest of the day and part of the next one. The guys worked to fix the door as best they could. We talked about what had happened—our shared experience I couldn't remember—but mostly we just got drunk and smoked a lot of weed. It wasn't the party atmosphere it had been before; the mood remained relatively sombre. Meanwhile, my parents, their friends and the police were all looking for me. I was supposed to have been home three days ago. Everyone now thought the worst.

After I left Macie's apartment the following day, I desperately tried to come up with a good reason for why I hadn't been home sooner. I made my way back to the park behind the arena where this nightmare had begun. My mind was muddled, and I was desperate. Maybe I could tell my parents I had been attacked? That would be a good excuse, right? But I would need some sort of proof. If I came home looking fine, they would know I was lying.

I found a shard of beer bottle on the ground. It looked sharp enough to do the job. I tore into the skin on the upper part of my left arm, my still-intoxicated brain believing this would pass for a knife wound. I didn't think beyond this to what would happen if I shared a story along these lines. Would my parents want to get the police involved? Would I need to make a statement? How detailed would I have to get, and how long would I have to keep up this lie? Nothing I was doing made sense.

The beer bottle shard cut too deep, I realized, and I was bleeding more than I had anticipated. Blood was dripping down my bare arm. Thankfully, there was a man shuffling through the back seat of a car next to Matt the dealer's house.

"Hey! Excuse me!" I called to him.

"Hey yourself," the man said, standing up. He looked to be around thirty, with patchy stubble and sunken eyes.

"I'm wondering if you have a Band-Aid," I asked. "I kind of cut myself." I shrugged when I pointed to my arm, trying to make it seem like no big deal.

The man looked at me and seemed to think for a moment. Then he looked around. The street was empty. We were alone.

"Uh, yeah," he began. "I have some in my car. Come on over."

My gut whispered to me: *Danger.* I didn't budge. I stood there, holding my arm and thinking about it.

"They're in here somewhere" he said. I could see that his car had a lot of stuff in it, as if he were in the middle of moving. "Come help me look."

Danger. I didn't like this guy. There was something about him, about how his smile didn't reach his eyes, just like Macie when she was trying to laugh about the break-in.

But I was bleeding, and I needed something to make it stop.

"Are you going to come help?" the man asked. Maybe it was fine, and I was just being paranoid after what had happened at Macie's. "You can look back here, and I'll look in the front," he said.

Fuck it, I thought, ignoring my gut. I started walking over.

Just as I got a few feet from the car, I heard my name being called in the most familiar voice I knew, strong and alarmed: *"Amanda! Come here right now!"*

I looked behind me. My mom had just pulled up. She had been looking for me for three days. How she ended up in that exact spot at that exact time, I don't know. But the man's smile faded immediately. He jumped in his car without saying a word and pulled away. I don't know if he had ill intentions or was truly just trying to help, but I'll forever be grateful that my mom showed up when she did and I never had to find out.

My mom barely spoke to me the entire way home. She was furious, but beneath that, the fear she had experienced while I was gone was undoubtedly bubbling to the surface. Still, she delicately patched up my arm and made sure to hug me too.

I couldn't bring myself to tell my parents what had happened in its entirety, but I did say I knew I needed help to stop drinking. A couple of weeks later, after I had one more night of uncontrollable binging and bad sex with a stranger, my dad dropped me off at a six-month-long live-in drug and alcohol rehabilitation centre an hour from home. At fourteen years old, I was its youngest client. I arrived full of attitude: sullen, defiant and angry. I would be made to sit with the uncomfortableness of sobriety and deal with my feelings without my usual escape hatch.

Rehab was strict. We rose at seven every morning and made our beds with hospital corners. If they weren't made properly, a senior resident—someone who had been there for at least three months and had taken on a leadership role—would strip them down and make us do them again. Staff would run their fingers up and down our bedroom furniture looking for dust. Every speck of dirt found after we did our chores was added up, and consequences for sloppy work were delivered at the end of every week. I once had to scrub the expansive kitchen floor with something only slightly larger than a toothbrush.

I hated my early days in rehab with a passion but feared my old life more than anything the staff could throw at me. If this would help me turn things around, I planned to tough it out for as long as I could. Besides, the people who had been there longer than I had seemed happier than me. Maybe they knew something I had yet to learn.

I miscarried Dan's baby within a few weeks of being there, crying on the bathroom floor at the shock of it. The staff drove me to the local hospital, where a doctor, an older man with grey hair and a scowl, examined me and then chastised me for my "promiscuity."

In the first few weeks, I was put on the hot seat again and again, as my attitude and unhealthy behaviours were challenged. Sitting in a circle of couches and chairs in the spacious living room, counsellors and fellow residents alike would take turns bringing up the things I didn't want to see about myself.

"You're very judgmental," a resident said in one of these sessions. "You think you're better than some of us because you haven't done the things we did."

While I denied it, a part of me knew it was true—on the surface, anyway. But deep down, I didn't think I was better. I was just angry about ending up in a rehab centre and needed to distance myself from the experiences of other residents. I was only a little bit broken. I was only a little bit addicted. I hadn't been in serious trouble with the law. I hadn't injected drugs. I hadn't lost my family to my addiction. Not like *them*.

After three months, I was given the role of a senior resident, supervising chores and acting like a mentor for newer arrivals. This role bolstered my ego, for good and for bad. I became controlling, smug and condescending, belittling other residents for failing to make their beds properly or leaving a smudge on the sink they had just cleaned. I talked down to everyone who was new, and my sense of superiority tainted the otherwise positive community vibe. I was drunk on power, having had so little of it in my life up until that point.

As a result, I was put in the hot seat again, and unceremoniously stripped of that role within a couple of weeks. In my time at the centre, I had never seen this happen to anyone else. The humiliation was unbearable. I watched as people who had arrived after me—the ones I had talked down to—became my superiors, stripping my bed when the corners weren't folded right.

But in that time, I started to pay attention to how the other senior residents behaved. They led with strength, not control. They led with kindness, not grandiosity. About a month after my eye-opening demotion, my senior role was reinstated, and I never abused that power again. I finally became the kind of leader I could be proud of.

I always had the option of leaving rehab and almost walked out several times. But I didn't. Ultimately, the decision to get sober would change my world in only good ways. In six months, I would emerge a very different person—one who was still wounded but could now see a future. I knew the benefits of talking to people instead of pushing them away. I'd learned to connect with the world instead of with a bottle. I was ready to start a new life.

But despite this early intervention, a lot had happened to me in a very short period of time, and my young brain still had no way to fully interpret it all. The "gun incident," as I called it, could have taken my life, but it also ended up saving it by being the catalyst that sent me to rehab. Nathan, who had caused much of the pain that led me to be in that dangerous situation in the first place, was the one who ultimately stopped another man from killing me. How does a teenager even begin to process that?

This would not be the last time Nathan entered my life in some capacity. Years later, I would find myself facing his chaos again in a different way.

THREE

keeping it all together

SOMETIMES, WHEN WE'RE NOT self-destructing from
the legacy of our pain, we run far and fast from it, hoping to escape
into a new life with no reminders of what we'd once lived through.
The first time I saw this in action was when my childhood friend
Nora repeatedly tried to push me out of her life.

Nora and I had been paired together in fifth grade for a school-
wide assignment, where we had to pick a foreign country, study it
and create a display for an open house to teach others what we
had learned. We were in different classes at school and had never
met before, but we bonded instantly, quickly becoming fixtures
at each other's dinner tables. Nora had come from the most
dysfunctional background I had ever known at the time. She told
me about her life, which included a history of abuse, in bits and
pieces, slowly unburdening herself from the weight of keeping
those secrets. Her friends were a haven for her, as eventually was

her boyfriend, Patrice, who she meet at fifteen. Patrice came from a completely different background and a stable family home. His parents had money, while Nora's mother, as a single parent, struggled to keep the lights on. His life was heavily influenced by his parents, while Nora, in many ways, was a second parent to her three younger siblings. At seventeen, she moved in with Patrice and his parents, finally enjoying a life with a full pantry, a car that didn't break down and adults she could depend on.

When Nora moved out, she cut off all communication with most of her friends, including me. I missed her, but with Patrice's family living in a different part of town, I figured she was busy trying to establish herself there and I didn't take her silence personally. She had supported me through my stint at rehab, and our friendship had survived my changing schools. I'd even moved out on my own before she did, and we had still kept in touch. I had changed a lot since my time in rehab, as had my relationship with my parents. I felt like I had already lived a whole lifetime, and living with my family was no longer a good fit. I left one morning two months after my sixteenth birthday, then spent the first few weeks at a friend's house before moving into downtown Ottawa in hopes of finding more permanent housing.

After about two years of no contact with Nora, I was with my partner and I ran into her and Patrice at the mall. In hindsight, I realize that Nora appeared immediately uncomfortable. She and I were eighteen by then, and I was so thrilled to touch base with one of my best childhood friends again that the vibe she was giving off went right over my head. It never crossed my mind that she might not be as eager as I was to pick right up where we had left off.

"Now that we're basically neighbours again, we should hang out," I stated enthusiastically. "Let's exchange numbers."

This was during the Triassic Period, when people had home phones, and cellphones were only for stockbrokers and other rich guys in movies. I took out a binder from my bag and wrote down my number on a piece of paper, handing it to her.

"Your turn," I said. "I'll write it down here." I tapped my binder.

Nora hesitated, casting a glance at Patrice. "Um, yeah. Okay," she replied, and listed off a number. Patrice returned her look with an odd one of his own.

The next day after school, I called the number she had given me and was greeted by a confused elderly woman who had never heard of Nora or Patrice. Assuming I got the number wrong, I apologized, hung up and tried again. This time, I was met with the more annoyed version of the same woman. Curious, I grabbed the phone book—we used to have those too—and looked up Patrice's last name. I found a number that nearly matched, but not quite. The last two numbers were off by one.

It finally dawned on me that Nora had given me the wrong number on purpose. She didn't want me to call her. The realization stung.

As fate would have it, Nora, Patrice and I ran into each other again at a bus stop a couple of weeks later. I decided to play innocent.

"I think you might have given me the wrong number," I said. "I tried calling it, but it belongs to someone else."

"Oh! That's weird. What number did I give you?" Nora asked sweetly.

I gave her the faulty digits.

She turned to Patrice. "That's our number, right, hon?" She gave him *the eyes*. I know the eyes. They're the ones you give your partner when you need them to lie for you.

There was a pause. Nora stared at Patrice, and Patrice stared back uncomfortably. Eventually, he nodded in agreement.

"Yeah, that's it." He was a terrible liar. It was all over his face.

"Oh," I replied. "I guess I dialed it wrong, then."

The rejection tore into me as I ricocheted between anger and sadness. Nora had once been my best friend. She had punched a girl who beat me up in the face. I had hugged her as she told me about the horrors she'd lived through—things no child should ever have to experience. I just didn't understand why she wanted nothing to do with me. Was it because I was poor, and she wasn't anymore? Was it because she thought she was too good for me? I fought back tears. Ultimately, however, I decided there was no sense in chasing a one-sided relationship.

The following year, Nora and I bumped into each other again at an adult high school where we were both trying to finish up our final few credits. She was always friendly, but often found reasons to be absent during our breaks, or to spend that time with other people. I got pregnant with my first child and dropped out shortly before he was born. Nora never called, of course. I discovered her again on Facebook a few years later and tentatively reached out. She seemed genuinely happy to hear from me at first. *Maybe she's grown*, I thought, *and is through whatever weird phase that was*. That was good, because not having Nora around felt like a hole in my life. She was a good person I knew at a time when there were a lot of bad people around. Couldn't she also be a good person in my life now that things were better? We had several heartfelt chats over many weeks and started talking about getting together in person soon. Our kids could meet each other. We could have coffee. I was very excited to finally reconnect.

Not long after our last exchange, I realized she had unfriended me. When I reached out to ask her why, she apologized and said Patrice or one of her kids must have done it by accident. This seemed like a strange excuse, but I accepted her new friendship request and we resumed our conversations.

When it happened a second time not long after, I gave up entirely. I haven't heard from her since, and I haven't tried to reach out. I should have let that friendship die years before.

Nora, I believe, was trying to shed her old life—a life filled with deep emotional wounds. And I, a reminder of that life, kept pushing my way back in, bringing with me difficult memories and emotions she likely no longer wanted. Nora was probably running. How well? I don't know. But I can't blame her for trying, because I spent a good deal of my life running too.

I was on a trail in Ottawa's Greenbelt a few years ago when someone behind me yelled, "Coming through!" and whizzed past on a mountain bike, upsetting a nest of yellow jacket wasps just ahead of me. When I rounded the corner, I was stung several times. I spent the next couple of minutes running as fast as I could up the trail, slapping the wasps that were still stinging me, and shouting, "Don't go that way! Angry hive!" to anyone I passed. I felt terrible for a solid twenty-four hours afterward, as my immune system fought off the venom. One of the stingers got stuck in my leg and infected it, which resulted in a trip to the doctor's office for removal and a tetanus shot, just in case. Even though this happened on the trail closest to my home and one of my favourites, I didn't visit it again for nearly two years. Every time I thought of doing so, my anxiety would spike. My mind had connected a frightening event to a path I had walked on dozens of times before with no issues, and now I couldn't bring myself to step foot on it.

We are hard-wired to absorb negative experiences more than positive ones. It's a survival trait that has served us well for millennia. If your ancestor nearly drowned trying to cross a river with a strong current, she would remember that incident more than all the times she had crossed in safer conditions. When she had children, one of the first things she would have taught them was not to try to cross the river when the current was strong. They, in turn, would have passed that life-saving knowledge on to their own children. We are all here today because these perilous instances our ancestors lived through became survival lessons.

Unfortunately, our brains are not great at deciphering between avoidance of actual threats and avoidance of the people, places and things we associate with those threats. Avoidance becomes a coping strategy. A soldier who nearly died from a bomb planted in a pickup truck while on duty overseas might be wary of any similar truck back home. A person who was mugged at an ATM might not be able to use another ATM for years. And a person who went through an awful time in childhood might avoid the best friend who saw her through it because of that unfortunate association.

I became a parent at twenty. By that time, the challenging situations I had already dealt with were piled high. In my teen years alone, I had been severely bullied, beaten up, set on fire in front of my school, taken advantage of by men too old for me, raped, held at gunpoint and treated for a substance use disorder. I had moved out at sixteen and hopped from friends' couches to shelters to stairwells to halfway houses, dealing with mistreatment, harassment and violence along the way.

One morning, when I was sixteen and staying at the downtown Ottawa YM/YWCA, a man called my room and told me that he had noticed me, and that he found me "pretty." He called me by name and told me my room number, then claimed he had almost knocked on my door more than once. "I'll work up the nerve to come see you soon enough," the man said. "I hope you'll let me in, Amanda." My blood ran cold as I hung up the phone. I immediately alerted the staff room downstairs and changed floors. I moved out of the shelter less than two weeks later, desperate to find a safer place to live.

Throughout all this period of turmoil, I had also gone to several different high schools and had no diploma to show for it. My life over the past few years had largely been a tumultuous mess.

The bright spot in those difficult few years was meeting Zoë. This is when things began to shift for the better. We met at a party on May 1, 1993. When we locked eyes that night, I knew I had found someone special. I had never had feelings rush through me like that before. I had never known what it was like to see only the person in front of you, tuning out everything and everyone else. It didn't take either of us long to realize we were both head over heels. After all I had gone through, finding this special person was my reward. I had someone who loved me fiercely. It was the start of something fresh—the new life I had been looking for since I left rehab a couple of years before.

On the day our son was born, in November 1996, I looked at his squishy little newborn face and decided I wanted to bring nothing from my old life into this new parenting role. To be there for this child in a healthy way, I concluded, meant shedding as much as possible from my past.

News flash from the future: being a Stepford wife is not necessary or even useful when it comes to parenting. But I didn't know that then. I felt the weight of societal judgment on becoming both a young mom and a bride in the same year. That feeling never went away. Even as I got older, had more children and became more established in the life I had chosen, I still felt like everyone was watching me, just waiting for me to screw up.

When I was twenty-two, I bought a home with my spouse in my hometown of Aylmer, Quebec. I always swore I would never move back there because it held too many bad memories. But the house was adorable and close to family, and the deal was spectacular for first-time homebuyers; we couldn't pass it up. We moved into a brand-new neighbourhood in an area I hadn't frequented when I was younger because at the time there had been nothing there but fields. Having no history with this part of town made me feel safer and allowed me to attach fewer unpleasant recollections to moving back. *I can do this*, I told myself. *I can make a new life here.*

Despite being wildly unpopular as a teen, I did have a small number of high school friends who had always been there for me.

When they got word I had moved back into the area, there was a lot of excitement about getting together and resuming our friendship. Whenever I bumped into one of them while I was out, I would make friendly small talk and promise we would see each other soon.

But I didn't mean it. I found reasons not to hang out and avoided most of them as much as possible. It wasn't because they were bad people. They were, and still are, great people, and I'm in touch with many of them today. They didn't deserve my avoidance. But spending time with them ignited painful memories of a chapter in my life when I had never felt so lost, scared or hopeless. I also worried that any old friends I had might still be connected to people I wanted to stay far away from, like Nathan and Dan—or heaven forbid, gunslinger Matt.

The truth is, my friends had moved beyond our teenage years, but I had not. A part of me was stuck there, and the pain of that time flared up whenever I saw any of them. So I did my best not to. I had switched roles: they were Amanda now, and I was Nora. I was running from the people who reminded me of what I was really trying to run from.

In order to heal, we must sometimes remove from our lives people who aren't good for us. But it's critical to recognize the difference between avoiding something—or someone, or many someones—because it's the healthier option, and doing it because we don't want to face something we probably should be facing. In my early twenties, however, I wasn't self-aware enough to see or understand that difference. I was desperately trying not to confront my demons.

Because guilt would consume me otherwise, I needed a way to justify avoiding these loyal friends. So to protect myself from feeling like an asshole, I became . . . well, kind of an asshole. I knew it was wrong to ghost the people who had been there for me during some of my worst moments; I even knew what it felt like to be on the other side of that ghosting. But rather than figure out what I was doing and work through that discomfort, I told myself I had simply "outgrown" these friends. Of course, we can and do outgrow people from time to time, but this wasn't what was going on; it was just a flimsy excuse. I had been through so much, you see. I had left this town and come back a different person, you see. I was married and had a child now, you see. I was just moving on with my life, and I needed new people who fit that life better, that's all. Nothing personal.

No good comes from comparing our lives to the lives of others, but if you were to hold mine up beside any of theirs, there was nothing about my life at that time that made it different or better. In fact, in many ways, I was worse off. I was both insecure and arrogant. This might sound like an oxymoron, but it isn't. I've often found arrogant people are quite insecure beneath the bravado. When there are parts of ourselves we don't like, some of us will prop up the parts we *do* like—or at least, the parts we believe others will admire—to try to make ourselves feel better. I didn't like my lack of formal education or what I saw in the mirror. But overcoming my teenage challenges, becoming someone's mother and starting a new life of peace and security were things I was proud of. In my mind, I had defied the odds to achieve all of this, and there's no harm in feeling a sense of accomplishment about that. But when that feeling is used as a perch to look down on others, that's when it becomes unhealthy.

Arrogance is an interesting thing. It's an attempt to create a narrative to wrap around ourselves. If you convince yourself you're superior to others, then you can't be *inferior* to them, right? That story becomes your control over the fear of feeling "less than." While the need for control can manifest in many different ways, trauma survivors will sometimes crave it in some fashion because, for a while at least, we didn't have it. Unfortunately, though, arrogance is often the sign of an uncertain ego, and all that acting doesn't protect us from the pain that lies within; you can't escape yourself. In my case, there was plenty of pain. No haughtiness could save me when I was slowly coming apart on the inside. Even while I judged other people's parenting styles and romantic relationships, I was chronically questioning my own. While I proudly boasted of home ownership and financial stability at such a young age, I did it only because I didn't believe I deserved the life I was living. I was behaving in the same way I had before my leadership role was stripped from me in rehab. Some of us need to learn a lesson more than once.

My fear that someone abusive from my past would enter my life through old friends wasn't entirely wrong, however. One day, I got a call from a friend named Kayla. We had been inseparable when we were younger and still tried to keep in touch.

"I wanted to let you know," Kayla said with a hint of hesitancy in her voice, "that I'm seeing Nathan."

ONE SUNNY AFTERNOON ~ 67

"Nathan?" I asked, not quite making the connection.

"Yeah, as in—" she began.

"As in *the* Nathan? Kayla—what?" I was incredulous. Kayla was one of the few people I had confided in about that horrific night with Nathan.

"I know you warned me about him. But that was a long time ago," she continued. "People change. Nathan has changed. He's so nice, Amanda. He has his own business and a kid, and he owns a house. He's really turned his life around. He told me to say hi to you."

It felt as though I had been punched in the gut. This couldn't be happening. There were many things I wanted to say to my friend, and they all began with "run." Run as far and fast as you can away from this man who raped me as a child. Run from this man who felt so little remorse for what he had done that he had the audacity to pass on a greeting. Run from this man who I didn't believe for a second could be trusted. But I knew Kayla well enough to know she wouldn't listen to me once her mind was made up. One of her best traits was a fierce determination, but now that was a problem. Dating Nathan was a choice she had made with the knowledge I had given her about our history—a history she still remembered—and I knew I would not change her mind.

I took a breath, steadying my voice. "Kayla, listen—I can't tell you what to do, but I want you to be careful, okay? Yes, people can change, but there are dark parts some of us just get better at hiding. I think that's what's happening here. I really do."

"That was years ago," she fired back. "You were kids."

I was a kid, I thought. Not both of us.

"I'll always be here for you," I said. "But I can't be around him. I *won't* be around him. If you need a friend, though, you know I'm here."

We ended the call, agreeing to disagree about Nathan's redemption arc. Our friendship felt suspended for a time. For my own wellbeing, I had managed to set a critical boundary, but it involved pushing away someone who mattered to me. Now, I resented Nathan not only for what he had done to me but also for what he had done to this friendship—and what I was all but sure he would do to my friend. Memories of the rape and our bewildering, addiction-fuelled days in his girlfriend's apartment came back to life again. Flashes of miscarrying in a bathroom at the rehab centre, curled up on the floor in tears, and getting lectured by the old man doctor who told me my "promiscuity" might have ruined my fertility forever. Nathan. Dan. Matt. A gun. The man with the car. The look my mom gave me when she saw I was alive.

When trauma isn't healed, it waits by the wall we've built to keep it away from us. When cracks occur—and they always do—the fear and terrible memories come flooding back in. For a couple of days after that call with my childhood friend, I was drowning in them.

It would be many months before I heard from Kayla again. And when I did, she was in tears, asking me to help her move her belongings out of Nathan's house while he was at work. He hadn't changed. He was controlling and abusive, and his rampant drinking only fuelled his rage.

I wouldn't recommend visiting your rapist's house under any circumstances—even years later, and even if he's not there. The stress can be overwhelming. But I was young, and I still had a hard time saying no to people I cared about. Furthermore, I felt like I needed to help my friend. I knew Kayla wouldn't have asked me if she had had any other options. Nathan's erratic behaviour and substance issues had all but cut her off from friends and family. Not everyone understands the radio silence that can come from abuse victims; some take it personally and are reluctant to rekindle that relationship. Kayla might also have been ashamed of getting involved with Nathan in the first place, knowing his history, and didn't want to admit to anyone that he hadn't changed his ways as she had hoped. I didn't ask, and I didn't judge her for it. I had fallen for his smooth talk once too. The Nathan who won over Kayla was likely far more skilled than the one I had met a decade earlier.

As Kayla and I walked through Nathan's house, I took in the chaos that was his life. His bungalow along a busy highway was filthy, with stacks of dishes on the counter that looked weeks old. Bugs crawled in the sink. Empty beer bottles lay everywhere, especially next to the mattress and box spring on the floor in his room. When he got blackout drunk, Kayla told me, Nathan would sometimes piss in corners around the house, which is why it smelled so bad.

This man, who had taken so much from me, was a wreck. I had spent years seeing him as this big, strong entity. But now, in this moment, I knew his reign of terror in my mind was over. I could see him for what he was: someone not to fear but to pity. I felt sorry for him and what his life had become, and I recognized that this was what my life had almost become too. I had been heading down this road myself before I got sober. These surroundings were a sad but powerful reminder of why I needed to keep heading in the direction I was going.

After we loaded the last of Kayla's boxes into the trunk of my car, I looked at Nathan's house and silently said a final goodbye to the man who had haunted the memories of my early life. I wished for him to get the help he needed so he could stop inflicting his pain onto others. I wished for his child to have a good life and not be pulled into this dysfunction. Nathan and I were not so different: we both carried pain. I mostly turned mine inward on myself, and he largely projected his outward onto others. But that pain is what had brought us together all those years ago, and it was the reason I felt empathy for him now.

Trauma keeps us stuck in fear. Again, I wouldn't recommend this unorthodox (and possibly dangerous) healing method, but for me, visiting Nathan's house allowed me to finally say goodbye to the fear surrounding his memory. In return, I was able to recategorize the terrible recollections involving him as "bad things that happened but aren't happening anymore." I would no longer have to relive what he had done to me in flashes of frightening detail. As much as it could be, the nightmare was over.

With this surprising accomplishment under my belt, I was able to start letting more old friends back into my life. I was able to recognize they hadn't caused my past pain and, in fact, had protected me from it as much as they could.

On a smaller scale, I used this same method years later, when I decided to walk the trail where I'd had that intimate moment with a nest full of angry wasps. By pushing past my fear, as uncomfortable as I was, I was able to confront it and rewire how I saw that situation. Yes, I had been stung there, but that didn't mean I was going to be stung every time. There was a lot to enjoy on that trail, and I needed to get out there again and explore it. Memory is an imperfect thing, and sometimes it's good to re-evaluate the stories we tell ourselves.

Recently, curiosity got the better of me, and I looked up Nathan's Facebook page. I will admit that I was surprised to discover he's still alive. I was even more surprised to see that he is now a family man. There were several photos of him posing with his wife and children, everyone smiling widely at the camera. I hope, more than I can put into words here, that these smiles are not an attempt to mask something painful, but a sign that he has finally turned his life around and contributes to the wellbeing of those around him. I don't know how likely that is, given his track record. But it is the hope I have for his family.

By 2006, I had found myself in the place I thought I wanted to be: married with three kids and living in a home on a quiet street. I had grown up with the goal of building a family and blending into society, and those goals had been met. But there were some things about this life that were more in line with what society expected of me than what I actually wanted for myself. Being closeted was taking a toll. I was now thirty years old and still living with the feelings I'd had years ago. My attraction to girls in school had evolved into crushes on women in everyday life. Even though I had everything I was told I should have, these feelings weren't going away.

Every day that I woke up was another day I had to put on a mask: I was Amanda, the suburban woman with a near-perfect life. I couldn't let that mask slip because if I did, that bubble would undoubtedly burst. So instead of admitting how I was feeling inside and doing everything I could to avoid setting fire to the family life I had built, I doubled down on being the best straight wife and mom I could be. I baked cookies for school fundraisers and jokingly complained about my "hubby" with the other moms. I attended ladies' nights and themed book club meetings to discuss what were often very dry books I only skimmed so I could pretend I had read them.

As hard as it was to be someone I felt deeply that I wasn't, there were some bright sides. For one, I loved being a parent more than I could ever have imagined. As the eldest of four siblings, I always viewed having a bunch of kids around as synonymous with family. I couldn't imagine a family without my own children, and the life I had made that reality easier. I also loved my spouse, even though there were clearly some issues going on under the surface for both of us. And many of the friends I socialized with at those book club evenings and ladies' nights were wonderful women who are still in my life today.

When it comes to these friends, a part of me now is glad that a part of me then wasn't more obvious to them—and I'm not talking about my queer identity. There was a darker side to me: an insecure side I wish hadn't been there. My friends appeared so together in comparison, so unbothered by things that certainly bothered me. I was constantly comparing myself unfavourably to others, while they seemed more confident in themselves. I was so unsure about my own feelings and choices that I would worry if my opinion differed from theirs, whereas they didn't seem to mind being challenged. What I found offensive, they often found innocuous—or at least less of a big deal. This was especially true on online forums and Facebook, where I would jump into debates on topics like parenting, vaccination, politics and other hot-button issues. Many of my friends did this too, but they didn't seem to interpret disagreement with their opinion as personal conflict. I did. Whenever someone disagreed with me, I felt attacked. If they did so publicly—and especially if they had a strong argument to counter what I was saying—I believed they were trying to make me look foolish, and instantly disliked them.

"Did you see what Sarah said to me on Facebook?" I might lament to a friend. "She trashed me for saying homemade baby food isn't better than store-bought."

"I don't know if she 'trashed' you," the friend might delicately reply. "I thought she just showed you that there's environmental waste with store-bought containers, and that making puréed baby food in ice cube trays at home solved that problem."

My friend would be correct. Unfortunately, I couldn't see that because fear was clouding my vision. When Sarah proved me wrong in front of my parental peers—the ones I constantly felt I didn't measure up to—it was exactly the same to me as if she were a bully mocking me in the high school cafeteria. Throughout my life, I always felt humiliated and at risk of being ostracized when some-one corrected me. Whether it was at school years ago, at my kids' playgroup last month or on social media that afternoon, it was all the same to me. My brain couldn't tell the difference, so my reaction was no different. I only saw danger. Sarah, the friendly mother of two, was suddenly a threat to me through no fault of her own.

Logically, I knew this didn't make sense. But when my hackles were up, I couldn't think logically. The shift in my thinking would happen so quickly and be so consuming that it blocked out reasoning. Instead, the parts of me that were hurt the most took centre stage. A resentment grew around someone like Sarah, who was simply trying to help me see her side of things, because I couldn't separate her harmless opinion from the harmful ones in my past.

I think it's safe to assume that most of us look back on our younger selves and wince a little at some of the things we said, did or thought. Well, I wince *a lot*. These are not proud moments for me. I was not at my best for years, and people like Sarah were the recipients of that. I would be passive-aggressive after exchanges like this, doing petty things like deliberately "forgetting" to invite the Sarahs in my life to events I was hosting. I doubt they noticed my pettiness, since I generally wouldn't confront them about how I was feeling; I knew I was being mean, and I was embarrassed by it. My insecurities led me to believe that everyone was either with me or against me. Being "against me" was sometimes the result of something that would seem small and meaningless, like a Facebook comment, to everyone but me. I couldn't possibly explain that to anyone else because I didn't even understand it myself. The world was black or white, with no room for nuance. Emotions ruled the day rather than logic. The disparity between my role as a mother and the immaturity with which I viewed far too many situations set me apart from most of my peers.

I've learned that trauma and anxiety can manifest themselves in many ways. At one point, I was pretty sure I had OCD, although I can't say for certain because I was never officially diagnosed. I was too ashamed to talk about it, let alone seek help. But the symptoms were there, and they all revolved around keeping myself and my family safe. I had to get up and check the locks on the doors several times before bed. I needed to inspect our old furnace throughout the day and make sure it wasn't going to overheat, explode or do whatever else I believed it might do. (I didn't know a lot about furnaces.) I checked the stove to make sure it was off, checked it again and then checked it one more time. I sometimes stayed up until two or three in the morning to make sure everything was safe, to convince myself we weren't going to die. This behaviour lasted a couple of years.

But the most debilitating manifestation was the sudden onset of health anxiety disorder, which also has the very clinical-sounding names of hypochondriasis and somatic symptom disorder. It's a form of anxiety that fixates on the idea that you're either gravely ill or will become so if you don't pay close attention to your health. I had never experienced this until a long-awaited pregnancy resulted in miscarriage.

After many irregular menstrual cycles and unsuccessful attempts to get pregnant in my early twenties, I decided to see a doctor about what was going on with my body. He did some blood work and took note of other symptoms—like my weight, an ongoing acne problem and excessive body hair—and diagnosed me with a hormonal condition known as polycystic ovary syndrome, or PCOS. Among other complications, PCOS is known to cause fertility issues, from conceiving to carrying a pregnancy to term. I soon realized how fortunate we had been to have one healthy child, given the odds, and I worried my body would never let us have another.

Eventually, with some medical support, I became pregnant again, and I was over the moon. I knew miscarriage was always a risk, but I was fairly confident that once I became pregnant, my body would take care of the rest. Six weeks in, I was already telling those around us our happy news and pricing out baby furniture. But my excitement was short-lived. The doctor told me that my hormone levels were not climbing as they would expect in a healthy pregnancy, and that we should perform an ultrasound. On the screen, I was shown what looked like an eggshell with nothing inside.

"Unfortunately, you have what we call a blighted ovum," the doctor explained. What an awful term. "A pregnancy began but didn't continue. That can happen for a variety of reasons. Very likely, the fetus wasn't developing properly, or you didn't produce the right levels of hormones to maintain the pregnancy. However, your body hasn't figured this out yet, so it hasn't started the miscarriage process. I'd like for it to happen on its own, if possible. If not, we'll schedule you for a procedure. But let's give you a few days and see what happens."

I left the office in tears. I remained in tears, on and off, for hours more. And not long after, when the bleeding began, I cried again. I mourned the baby that I knew for sure was meant to be. I couldn't understand why my body had produced such a beautiful child four years earlier but couldn't repeat the process. Secondary infertility isn't discussed very often, but it's a heartbreak many families live with.

A piece of me broke the day I found out our baby would never be. This wasn't like the miscarriage I'd had in rehab, which left me sad but relieved. This was a wanted pregnancy that we had been trying to achieve for a few years. But whenever I brought up my loss to medical professionals or some of my friends, I was told that many people have miscarriages, and that it was a good thing it happened early on. I was told I was young, and we could just try again. I was told that at least I had one healthy child, so I should be grateful. I was told that at least there was never a baby in there to begin with.

Well, there had been a baby for me. That phantom baby, who would have arrived in November 2001, was *my* baby, the one I would now never hold or get to see grow up. The loss was profound, but I felt I couldn't share exactly how much it hurt without being dismissed by well-meaning folks who just wanted me to feel better. So I stuffed the sorrow down and tried to move forward in my life. Unfortunately, my mind had learned something and would hold on to it: bad things happen in your body when you least expect them to.

One year later, almost to the day, I became pregnant again. Rather than be elated, I was gripped by fear. Surely this would also end in disaster, right? I couldn't be so lucky as to have another child. That gift was reserved for other people. I had a body that didn't work right. Maybe that doctor who'd chastised me during my teenage miscarriage was right: I had somehow done this to myself. Maybe becoming a mom had just been a stroke of luck. This pregnancy was likely doomed.

Bad things happen in your body when you least expect them to.

I waited and waited for the bleeding to start, checking for it several times a day. I begged my doctor for an early ultrasound, which I thought would make me feel better. It did, for a short while. Seeing my baby at eleven weeks with a strong, beating heart filled me with hope. But then I remembered all the stories I'd heard of people losing pregnancies after the first trimester and became convinced that would happen to me.

Bad things happen in your body when you least expect them to.

When my worst fears didn't happen and I gave birth to a healthy full-term baby in November 2002, I then convinced myself that something would take that baby away from me. Childhood illness was my top concern, and the first few months of that poor child's life were spent seeking reassurance from pediatricians that yes, it was just an ear infection, yes, it was just a cold, and no, there was nothing more sinister going on. Finally, I accepted that our little one might in fact be absolutely fine. With that, the fear should have gone away. Except it didn't. The anxiety over my child's health morphed into anxiety over my own. Because if bad things weren't going to happen in my child's body, they would certainly happen to mine.

Soon, I was convinced I had every kind of cancer, several auto-immune disorders, heart disease and a host of other far rarer medical conditions. I would look up a symptom on the internet, and the internet, of course, would inform me I might be dying. A stuffy nose could be allergies, a cold or sinus cancer. I probably had sinus cancer. If my stomach was upset, I didn't have indigestion, I had stomach cancer. If I was tired, I had a heart issue or multiple sclerosis. I lived in fear every day, checking and rechecking my symptoms, asking for endless reassurance from my spouse, my friends and my doctors. But that reassurance was merely a Band-Aid. It would do for a short while, and then the fear would return. I needed constant reminders that I wasn't dying.

I lived like this for about three years, but I wouldn't call it living. I had created a prison in my own mind, and that's where I remained. I missed out on serenity or any real joy. Instead of getting help from professionals, I once again stayed silent. I didn't want to tell anyone how obsessed I had become with my health because I knew it didn't make logical sense. But as I've mentioned before, a brain in an unwell state doesn't often care about logic. Thoughts of illness tormented me and played out in my mind in terrifying scenarios I couldn't seem to control.

What put this nightmare to an end, at least for a few years, was finding out I was pregnant again. Zoë and I were shocked. I had come to accept that my body would likely never do its part in conceiving another child without significant help, and the stress of fertility treatments didn't seem worth it. We already had two children, after all. But I had always wanted three, and suddenly, it seemed like my dream would come true.

As I stared at the pregnancy test, fear began to overwhelm me. This was a fluke. I would miscarry again. We would be devastated again. This was sure to happen. I was already mapping out how I would handle my grief.

Bad things happen in your body when you least expect them to.

"Enough!" I whispered in the bathroom, surprising myself. Frustrated by my mind's decision to catastrophize what should have been exciting and joyful, I felt an anger rise inside me. I was suddenly resolved to stomp it out. I stared at myself in the mirror above the sink, determination on my face. "That's enough. You're not going to do this to yourself again."

I hadn't enjoyed my previous pregnancy, which I spent so gripped by terror that all I ever thought about was whether my baby was still alive. Anxiety had robbed me of what should have been a special time: what I was sure would be my last pregnancy. And now that I had an unexpected chance at a do-over, I wasn't going to let anything take that away. In that moment, I made myself a promise to enjoy this child growing inside me, whether that experience lasted for nine days or nine months. I would actively choose to be happy. It was an easy decision to make and a harder one to keep, but I was determined not to waste this moment in worry.

While the experience was by no means perfect, it was a significant improvement over the last time I had carried to term. I loved being pregnant—minus the nausea, vomiting, sore back, fatigue and moodiness—and I had far more good days than bad. When the fear set it, I would remind myself I had no control over the situation, only my reaction to it.

Three days past my due date, I gave birth to a healthy baby boy. I now had three children and not a hint of health anxiety.

What I've come to realize is that the type of anxiety I was experiencing around my body isn't really about health at all. Once again, it's about control. I was trying to control situations I had no control over: whether I would miscarry, whether my child would be healthy and whether I would live to watch my children grow up.

Health anxiety is also about distraction. Rather than focus on what was really going on—like all the past trauma I hadn't dealt with, the struggles in our marriage and the pressure I felt to conform to societal norms—I subconsciously directed my attention to something else: my health or the health of one of my children. This put the focus on fabricated what-if scenarios instead of actual problems. In some ways, this was far less scary than dealing with my real issues. I had no idea I was doing this at the time, but it's easy to spot now.

I tried to control the pain inside. I tried to distract myself from it. But it would all come crashing down. You can't outrun your past.

avalanche

EVERYONE HAS SEEN THOSE CARTOONS where a snowball rolls down a hill, getting larger and larger as it collects more snow along the way, until it becomes so big it can take out a house. I've always wondered if a snowball tumbling down a mountain could trigger an avalanche. So I looked it up. As it turns out, it's not very likely, although it could happen under just the right conditions. That is how May 2020 was for me. It was a perfect combination of the right conditions—or the wrong ones, I suppose—to create something terrible.

Life had taken many different turns since our third child came along. I left my job as a part-time personal assistant to become a full-time freelance writer and built a career penning parenting articles for different online and print publications. In February 2014, our middle child came out as transgender. The following year, in July, my partner came out as a trans woman. My social media presence grew as I used it as a tool to advance LGBTQ causes. I mostly put aside the parenting articles and devoted the days and years that followed to advocacy for trans kids and families. By sharing our family story, we wanted to normalize the trans experience for more people.

My memoir, *Love Lives Here*, was an extension of that work. There were aspects of our life that my family and I felt could be discussed only in long form because they required detail, explanation and nuance. Writing that memoir was the work of a lifetime; I poured everything I had into it, making sure to approach the subject of affirming trans loved ones delicately and respectfully. I wrote the past without using my family members' old names, as the practice of "deadnaming" can be disrespectful and even painful for many trans people. With careful gender-neutral wording and a bit of creativity, I still managed to bring readers into the chapters as if they were witnessing events unfold in real time. This took countless hours of careful storytelling. I didn't mind. It was important to me to get it right.

In the end, all that work paid off. *Love Lives Here* was, by any measure, a success. It was published in July 2019 and hit the bestseller list in its first week on sale. It remained there for several more, even reaching number one. It received many accolades and was featured on a number of must-read lists. Even now, I hear nearly every day from readers who say how much our family's story has positively impacted their lives as trans people or helped them in their learning journey to become stronger allies.

This was a dream come true for someone who'd always hoped to publish a book one day. Recently, my sister sent me a screenshot of something I had written on Facebook in 2009, a full ten years before *Love Lives Here*'s publication. It was a list of sixteen hopes and dreams. For number twelve, I wrote: "I want to be a bestselling author one day, although I haven't the slightest idea what I'm going to write about that will be worth reading. I figure it'll come to me someday."

It's wild to read that now. I had no clue that the first book I wrote would be about loving the trans people in my life. By that time, my perspective of the world had changed greatly. Ultimately, the issues I was writing about were far more important than any accolades. The only reason I wanted my book to be a bestseller was so our family's hopeful message—you can come out and be loved, and you can love someone who comes out—would reach as many people as possible. To be frank, though, I didn't expect it would go on to be the success it was. This book about trans people, I surmised, would not gain a foothold in larger society. It probably wasn't sad enough. Tragic stories about marginalized folks were still largely dominating bookstore shelves. How would our happy ending go over? Probably not very well.

Except it did. Our story resonated not only with many members of the trans community but also with plenty of cisgender people who had no personal connection to a trans individual. They just wanted to learn more or be better allies to trans people in general. Through word of mouth, *Love Lives Here* became a book club favourite, especially during Pride Month. I was floored by the attention my memoir received.

I started attending book launches and writers' festivals, and I did more media appearances than I could count, both with and without other family members at my side. (I have always left it up to my individual family members to decide how public they wish to be.) My calendar filled up with speaking engagements, and I found myself travelling more than ever to attend various conferences. In many ways, I was at the height of my career, doing work that felt meaningful. Our little love story was helping to open hearts and minds around the country and even the world. This was more than I could have ever dreamed possible. It was an exciting time—one that should forever be top of mind when I conjure up fond memories.

The entire time I was writing the book, however, I worried what other people would think of what I was doing. Was it really my place, as a parent and partner, to write a story that centred largely around the trans people within our family? They believed so, and gave their blessing and had a big hand in constructing that story to include everyone's viewpoints. But Twitter didn't always agree. Rumblings began even before the book's publication that it was simply not okay for me to be the primary storyteller in this case. I was cisgender and should not be blocking my trans family members from telling their own stories. The first time I read a thread about this, a handful of people were discussing going to my Ottawa book launch to ask me why I wrote a book I had no business writing in the first place. As I scrolled through the upset comments, I felt as though my worst fears about this project were being realized. (They never did show up at the launch, but my stomach was in knots the entire time.)

My biggest fear as an advocate was that I might inadvertently cause harm to the trans community while trying to help. Intention matters, and my intentions were certainly good. But even well-intentioned people can cause harm. What if I took up space where I didn't belong? What if I said the wrong thing and helped set back some of the progress that had been made? These worries would sometimes keep me up at night, both before I agreed to write the book and as it came to fruition. I believe it's always a good idea to take a step back and consider your own voice on an issue and where it belongs. In this case, I ultimately decided that the pros of writing *Love Lives Here*—the effects of providing an affirming blueprint for loved ones of trans people, and the ripples this could have in society's strides toward acceptance—far outweighed any cons. And given all the good the book has done since its publication, I stand by that today. It was a story that needed to be told, and as the writer in the family, I was best positioned to tell it.

But when the book started receiving more attention than I had anticipated, it made my worry grow. Was my voice too loud now? The chatter on social media grew louder to match. Only a handful of people spoke to me about it directly, leaving the occasional upset comment beneath something I had said. But there was a lot of talk *about* me and how I had somehow taken advantage of the community for profit. To some, I was nothing more than a grifter, making a quick buck off the backs of trans people. I was exploiting my family for money, some said, and deliberately taking opportunities away from the trans community. Eventually, a few people argued, I would show my true colours and those who respected my work would be sorely disappointed.

Not only was this idea of who I was in itself upsetting, but it also reopened those old wounds from childhood. In the past, public shaming in school and elsewhere had escalated to violence against me more times than I could count. It had also affected me in subtler ways, leading to avoidance by peers and even complete ostracization. This had in turn led me to feel depressed and even suicidal from all that isolation. I was beginning to feel incredibly alone at that moment.

Social media had always been and continues to be a big part of my work. As a writer, I had to have an online presence. As an activist, even more so. Ideas are shared more widely and connections made more easily through sites like Twitter, Facebook, Instagram and TikTok. I could have a conversation with a politician about inclusive policies or speak directly to an employee of a large corporation about diversity, and the eyes on our conversation would keep the pressure on. I have challenged more than one company for proudly proclaiming inclusion during Pride Month, then quietly donating to anti-LGBTQ groups or political parties the rest of the year.

But being on social media was always more than that. It was, and is, about forming friendships, and I had made and maintained plenty of them over the years using various platforms. The pros of being regularly online had always outweighed the cons.

But now? I wasn't so sure.

Worse still, was that I now had a family to think about. Everything I did and everything people said about me as a public figure affected those I cared about most. I felt a deep responsibility to protect them from much of what was being said. But that was impossible. Our kids were teens and young adults with their own social media accounts. They read everything. While most of the anger was directed toward me, some of it spilled over onto them. My family was greedy, people said. My wife was a pushover who let me hog the spotlight. My kids would inevitably be harmed by the visible work I was doing. I was taking advantage of all of them so I could be famous. I was nothing but a stage mom.

I told my kids to ignore it and did my best to do that too. This is the life of a public figure, I explained. There is always scrutiny, there are always accusations. Some people believe they have the whole picture when all they really have is a view from a singular angle. For these reasons, it's best to ignore inflammatory comments.

But this online chatter was hard to ignore. The anxiety disorder I had lived with all my life only got worse after the book's publication. It felt like I was experiencing more pressure, more community politics, more negativity. It wasn't the criticism itself, but how it was taking place. It felt like personal attacks rather than constructive criticism. It seemed those with the biggest bones to pick with me had no intention of getting in touch for an actual conversation but preferred to talk about me publicly and from a distance. They wouldn't usually tag me into these Twitter discussions, but I would still end up seeing many of them, and the comments were often worse than the original post. Rumblings were getting louder, and my mind was getting louder too.

Love Lives Here was released in July 2019. By September, my doctor had doubled my anti-anxiety medication to the maximum dose. It still barely made a dent; I fought waves of nausea and dealt with heart palpitations every day. And that's because there were other, arguably far more important things going on in my world.

Back in the winter of 2013, as my family was getting ready to sell our home in Gatineau and move across the river to Ottawa, my friend Liliane texted me two long-awaited words: "It's time!"

I was laying tile in the kitchen and immediately dropped everything. "I've got to go. Lil's in labour!" I said to my spouse, and then dashed out the door, car keys in hand and still fighting with my coat. I made my way to the Ottawa General Hospital to welcome a baby into the world.

After a long night of painful contractions, Sophia was born. She had a full head of dark hair and the cutest little feet. She was beautiful—the third child and first daughter for our friends. They'd had a rough go in the parenting department, and Sophia's arrival was the spark of joy they needed. Several years earlier, their eldest son was diagnosed with brain cancer at the age of five. The type he had was rare and extremely aggressive, and it had a bleak outcome. Only 10 percent of children with this cancer are still alive five years after their diagnosis. But he defied the odds. His mother gave birth to his younger brother when he was still in the hospital undergoing radiation. A few years later, they decided to have a third child, and that is how this sweet baby girl came to be.

Sophia's family is, in our minds, a part of our family. They have supported us through each transition and each challenge uncon-ditionally. For this reason, Sophia felt more like my niece than a friend's daughter. The moment I held her, I felt nothing but love.

Sophia was pure sunshine. She loved to dance, play dress-up and give big hugs. Everything she did, she did with style. She was quick-witted and could make you laugh in a heartbeat. Unfortunately, she also had the same genetic mutation as her brother—a hereditary condition only recently discovered. Devastatingly, this resulted in a brain tumour for her as well. Sophia, now a preschooler, fought hard through a twenty-four-hour surgery, countless hits of radiation and numerous rounds of chemotherapy. She was a warrior who never seemed to lose her joy. But eventually, her tumour came back, this time more aggressively, and not even the best medical care could save her.

Grief is a terrible thing to navigate, especially when it involves a child. But during a pandemic, it's even worse. With so many precautions in place, only a few people were able to say goodbye at the palliative care home where Sophia spent her final days. In the few minutes I was able to have with her, I held her tiny hand in mine and whispered to her that she could go when she was ready. I told her all about the day she was born, and how much we all loved her from the beginning. I shared stories from her toddler years, including the time she told me to "get in the garbage" because she was angry with me. As heartbreaking as it was, this was a moment I will always cherish—and one that many people who lost someone they loved were not given at that time. Most were saying goodbye on iPads while nurses held their loved ones' hands.

Hours after I left, Sophia passed away, surrounded by her family. She was seven years old.

May 2020 was a challenging month, filled with sorrow and lost rituals meant to help us make our way through grief. Sophia's funeral could have only five people in attendance. There would be no memorial service until well into the summer, when gathering restrictions lifted enough for it to happen more safely. Lil's family lived on the Quebec side of the Ottawa River and mine lived on the Ontario side. For several weeks, the border was closed, and most cars were turned around on the bridges connecting the two provinces. I felt largely cut off from my friends at their worst time.

Nothing I could personally experience would come close to what Liliane and her family were experiencing. Still, the weight of the pandemic, coupled with these barriers to grief and healing, were taking a serious toll on my own mental health. You know how they say, "It's okay not to be okay"? Well, I was really not okay.

So when I started noticing the hostility toward me and my family online, I didn't know what to do. I barely had the energy to manage what was happening around Sophia's passing, and I couldn't cope with this outrage that had now hit its boiling point. My social media notifications were coming fast and furious, and nearly all of them were about what a bad person I was. I didn't have the strength to challenge much of what was said, even though a lot of it went well beyond criticism of my work and into mischaracterizations and outright lies.

It took me a long time to understand why I felt the need to keep looking at my notifications when I knew they would be filled with ugliness. Why wouldn't I choose to ignore them instead?

Once again, it came down to control. I needed to know what was going on so I could feel some sense of it. Not knowing was worse than knowing, even if what I found out was bad. When I was younger, there were a few times when rumours about me had gotten out of control. By the time I found out about them, they were all over the school: Amanda was a drug dealer or slept with any boy who asked. Amanda was a pervert and would try to seduce any girl who talked to her. These were damaging accusations at the time. What if that happened again, on a much larger scale, and by the time I saw it, it was too late to react? If I found out right away, maybe I could nip it in the bud. I knew I couldn't handle anything more than I already was, and this was my foolish attempt to ensure that.

Rather than get off the internet like I should have, I pleaded for space and time to work through my grief. I openly shared on my social media platforms that my mental health had not been good for several months. I hoped my transparency would be enough to calm the storm, at least temporarily. Instead, my pleas sparked further demands to respond in a way deemed suitable to people who didn't even know me. I was an example of "fragility," some said, unable to handle simple criticism. I was making up excuses to avoid accountability. I was trying to "tone police" marginalized people. Not only was I attempting to hide behind grief, one person stated, but my grief was nothing compared to what trans women go through and I needed to suck it up. I must address this *now*. I must take responsibility *now*.

I couldn't do any of those things. First, it wasn't entirely clear to me what everyone was upset about—it seemed like a multitude of different issues from a multitude of different people. This is often what happens in a social media storm: it creates a snowball effect. This snowball began with me taking up space in trans advocacy and got bigger from there. It was the book. It was the attention the media gave me. It was that I had blocked a few trans people I found to be pretty toxic (to some, it was wrong of me as an advocate to block trans people, as this was seen as making myself unavailable to those I was supposed to be advocating for). Even if I had been in a great headspace to begin with, I wouldn't have had the slightest idea how to address everything coming at me. And the accusations were growing by the hour. Also, addressing issues online is sometimes the last thing you should do—with everyone already upset, words are taken out of context, intent is assumed and the outrage grows.

But now more than ever, this groundswell of discontent wasn't something I could handle. When I saw that the Monday morning explosion wasn't going to end anytime soon, I did the only thing I could think of: I hit the emergency brake and shut down my Twitter account. This decision wasn't taken lightly. Twitter was my largest platform, and the one I did the most advocacy on. I had spent years building up a following that I was proud of. I had made friendships there and had learned a lot from experts I couldn't easily have found elsewhere online. To deactivate Twitter meant losing many connections. But that still seemed preferable to trying to manage the pile-on.

Besides, Twitter was also where I dealt with the vilest comments and personalities, and where trans-exclusionary radicals, fascists and bigots of all kinds ran amok. Nobody can adequately prepare you for what happens when an alt-right personality quote-tweets you to their audience of millions and unleashes several days of hate upon you. I was barely able to handle the influx of intolerance before the book's publication, let alone what was happening now. Twitter had become a toxic place for me, and this was merely the final straw. If the community I was trying to support didn't want me there, it made no sense for me to stay. I put out a tweet sharing where else I could be found online and then deactivated a few hours later.

Unfortunately, leaving Twitter only added fuel to the fire. It wasn't long before users were sharing screenshots of my shutdown account, and this news made a lot of folks angrier. Within minutes, I started hearing from well-meaning friends about more attacks on my character. I was labelled a coward, someone who runs rather than take responsibility. I was called a manipulator and accused of trying to make the people who were only attempting to hold me accountable look like bullies. I was charged with hiding behind the excuse of mental illness. People said that leaving Twitter was my attempt to look like the victim, rather than the person who had victimized others.

I was angry, hurt and scared. After months of feeling worn down by life and coping with responsibility, bigotry, grief and now a huge influx of personal attacks, my emotional armour had worn through. I needed space from the situation, and leaving Twitter was what I'd hoped would do it.

I was wrong.

I deactivated my Twitter account on a Monday. By Tuesday, a friend warned me that screenshots of things I was saying on my personal Facebook page were getting published on Twitter. Some of these posts were set to be visible to "friends only," meaning that one of my "friends" had decided to send my thoughts off to the people publicly criticizing me. One post was about how upset my children were to read what others were saying about me and our family; it was distressing to them to watch us get torn apart by countless strangers. Some of the people on Twitter who were vocal in their opposition to me and my advocacy work were getting publicly shamed and even receiving threats, which some were now blaming on this post I'd made about my kids. I was contacted by a couple of them to say I should release a statement calling for an end to these attacks.

I had never asked for or even alluded to retaliation, and anyone who knows me knows that I don't condone violence, whether physical or verbal. It was also clear to me that a lot of the harassment and threats were coming not from anyone who respected me or even knew me, but from alt-right accounts, bots and anti-trans trolls. They saw an opportunity to do what they do best, which is to try to silence marginalized people, and jumped on it. That had nothing to do with me. Still, I released a statement without hesitation, just to be sure; threats are never okay, no matter who is responsible for them. In the statement, I said the last thing I wanted anyone to do on my behalf was hurt trans people.

By mid-week, I'd started getting hateful Instagram comments and messages, and each morning I would wake up to horrific emails, sent anonymously through my website, telling me, in many creative ways, how I deserved everything I was getting. There might be some people in the world who can handle this continuous stream of vitriol. I was not one of them.

But the internet was right about one thing: I was fragile—just not in the way they assumed—and I was getting more so by the hour. I was a wreck, eating next to nothing and living on broken sleep that felt more like a couple of bad naps strung together. I wanted to get updates from friends about what was happening online and simultaneously felt crushed by everything they had to say when I asked.

"It's bad, Amanda," a fellow parent of a trans kid told me. "It's been days, and half my Twitter feed is still people talking about you." Some more ideas of who I was had begun to emerge. I was wealthy from all the money I had made talking about trans people. My family and I lived a luxurious life because of it. I had exploited the privacy of my trans teen, who could in no way consent to my writing about them so publicly. I was addicted to fame and not willing to share the mic with other activists or even my own family members.

Greedy. Deceitful. Exploitative. Narcissistic. Harmful.

These opinions of me were being shared not only by people within the LGBTQ community but also by activists in other areas who I had never even heard of. It was overwhelming to consider the fallout from all of this. How would this affect my family in the long term? What did this mean for my own future? Did I even have a future?

It's hard to find reasons to keep going when it feels like everybody hates you. There is no safety, no reprieve. I was afraid that if I left the house, I'd face some kind of offline confrontation. I avoided speaking to all but a select few people. Because someone had sent screenshots of my friends-only posts and comments to others, I didn't know who I could trust anymore. Who were my friends? Which ones were just pretending? I had no idea.

If you wait long enough, every storm passes. Somewhere, deep down, I must have still known this. But in the moment, all I could think of was how I was living my worst nightmare all over again.

Everything I thought I had left behind had found me. I was the kid in the schoolyard again, except this yard was a lot bigger and the people in it meaner. My world was collapsing.

See, Amanda? a little voice inside me said. *This is what you've created for yourself. You can never escape it. You will forever be this person everyone hates. Nice going.*

As I was about to be reminded, there is no time more unpredictable or dangerous than when we think there's no way out.

breakdown

IS THIS A BREAKDOWN?

I was almost okay this morning, on this sixth day after leaving Twitter. For the first time since then, there were no hate emails waiting in my inbox. There were no frantic texts from friends trying to warn me of what was said about me overnight online. I thought I might actually have a nice morning. I told Zoë I would try to get outside and maybe do some late-May gardening. It was sunny out there, and it was almost sunny in here too—my head, I mean. Maybe not *sunny*—that's a bit of a stretch—but not stormy either. A little overcast, perhaps? Yes, that's it. Things were overcast. Drying out after a rainy week, if you will.

And then social media happened, of course. I opened up Facebook—the place I'd once thought was safe—and a friend had tagged me in a post accusing me of all the same stuff people were proclaiming on Twitter: I was exploiting my family, keeping opportunities from the trans community and doing it all in the name of my own self-interests. Mocking me. Belittling me. Telling me that I should tell my "PR team" what a bad look this all is for me. And other people were commenting, agreeing with what my supposed friend had written, or saying how surprised and disappointed they were to hear this about me. They hadn't known I was someone who would mistreat trans people like I had, but now they did. I should consider myself no longer welcome in their circles.

Well, I had enough of staying quiet. I commented too.

I asked why these accusations were resurfacing. I said they had been levelled days ago, and I had said everything I needed to say in response, and could everyone just leave me alone for a bit? I'm not well. My mental health is bad. I'm grieving. I really need some space and empathy right now. I've said all this too. Why isn't anyone listening?

Well, that "friend" who had posted didn't listen, and neither did most of their friends. I got piled on again. And after I read about half a dozen replies largely agreeing with the original statement, something . . . snapped. It broke inside of me. I could almost hear it.

And here we are. There's no going back now. The avalanche is coming down the hill at top speed, and all I can do is look up at it.

I think this is a breakdown.

I can recognize it happening, but I can't do anything to stop it. This is now a runaway train, beyond my control. Avalanches. Trains. Circuits. How many metaphors am I going to use to describe what's happening? My mind is throwing them overboard as if it's bailing water out of a sinking boat. Oh, look: another metaphor. They're tumbling out of me now, making room for the ugliness that is quickly filling up that space.

Yes. This is a breakdown.

Speaking of ugly, the ugly bookshelf in the corner of the bedroom holds my attention. I can't stop looking at it. We got it second-hand from friends twenty-five years ago. It consists of cheap pressboard clinging to an increasingly scuffed-up oak veneer. I'd always said I would paint it, but I never did. Now it's too full to paint, straining under the weight of too many books, its individual shelves slightly bowed. Despite its valiant fight against gravity all these years, it could break at any minute.

I'm breaking right now. Everything I'm thinking is dark and hopeless. I'm convinced that things will never get better. This pain will never leave me. I am all the things that have been said about me, and I am everything they said to me at school when I was younger. I am the sum of it all: worthless. My mind has too many thoughts, just like a bookshelf with too many books. I keep staring at that damn piece of furniture, drawing comparisons. The shelf is the ugly wood version of me, isn't it? Uglier, but better than me in the most important ways. What would it think if it knew I didn't like it? Trick question. It wouldn't think anything because it's a bookshelf. But *I* care that people don't like me. I care what they're saying about me and thinking about me and judging me for. I care so much that I don't believe I can do this life thing anymore. And then there's the shelf, perfect in ways I will never be. Despite everything it's weathered over the years, it continues to carry its load. I used to think I was like that too, but I'm not. I'm officially worse than furniture. How about that?

This is a breakdown this is a breakdown this is a breakdown.

That little voice in my head keeps telling me the same thing, over and over. Why is it being so loud? Everything is loud right now. My thoughts of hopelessness and self-loathing are loud and the dog obliviously snoring on the bed is loud and the neighbour mowing his grass is loud and the TV on the wall is loud too. It's as if everything is screaming at me.

"Babe?" my wife says too loudly, even though she's probably being quiet. She's looking at me with her concerned face. She pulls that out only for special occasions. "Are you okay? You don't seem okay to me."

"Yeah, I'm fine," I lie without a second thought, looking at her for a brief moment before going back to staring at the shelf. Imagine if I put one more book on there. A really heavy one. Would the whole thing crash down in front of me? Now *that* would be a metaphor for my life.

"I know this has been hard," she says, "but try not to let it get to you, okay?"

"I'm not letting it get to me," I lie again. Or maybe I'm not lying anymore. See, I had all these horrible feelings about what was going on, and suddenly I don't seem to have any. They're gone. That's surprising, since I've had nothing but big feelings for days. Now I'm numb and calm, as if I've resigned myself to what's awaiting me. The only thing I'm feeling right now is *done*.

This is it, I guess. This is the end of the line for me. This runaway train has met the end of the tracks. The boat is sinking. The circuits are fried. The avalanche has buried me. The shelf is collapsing.

I can't take anymore, and I'm out of metaphors. This pain is never going to stop.

It's never going to stop.

It's never going to stop.

It's. Never. Going. To. Stop.

"I'm going to shower," Zoë says. Her words come at me loudly but also from far away. She's beside me, but I'm also alone. Everything she says is clear to me, but it's also fuzzy like a broken speaker. "Are you sure you're going to be all right?"

Amanda, you're having a breakdown.

"I'm fine, really. You go ahead and shower. See you in a few."

Amanda, you're having a breakdown.

She looks like she doesn't want to leave. She's still wearing her concerned face. She knows me too well and can read every bit of my body language, I'm sure of it. I think I'm smiling at her, but it's not reaching my eyes. I'm just like Marcie after the gun incident and the guy with the car who might have had Band-Aids. But I don't want Zoë to worry, so I need to try harder. *Just go shower,* I try to make my eyes say.

There's nothing you can do anyway. I'm already gone.

Amanda. You need to tell her you're breaking.

I'm the bookshelf, Zoë. See? I've been around forever, and I'll still be here when you get back. I'm strong just like the bookshelf. That's why I'm smiling. I'm smiling at you so you'll always remember me smiling.

If you don't tell her, you're going to do something bad.

"I'll just hang out here and watch TV with the dog," I say, patting the bed. "And try to forget what I just read on Facebook." I laugh a little and it sounds empty. It echoes inside of me because I'm empty too. Zoë gives me a kiss on the cheek and disappears into the bathroom. I can hear the water running.

As soon as she leaves, I start planning how I'm going to kill myself. The bookshelf is still standing tall, mocking me. I feel like the whole world is mocking me. But not for much longer.

I'm having a breakdown, and I'm not going to make it out.

Cars break down sometimes, and depending on who you ask, so do human beings. But when it comes to people, "breakdown" isn't an official medical diagnosis. In fact, there are plenty in the mental health field who wish we would do away with this wording altogether. They don't like it.

I'm not one to resist change, but here's the problem: I have searched high and low since my own breaking point and have yet to find another succinct way to adequately describe the experience. "Mental health crisis" and "state of extreme emotional distress" mostly fit the bill, but not quite. Also, try saying "I experienced a state of extreme emotional distress" ten times fast. It doesn't exactly roll off the tongue.

On the other hand, saying "I had a breakdown" encompasses the totality of that horrific experience perfectly. My mind effectively broke like an engine would; the pieces couldn't work together anymore to keep things running smoothly, and I was no longer able to function. Smoke poured from under the hood, so to speak, leaving me in desperate need of repairs.

The issue, for some, is that the term "breakdown" can be seen as stigmatizing, and I understand why. Advocates have been trying to curb harmful stereotypes of mental illness for years, denouncing the idea that those of us who are unwell are one bad day away from turning into Ted Bundy. To some, the term "breakdown" might imply that we've reached a point of no return, that we've lost ourselves completely and goodness knows what we're capable of now. This idea of us "snapping" is often wielded as a weapon of intolerance against the mentally ill. It's been used as a reason not to trust us, house us, hire us or have us around your children—and sometimes even our own.

Of course, the idea that mentally ill people are more dangerous than everyone else is a bogeyman. Research has repeatedly proven that in the majority of violent crimes, mental illness plays no role. Furthermore, those living with severe mental illness are more likely to be the victims of a violent crime than the rest of society.[1] This has to do, in part, with the situations mentally ill people experience more regularly, such as poverty and housing insecurity. The stigma surrounding our mental health makes us more vulnerable to violence—ironically, one of the very things we're stigmatized for.

The earliest use of the term "nervous breakdown" that I've found is in a medical publication from 1901 entitled *Nervous Breakdown: Its Concomitant Evils: Its Prevention and Cure, a Correct Technique of Living for Brain Workers*. (Side note: "Brain worker" is quite possibly the coolest job title on the planet, and I'm wondering why no one uses it anymore.) Also known throughout the years as an "emotional breakdown" or "mental health breakdown," it's been used to sum up a state of distress so severe as to make everyday life impossible. The ability to function breaks down as the person becomes psychologically overloaded.

This can look a little different depending on who is experiencing this overload, and that's another potential issue: perhaps we're trying to describe too many predicaments with the same words. Is staying home from work for a few days due to mental distress the same as spending that week in the hospital for the same reason? Both examples might be described as a "breakdown," but a person's ability to care for themselves and carry out daily tasks is different. In both instances, a person would likely argue they couldn't function well at all, but one of them could still care for themselves in some capacity, while the other would need around-the-clock care from professionals.

Personally, I don't have an issue with either of these scenarios being described as a breakdown. We don't have to be in an acute crisis to be unable to function in some critical ways, and only we can know how deeply we're suffering at any given moment. Just because someone doesn't need emergency help does not mean they're not experiencing an extremely difficult time.

This and other kinds of gatekeeping for words that don't have a specific meaning anyway can leave many excluded from the support and services they require to get well. If someone wants to call what they experienced a "breakdown" and someone else would prefer another term, let's make room for that. What's most important is that we keep people talking so they can find their way out of the darkness. These moments are extremely challenging, no matter what we choose to call them, and the last thing we should do is make them harder.

———

There was a time not too long ago when my thoughts were mostly happy. I was the sunshine person in the spaces I entered. I brought light into the room. "You're always smiling," one of the trainers at the gym used to tell me. "It's really uplifting whenever I see you."

Knowing that my positivity begot more positivity only fuelled the vibes I was giving off. On those good days and in those moments, I really *was* that happy, and I exuded it freely. Friends came to me when they needed cheering up. They would invite me out knowing I would make them laugh when we were together. When someone tells you they feel better about life after they spend time with you, that's an honour.

I can't imagine feeling that way now. Over the past few days, I crossed a wide bridge of difficult emotions to get to where I am. My happiness turned to distress, anxiety and sadness. It turned to tremors in my hands, sleepless nights, and racing thoughts.

I welcome this nothingness, this numbness. It relieves me from the immense pressure I've been under. It tells me I can stop fighting now and finally rest. It whispers that I don't need to try to keep going anymore. We can put an end to this. Doesn't that feel good to hear? There is a way out. Let me show you.

I make my way out of the bed, knowing this is the last time I will ever lie in it. I get dressed, knowing this is the last time I'll be picking out my clothes. I pet the dog to say goodbye. The kids and I found Blue in a shelter in 2017. He was scrawny and anxious, with what looked like a cigarette burn on the top of his head. But I could tell he just needed a little kindness and security to be the perfect family pet. I love this dog. Blue looks at me, and I know he loves me back. I'm not going away because nobody loves me, I want to tell him. I've just finally accepted what I've been told my entire life: I'm not deserving of that love. I've never been deserving of it. I don't bring people happiness; I bring them anger and disgust. I've heard that message, loud and clear, many times in my life. I'm a terrible person. Now that the veil has been lifted and I see myself the way they see me, I can't continue to live.

I don't have much time. Zoë will be out of the shower soon. I have to act fast. Everywhere I look, there's an idea. A plan is beginning to come together. We have prescription pills in the kitchen. There are also knives. What's easier? Less painful? What will get the job done quickly, so nobody can stop me?

Keep listening.

Maybe hanging myself in the garage would be the best thing. I'm guessing it's not as messy as the other options. I don't know how to do that, but I can look it up. I grab my phone and put it in my pocket; a quick online search will help me figure out how to tie the noose properly and ensure I never wake up. I don't want to end up in a vegetative state for years with worried family members taking turns by my bedside. This is already going to be hard for them. I don't want to make it worse. They don't deserve any of this. They don't deserve a parent this broken, a partner this pathetic, a child this embarrassing, a sibling this weak. They don't deserve a mess when I go either. Yes, doing this will hurt them, but it won't hurt them as much as if I keep living and adding this burden to their lives for years to come.

Remember when you used to be happy? Were you ever happy? Come to think of it, probably not. Hold on to that realization as you walk into the garage. Hold on to it as you look around for what will get the job done. Hold on to it as you figure out how to loop the rope. As you find the stepladder. As you position yourself.

As you say goodbye.

It's going to make it a lot easier if you remember that the goodness you thought was in you is a lie. It makes it better when you see what you will never be able to give to the world because you're nothing but a fraud. They'll be upset that you did this, but they'll understand. They'll forgive you. They'll move on without you. This is best for everyone.

Remember when you used to be happy? That was a fucking lie.

Hello, Amanda. I'm glad you're listening. Let's get this done.

Every forty seconds, someone in the world dies by suicide.[2]

This amounts to 800,000 people a year.[3] On average, 11 people lose their lives to suicide in Canada each day—or 4,000 annually. In the US, those figures are 123 people and 48,300 people, respectively.

Suicide is pervasive. It's the second-leading cause of death worldwide for those aged fifteen to twenty-four, with 45 percent of suicides occurring in middle-aged people.[4] According to the website save.org, a US organization dedicated to suicide prevention, women are twice as likely as men to experience depression and are more likely to have suicidal thoughts. They are also three times more likely to make an attempt on their lives. But actual suicide rates in men are three times higher than in women, in large part because of the more violent methods they employ, such as firearms. (The preferred method for women is poison.)

Yes, these are very unpleasant facts to read. But if we love the people in our lives, they're also important.

We don't like to discuss suicide because for most of us, it's incredibly uncomfortable to even think about. As living beings, we have an innate desire to remain . . . well, *alive*. The will to live is the default for a well-functioning brain, and this instinct drives us to any lengths possible to keep breathing. When someone's default switches to a desire for death, this is an alien concept for most of society. Yet just under 12 percent of Canadians have reported thoughts of suicide.[5] I expect the real number is higher, but stigma prevents us from getting the full picture. Then there are the planners: roughly 34 percent of those who have had thoughts of suicide—also known as "suicidal ideation"—report having made a plan to end their lives.

As someone who falls within these statistics, I will emphatically state that we need the space, safety and understanding to be able to talk about suicidal ideation more openly—because it's not that uncommon. If we crunch the numbers, we will see that there are roughly 1,520,000 Canadians who have reported planning their suicide. This likely means everybody in Canada knows at least one person who has thought so seriously about ending their life that they fit into this statistic. These stats are persistent throughout much of the world. No matter who you are or where you live, you either are someone or know someone who was very close to not being here anymore. You may also know someone who is no longer here. And if that's the case, I'm so sorry.

These are the reasons we need to get more comfortable having uncomfortable discussions. Because behind all these suicide stats are real people who lost their lives and left grief in their wake. What could they have done with more time? What would having them still here mean to those who loved them?

It will take empathy from all of us to have these conversations, and I believe that empathy is largely built through listening to personal stories and finding ways to relate to them. This is why I'm telling mine, as hard as it is to tell.

Just go left.

I'm standing in the main-floor hallway, which has become my proverbial fork in the road. If I go left, I'll find the door to the garage. But if I go straight, I'll get to the front door instead.

Get it all over with. Go left.

I want to go left. My mind is screaming at me to go left. I can end the pain right now and never have to worry about anything again. It won't matter what people think about me anymore because I won't be around to hear it. It won't matter what they say about me because their opinions will be about a dead person who can't read their words. I won't be a problem or an embarrassment for my family anymore. I will no longer take up space in this world, and the world will be better for it.

All you have to do is go left, Amanda. The garage is right there.

But for some reason, as sure as I seem to be that this is the right decision, I can't move from this spot. I keep staring at the front door a few feet away. What if I go that way instead? What if I grab my keys and jump in the car? What if I go to the hospital and ask for help? Would that even do anything? Would that help? Would I want it to?

I'm suddenly reminded that this is an option. I have been the support person to family, friends and even strangers in crisis before. I have gone to the hospital with them and helped them get care. Why have I not thought of this for myself until just now?

Maybe my brain is lying to me when it tells me I want to die. Maybe I'm listening to something that doesn't make sense. Maybe I'm . . . sick. Maybe—

GO LEFT, DAMMIT! WHY ARE YOU DOING THIS TO YOURSELF, YOU STUPID PIECE OF SHIT?! GO TO THE GARAGE AND DO WHAT YOU WERE GOING TO DO!

No.

I need to go straight. I need to get to the car. Right now.

Before I can think about it anymore, my feet are moving toward the front door. I'm almost there. But that's when I remember I have to pass by the kitchen first. The kitchen that holds pills and knives. The kitchen that has other perfectly good means to do what my brain wants me to do. The kitchen that is only a few steps ahead of me now. I start to reconsider heading for the car. Maybe I should just give in. The urge to do something I can't take back is strong, much stronger than me.

JUST DO IT, YOU WASTE OF SKIN! YOU DON'T DESERVE TO LIVE.

I darken the kitchen doorway now. I'm about to enter. But there are people there. My people. Two of my children. Seeing this stops me in my tracks.

"Good morning, Mom!" one of them says as I stand in the doorway, frozen. She's cooking brunch while her brother hovers nearby, chatting with her. There's music playing on the Bluetooth

speaker. The sun is shining warmly through the window, bounc-
ing off the bright white cupboards. It's a happy scene.

Remember when you used to be happy?

WHAT ARE YOU DOING? STOP IT.

"Good morning," I reply robotically from the doorway.

I can't do anything while they're here. That wouldn't be right.
And suddenly, I'm reminded of why I maybe shouldn't do anything at all. What am I thinking? These kids need me.

I keep going to the front door, knowing I can't stop again for
my own safety. I grab my keys and handbag. I slip on my shoes. I
feel rushed to leave this house, like something bad will happen if
I don't. Because something bad *will* happen if I don't.

"I'm just going for a drive," I say quickly. And before anyone
can ask me where I'm going or if they can come, I'm out the door.
I'm in the car. I'm pulling out of the driveway. I'm making my way
down the road.

I have just decided, however precariously, to live.

on a fine spring day in may

THE DRIVE THAT MORNING was both literally and prover-
bially bumpy. It's a straightforward route from our house to the
Queensway Carleton Hospital in Ottawa's west end—one long
stretch of road that requires little thought, except for the spring
potholes. Normally, I would weave my way around them like a race
car driver, slightly annoyed at having to do so while simultaneously enjoying the challenge. But this drive was different. I didn't
even see most of the potholes and would realize I had hit one only
when the whole SUV bounced. My muddled mind was focused on
one task: getting to the hospital. I had to get to the hospital.

No stops.

No detours.

No second thoughts.

I remember repeating the words "No, I am not crashing the
car—I am going to the hospital" out loud to myself to fight back

the intrusive thoughts inside my head. It seems surreal and overly dramatic that I would need to say something like this, but break-downs are not exactly times of logical thinking or doing.

In hindsight, I probably should have asked my wife to drive me, or maybe called 911. But I didn't like the thought of an ambu-lance showing up and scaring my kids. And with Zoë in the shower and my brain screaming at me to find a quiet spot in the garage, I felt like getting help as soon as possible was the best option. I knew the route to the hospital well and it wasn't far. I could do this, I told myself. And miraculously, I did. I pulled into the park-ing lot, turned off the engine and took a few deep breaths before making my way toward the building.

The front doors of the emergency department looked different than the last time I was there. As per provincial COVID protocols, tape strips had been placed six feet apart on the sidewalk outside the automatic doors. I stood in line behind two other people, who themselves were behind three more people standing inside the double doors.

In the warm spring air, I planted my feet firmly on the tape and tried to drown out the noise in my head. These legs weren't going anywhere. I had come this far, and I was going to make it inside the doors. Eventually, the line moved. I walked a few steps forward. A few minutes later, the line moved again, and the doors opened. I shuffled inside. A large sign stood in front of me, ask-ing me to tell the clerk if I had any known COVID-19 symptoms. Another advised me to wear a mask at all times.

An elderly man and his wife were at the desk in front of me, explaining his health concerns and accompanying disabilities. He was deaf, visually impaired and had dementia. His wife explained he would need extra support to navigate this hospital visit. Normally, to give them privacy, I would have tuned out their chat with the receptionist by using my phone. But my phone terrified me at the moment; I was afraid to even take it out of my bag. What would I see? Would there be a fresh batch of personal attacks on Facebook? More hate mail, perhaps? I wasn't ready to touch anything with an internet connection. Instead, I fidgeted with my empty hands and stared intently at the COVID-19 sign, reading off the symptoms, over and over: cough, fever, headache, nausea . . .

"Next, please!" a slightly muffled voice called from behind the plexiglass. The elderly man before me was walking into the waiting room while his wife made her way back outside. Despite his myriad of health issues, she wasn't allowed to remain with him due to current restrictions. He looked back, slightly worried. My heart hurt for both of them. Even though I didn't have much empathy for myself at the moment, I apparently still had some for others.

The receptionist took down my information, squinting as I held my health card up against the plexiglass for her to read. She pulled up my file. "Reason for your visit?" she asked.

I paused before answering.

There were two more people behind me now, in this small reception space between the sets of double doors. Two people who could hear every word.

"I'm here because—" I began, before my brain chimed in, for the umpteenth time, to tell me that I was needlessly taking up space in this ER and should just go home.

Hey, brain? Fuck off for five seconds, will you?

I took a deep breath.

"I'm here because I'm a danger to myself right now."

Just like that, the receptionist's automatic nature changed. Her voice softened. Her eyes looked kindly into mine. "Okay," she said. "That's okay. I understand. I'm glad you're here."

She handed me a bracelet with blue on it, to indicate what part of the waiting room I should sit in. "Put this on, switch your mask with this fresh one and go take a seat. They'll help you really soon, I promise."

"Thank you," I replied, knowing full well the people behind me had heard my reason for seeking help today. I didn't care anymore. I *couldn't* care anymore. I was busy trying to save my life.

Hello, and welcome back to where we were at the beginning of this story. I told you we would get here again.

As I sat in the waiting room with half its plastic chairs taped off to aid with social distancing, I knew I had just made an active decision to live. I had no idea what that entailed exactly, but I understood that I needed to stick by it. It would probably have been easier to stop living—easier for me, anyway—but I had chosen to keep going, at least for now.

"Amanda?" a triage nurse called. I don't remember what her name was, but I'm going to call her Amelia because I have never met an Amelia I didn't like.

Amelia was around the same age as me, with a fair complexion and kind eyes with plenty of laugh lines. I couldn't say what the rest of her face looked like because like everyone else, she was wearing a mask over half of it, and on top of that was a plastic face shield. But I will never forget those eyes. She sat at a desk across from me, reading over what was on the computer screen in front of her. Amelia knew why I was there, no doubt; she would have scanned my chart before she even called my name. I watched her carefully for signs of judgment and thankfully found none.

There are many ways someone can respond to a suicidal person. In my opinion, the best way is with compassion. But some will take a more standoffish approach, often in the name of professionalism—a "show no emotion" stance. I received this icy treatment once when my parents took me to the children's hospital late one night to meet with a psychiatrist during those terrible early teen years before I went to rehab. The psychiatrist was cold in her behaviour and watched me in a calculated way, as if I were a rat in a maze rather than a teenager in crisis. This left me hesitant to open up to her. How can anyone feel safe with someone who demonstrates no empathy? I can say it is the least helpful way to be around me when I'm in crisis. I need an actual human being, not a robot. I need someone calm but with feelings. I need someone who demonstrates empathy at the worst times of my life. Amelia was that someone for me. As I sat there with a blood pressure cuff on my arm, she asked me if I could tell her what brought me to the hospital.

"I think I'm having an actual breakdown," I said. "I don't know how else to put it. I just snapped under pressure, and I'm suicidal right now. I can't believe I'm even saying that out loud." I paused before continuing. "I almost killed myself less than an hour ago. My options were to come here or to go through with it, so I decided to come here. I still don't know why I made that choice, to be honest."

"You made a good decision," Amelia replied. "This is the right place for you to be."

"I had it all planned out. I knew exactly how I was going to do it," I said. "I feel like I'm coming out of a haze or something, like I haven't been myself for a while. Being here makes it all so real." I suddenly felt overwhelmed and began to cry. The numbness was melting away.

"It's okay," Amelia said, placing her gloved hand on my arm. "You're going to be okay."

"Do you want to know what the worst part is?" I asked and lowered my voice in the hopes no one else would hear me. "I'm a mental health advocate. I'm a *mental health advocate*, and I'm here because I'm suicidal. Can you believe that? I feel like a complete failure." Tears ran down my cheeks and onto my paper mask.

"You are *not* a failure," Amelia said to me, her eyes meeting mine. "You're doing for yourself what you would probably tell someone else to do in your position, right? You're demonstrating what people need to do when they're in crisis. That's part of advocating, isn't it?"

"That's true," I conceded.

"And look—because you made this choice, you're still going to be around to help more people. It's going to make a difference to others that you went through this. But right now, you need to take care of yourself—just you and only you. So let's get you back into the waiting room so you can see a doctor, okay?"

"Okay," I replied, getting up from the desk. "Thank you."

"You're welcome. And, Amanda," Amelia said as I was about to leave her cubicle, "I'm really glad you're here. I am."

I would have hugged her if I could. It was her kindness that pushed the self-destructive voice out of my head and kept me in the waiting room that day. I stayed because she reminded me I was worth staying for.

Amelia with the kind eyes. An actual hero.

I don't remember how long I sat in the waiting room, but I do remember spending a lot of time looking outside. It was a beautiful day, the kind Ottawans wait months for. By November in this part of the world, the leaves have fallen and garden flowers have perished in the frost, and residents know we have nothing but snow and bare branches to look forward to until April. By May, we're eager to get back outside into the warmth and greenery. What were other people doing while I sat here, miserable, in this sterile waiting room? Were they taking out their patio furniture? Raking leftover leaves from autumn? Planting flowers on their balconies? If I went to Facebook right now—and I certainly wasn't going to do that—I would undoubtedly see a flurry of smiling selfies as friends enjoyed the sunshine. The juxtaposition between what was undoubtedly a perfect Saturday for many and a terrible one for me was weirdly fascinating.

I had decided to live. But for what? My family, certainly. But beyond that, I hadn't the faintest idea yet. I couldn't think past this moment; everything on the other side of it still felt hopeless. What would I return to after I left the hospital? I had spent my life running from rejection. I had spent years trying to fit in and had

just been shown, by way of countless angry comments and messages, that I would always be an outsider. I was still the same kid
trying to escape the same pain, except I was now forty-three years
old and should have been beyond that. What a failure that was.
What a failure *I* was. I couldn't even begin to reconcile it.

So I didn't try. I just stayed in the moment. One thing I've
known throughout my life is that the mind doesn't always tell us
the truth when it's sick. My perception of events might be completely skewed, and I would have no idea. In the past, anxiety had
convinced me I was dying on many occasions, while depression
had left me feeling alone even when surrounded by people who
loved and cared about me. I couldn't know if I was seeing things
clearly, but I had a suspicion I wasn't. I tried to drown out all
these thoughts—the ones that highlighted words such as "failure"
and "disappointment"—and just focus on the moment at hand.
What did I need to tell the doctor? How could I advocate for
myself right now?

I'm a big believer in having a medical advocate with you in
times of crisis. When we're in pain, be it physical or emotional,
we are vulnerable and not in the best place to relay information. It
can be easy to forget something important or not get our concerns
across clearly. Having someone to push more assertively for the
medical care we need or to ask the questions we might forget is
paramount in those times. Normally, I would have asked Zoë to
come with me—she's always clear-headed and with my best interests in mind. But the pandemic prevented that option. Even the
man who had come in just before me wasn't allowed to have his
wife accompany him. We were both on our own in here, which

was far more worrisome for him than it was for me. Still, I had to
ensure I got what I needed by fighting for it if necessary.

The emergency department waiting room was quiet for a Saturday.
I assumed the pandemic was the cause. Who wants to go to a hospital during an outbreak unless they absolutely have to? It took
less time than expected to be shown to an examination room. It
was your standard fare—uninspiring room with a couple of chairs,
an exam table and a counter with a sink. A nurse came by to ask
how I was feeling and let me know the doctor would be in soon.

I'm going to call him Dr. Friendly because when he entered
the room, that's what he immediately was. Young, compassionate
and genuine, he sat on the edge of the exam table, and I stayed in
my plastic chair against the wall. I was getting quite used to plastic
chairs by that point.

I didn't hold back with Dr. Friendly. I told him I was suicidal. I told him I had been minutes away from not being here
today, and I still didn't quite know if I had made the right decision because I couldn't see a way through this yet. But I also said
I was determined to get out of this because I had a family who
loved and needed me.

"Was there a specific event that brought all this on?"
Dr. Friendly asked.

I gave him a rundown of everything that had happened, from
Sophia's recent passing to today's tag on Facebook. He shook his
head in disbelief.

"That alone is enough to cause severe distress," he said. "But
I'm curious if there's anything in your past that could also have

contributed to how you're feeling right now. Does this remind you of something from before?"

Smart doctor.

I told him that on top of other traumatic events, I had been relentlessly bullied when I was younger, then I shared some key experiences, including times when I had been beaten up and the day I was set on fire in front of my school. I said that, yes, years of persistent harassment from my peers had caused a wound that opened back up again when the online bullying occurred. All those painful childhood memories, compounded by grief over Sophia, had left me particularly vulnerable. It's not that I couldn't put the pieces together—I just didn't know the significance of the finished puzzle.

Dr. Friendly sat silently for a moment, thinking about what I had said.

"Amanda," he began gently, "has anyone ever discussed PTSD with you?"

"Sort of," I replied. "I've just started learning about complex PTSD and how it can affect people in some research I was doing for work. To be honest, I wouldn't be surprised if that's what I'm dealing with."

"I would be inclined to agree," Dr. Friendly said. "You probably do have some kind of trauma disorder, and I think you need to get the right help for it. So let's figure out how we can help you."

And with those words, Dr. Friendly changed my life for the better.

Has anyone ever discussed PTSD with you?

At a moment when I felt I had nothing to live for, that question was hope with a giant bow on it. It presented a possibility: that something big going on inside of me had been overlooked and was causing me so much pain. And that maybe, with the right diagnosis and treatment plan, I could see my way out of this crisis and into better days—whatever those might look like. I had a hard time believing that things could get better, but it was worth a try. Possibility could keep me going for now. Everyone needs the promise of a light in the darkness, and this hope of a diagnosis and treatment was mine. Maybe, if I followed it closely, I would find my way. I knew I couldn't keep living the way I had been, but perhaps I could keep living if things were different.

I had come to the hospital to ask the doctor to admit me because I didn't trust myself. I still had that option if I wanted it, Dr. Friendly explained, but it wasn't going to be imposed on me at this point. After chatting with me for a while, he felt it was safe to give me the choice, rather than make it for me. We worked through the pros and cons of staying at the hospital or going home. There was a mental health bed available, and I could be assessed by a psychiatric team while admitted. However, Dr. Friendly also said that he believed I was sound of mind enough to go home, and that it seemed to him I had a great support system there.

He wasn't wrong. When I was in the waiting room, I had fired off a quick text to my wife. "Hey, just want you to know I'm safe. I went to the hospital to ask for help. I'm really not okay, so it's best if I'm here. I love you."

Her reply came quickly: "I figured that's where you went. I'm glad you're there. I love you too, and I know you're going to get through this. You're strong as hell. I'm here for anything you need."

Zoë is my most important support person. We have been married for over a quarter of a century, which is a very long time to get to know and trust someone. But thankfully for her, she's only part of a larger support team because I can be *a lot* sometimes. I mean, can't we all? My friends and extended family always seem to show up when I need them most. Even my kids have seen me through bad days in some ways, just as I've seen them through theirs. Children give us an extra reason to get up in the morning and try a little harder. When I felt completely alone a few hours before, why hadn't I remembered how much love I have in my life? The unwell mind can lie, and it can conceal. I could see it now. The truth had been filtered through a distorted lens, creating a false and dangerous reality. It can tell us we don't have anything to live for when we really have so much. It can tell us we are unlovable when we are anything but.

"Whether you stay at the hospital or not is entirely up to you," Dr. Friendly stated. "You seem pretty self-aware, and I think you'll be able to decide what's best for you. I'm not going to hold you here, but I'm also not going to push you out the door. If you stay, you'll see the team at some point tomorrow. If you decide to go home, I can set you up with an outpatient psychiatrist and put a rush on it. It might still take a few days, mind you, so that's the downside."

I thought about it, and I thought about it some more. Staying at the hospital felt safe in a way. But going home to my wife and kids, who I suddenly missed and needed hugs from more than anything, felt safe in a different way. If I was honest with my family and asked for their support, home—familiar and comfortable—might be the best place for me. I no longer felt like an immediate danger to myself, so I opted to go home to the people who loved me.

The doctor helped me draft a quick safety plan for home. What would I do if I found myself in crisis again? Who would I talk to? When would I know it was time to return to the hospital? Safety plans are paramount for many of us with thoughts of suicide. According to the Centre for Suicide Prevention, a safety plan is "a document that supports and guides someone when they are experiencing thoughts of suicide, to help them avoid a state of intense suicidal crisis." The plan can contain many pieces of information, including warning signs, coping strategies, reliable support people to lean on and a list of reasons to keep going. It's made with the help of a trusted person, whether a professional or loved one. What Dr. Friendly and I came up with at the hospital was rudimentary at best. Whenever possible, these plans should not be created in crisis. I was just on the other side of nearly taking my life, so it was not the best time to pick my brain for details; it was worn out. Still, the doctor wanted to make sure I had everything I needed when I left. And you know what? I did. I had a compassionate response to my crisis, a plan I could implement if I started to feel I was a danger to myself again and incoming help from a psychiatrist.

I could do this—maybe. With a hint of hesitancy, I thanked the doctor, waved to Amelia the triage nurse and made my way out the double doors.

Here goes nothing.

—

It was one sunny afternoon as I left the hospital. I saw two robins hopping around on the grass, looking for a meal. I could hear two people laughing on a bench behind me as they engaged in conversation. An ambulance pulled away gently, its lights off. Just an ordinary sunny afternoon for everyone and everything around me. I could sense it, but I couldn't make sense of it. How could everything be the same when *I* wasn't the same? It felt like I was experiencing a deep level of suffering to which everyone else around me was oblivious. I pondered this in my blurry mind as I made my way back to the car.

My phone rang.

I didn't recognize the number, and it was from out of province. *Probably a scam call*, I thought to myself. But something told me to answer it anyway. I'm glad I did.

It was Marie, a trans woman I had met in person only a couple of times through our mutual advocacy work. Marie was an incredible person. She had tackled several large advocacy projects over the past few years and had broken some glass ceilings once thought impossible for trans women. I had always admired her. We got along well—we had even met for drinks the last time I was in her city—but she had never called me before. What a time to do so now. When I answered, however, she told me that was exactly why she was calling.

"I've been watching what's happened to you this week," Marie said. "I wanted to make sure you were okay."

Oh, Marie, you couldn't have asked me at a much worse moment, I wanted to say, but I didn't. I didn't want to stir up more drama. Goodness knows there had already been enough. I just wanted it all to go away, and yet it kept finding me. What should I say? I thought about telling her everything was fine but guessed she would hear the lie in my voice. I knew I sounded tired and weak, a far cry from the loud and outgoing person she'd met before. At this point, I figured, honesty remained the best policy. Besides, it's not like I had anything left to lose. This was my bottom, and Marie had just happened to call shortly after I hit it.

"Well, I just left the hospital," I told her. "So I'm not great." My voice shook.

Don't cry, don't cry, don't cry.

I cried.

There was a pause on the other end of the line. For a second, I imagined Marie rolling her eyes and telling me that I deserved to feel this terrible after what I had done. Instead, she said softly, "I'm so sorry, Amanda." Her empathy broke me. I started crying even harder in the parking lot, on the strip of grass in front of my SUV. Cars drove by as the tears flowed, but I was beyond caring about what people thought. Hell, I had spent the entire week caring about what others thought of me, and that had led me here. It was not lost on me, either, that big conversations in my life seemed to happen in parking lots lately. A few years earlier, my wife and I had our pivotal chat about her being trans in a Walmart parking lot as the rain rolled down the windshield. It was the most unremarkable suburban setting for a most remarkable conversation. Now I was standing in another parking lot talking to a different trans woman about another pivotal moment. Life had a funny way of repeating itself.

"I'm sorry," I said between sobs, trying to compose myself. "It's just been a really long few days. I'm pretty worn out."

"Of course you are," Marie agreed gently. "To be honest, I'm not surprised you ended up in the hospital. But I'm glad you're safe. You *are* safe, right? Did you hurt yourself?"

"No. Almost," I confided. "Marie, I got so close. *So* close. I never thought I would feel this way again. I can't believe I'm here."

"I can," she said. "Would it surprise you to know I've been there? I've had something similar happen to me a couple of times, where parts of my own community turned against me. When it's happening, it feels like the whole world is against you."

"They all hate me," I whispered.

"No, they don't," Marie stated. "They don't all hate you. It just feels that way. Look, I'm calling you, aren't I? I'm a member of the community, aren't I? It's a small group of people, really. Some are just very loud in their disagreement, and the loud ones get heard. They're upset, and this is social media, so things got out of control. You know how it goes. I bet half the people saying things right now don't even know who you are—they're just seeing an opportunity to troll. But listen, a lot of people appreciate what you do, even if they're scared to say it publicly right now."

I understood that. When someone is getting heavily criticized online, it can be hard to stand up for them, even if you support them wholeheartedly. Nobody wants to be the next target, and that can quickly become the case. Goodness knows I had stayed quiet at times in the past when this exact thing was happening to someone else.

We talked for over an hour. Marie shared times when other LGBTQ people had been upset with something she had said or done, and she told me how that had impacted her and how she had learned to deal with it over time. "It's an inevitability in this work," she said. "You have to learn to expect it." She told me about being in the dark place I was in now, and how she got out of it. She strongly encouraged rest, time off and good therapy. By the end of the conversation, my tears were mostly used up, and I had even managed to laugh a few times, however weakly. I will never forget that conversation; everything about it was impactful, from the timing of it to the words that were spoken.

"The thing you have to remember," Marie imparted before we ended our call, "is that you're never going to make everyone happy. Nobody can—not even you. If there was any constructive criticism in what was said, take that with you and leave the rest. There will be a lot that isn't worth holding on to."

That was certainly true. But for now, hope was what I needed to hold on to most. That was what would get me through the next few hours and days until I could see the psychiatrist. I also had a lot to think about in terms of immediate next steps. I was about to go home to my family after many hours in the emergency department. What would I tell them? What would I say to my children? There is no manual for this. Thankfully, I had a bit of time to mull things over as I dodged potholes on the drive home.

In a welcome turn of events, my brain didn't yell at me once.

Zoë was waiting for me when I got home. She wrapped her arms around me and held me tightly. I could feel the tension in my body start to release. We often talk about how much our minds are impacted by heightened anxiety, but less often about our bodies. Our bodies hold on to stress. The nervous system, when activated, tightens our muscles to prime them for use. If our ancestors encountered a great cave bear—yes, that was a real animal—they needed their muscles ready to escape or fight. Our nervous and cardiovascular systems react in the same way to other kinds of stress, including the acute emotional kind. One of the ways to release some of that stress naturally and begin to regulate our primitive system again is to get a good long hug. According to current science, twenty seconds or so should do it.[1]

Zoë held me for longer than that, I'm sure. It felt like she might never let me go. I'm immeasurably grateful to have someone who loves me this much, and who takes care of me when I'm not able to care for myself. When she came out to me, those who knew us put a lot of emphasis on how supportive I was of her. I understand why, since many partners don't stay in the relationship when the other one transitions, and even some of the ones who do stay aren't always kind. But Zoë shows up for me too, even more so since the burden of living in the closet is behind her now. And in this moment, she was my rock.

"What do you need from me?" she asked as she made me an herbal tea. Rather than assume, she likes to ask me this question when I'm hurting. It's a kindness I appreciate.

"I need to not be alone right now," I said. "But I'm really tired and have to rest. I might take an edible and curl up in bed. Would you watch TV with me? And maybe just let the kids know I'm not feeling well and I'll talk to them tomorrow?"

I rarely get high. My asthma doesn't play well with smoke or even vapour, and edibles often surprise me with how little or how much they kick in. Also, given my history of addiction, I like being in control of my body most of the time. After twenty-five years of sobriety, I made the decision, with the help of trusted health professionals, to try to drink socially again. Getting sober at fourteen and staying that way for many years was the best thing I could have done. But drugs and alcohol were my only somewhat effective coping mechanisms back then, and I had plenty of better ones now, including being able to communicate my feelings and ask for help when I needed it. As it turned out, I generally preferred being sober. I drink only occasionally—a beverage or two every couple of months at most. It was nice to have the option to enjoy a glass of wine with dinner every now and then.

Right now, however, my body was out of control with anxiety, and it urgently needed to relax. So I decided this was a good time to try one of the gummies a friend had given us a few weeks earlier. I took half of one. And when that didn't work after a little while, I took the other half.

Pro tip for my future self: Never take the other half when you think you should. *Wait longer.*

Not long after, the THC hit me like a bullet train. I felt *mellow.* Zoë was playing an episode of the animated series *Rick and Morty* that I had never seen before, but I was so stoned that I couldn't even open my eyes to watch it. That was fine, though, since my brain had decided to create its own animation to go along with the audio I was hearing. Every scene came to life in my head. I discovered later, upon rewatching that episode, that what I had imagined turned out to be far more colourful than the original.

At some point, I drifted off to sleep, then stayed that way for over twelve hours. It was peaceful and uneventful. After several days of exhaustion, this was the rest I needed.

The next day, I thought a lot about what to tell our kids. When your children are little, you can protect them from the harsher realities of the world. But at the time, ours ranged in age from thirteen to twenty-two, and they had just watched my reputation go up in flames online. They stayed on Twitter after I deactivated, reading things I wish they hadn't, and they had been hurt and angry on my behalf for days. Meanwhile, they had also seen me become a shell of the person I usually was. Being a parent means always having to think of others, even during your worst times, and I was worried about whether my kids were okay. In many ways, I was more upset for them than I was for me. My job was to protect them, and it felt like I had failed in that department. I still wonder to this day how seeing what gets written about me impacts them. I can only imagine how it would feel to read those things about my own mom.

Now this situation had nearly driven me to suicide. How would I even begin to approach that with them?

After a chat with Zoë, the hard answer became the only good one: be honest.

There are times when it's best not to tell your children the truth; maybe they don't need to know all the reasons for their parents' divorce, for example. But in my opinion, those instances are rare. It's especially important to be honest when we're discussing mental health. There is plenty of evidence to show that mental illness can be multigenerational, which is why health professionals will ask if there is a history of it in the family. In my family's case, mental illness is a part of our story. I know my biological father had some demons he was fighting, and multiple generations on my mother's side have a history of anxiety, among other things. Because of this, my children have a greater chance of experiencing the same types of struggles I have, and my silence won't make that any less likely. Why hide this from them when I could use it as a teaching tool? But I had to be ready because I wanted to say the right things—the things that could help them in the long run, not hurt them.

As usual, however, the kids already knew something serious was up. I'm not very good at hiding things. When I made my way downstairs that Sunday morning, they began asking me if I was okay before I had any time to prepare what I was going to say. I would have to wing it, like I had many times before. I gathered them all in the living room less than twenty-four hours after my trip to the ER. This room had become ground zero for our deepest discussions. It was where their sibling had come out to them in 2014, where their other mom had done the same in 2015 and where I was about to tell them about my own inner struggle.

"I was at the hospital yesterday," I began. "I was feeling suicidal, and I made the decision to get help instead of taking my life."

You could hear a pin drop in the room. I immediately wanted to take back what I'd said, out of fear I had hurt them even more. But you can't put the genie back in the bottle, so I pushed on.

"I'm sorry if this is a lot to take in. I thought about not telling you, but ultimately I decided you need to know that I'm not okay right now. I'm in a pretty bad place, and I think it's going to take me a while to come back from it. But I promise you: I *am* going to come back from it. I'm going to be okay."

It was the first time I had said that out loud. And now that I had, I needed to make sure it was true because I had just made a promise to my kids. I take those seriously.

"What I want you to know, more than anything, is that things can seem hopeless and there can still be hope. Yesterday, I thought my life was over, and today I have a sneaking suspicion it's just beginning, in a way."

Our kids said kind things to me. They hugged me. They asked good questions. They made their own promises to do what they could around the house while I got better (and in true teenage fashion, kept those promises only to varying degrees). They didn't seem significantly upset by what I had said, and I attribute that to a history of hard conversations in this family. Each time we have them, we always rise to the challenges and come out stronger. That is the lesson the Knox kids have learned. Unfortunately, they still haven't learned how to load the dishwasher regularly. One thing at a time, I guess.

I will not discuss my children's mental health struggles here. But I will say they've had them, and my openness that day and on many other days has helped them be more open themselves about what is going on in their own lives. We have never been a family to associate shame with mental illnesses—they're illnesses, after all, just like any other kind. By making them easier to talk about, it removes a significant barrier that many face in asking for and receiving help. In turn, we can sometimes prevent an issue from reaching a crisis before that help is sought. This is the gift of transparency. I would much rather our kids under-stand that all humans struggle, and it's okay if they struggle too.

Now that I had made a commitment to these four amazing humans I love, I had to get better. It was time to get on with that.

hope in diagnosis

I HAD DEACTIVATED TWITTER with the intent of never going back. But I'd kept my Instagram and Facebook accounts open. These were friendlier social media sites overall, and I'd hoped they would allow me to keep doing my advocacy work in some capacity. Still, I was almost terrified to log back into Instagram for the first time. My emotions were raw and my nerves shot. When I saw that someone had sent me a link to a podcast on trans issues, I didn't know what to think. "You were the topic of this week's episode," that person wrote. "I think you'll like what they had to say."

What did that mean, exactly? I wasn't sure if I was ready to hear any commentary about what had transpired a few days ago, good or bad. But curiosity got the better of me, so I loaded up the podcast and had a listen. This is when I was first introduced to Maya.

The episode was a roughly ninety-minute conversation between the two hosts, Maya and Laura, both transgender women. They spoke about what they saw as community "cannibalism"— essentially, how small factions within a marginalized group will attack other factions or group members until there's no cohesiveness or energy left to fight much larger issues stemming from outside the group. They believed that this social cannibalism was detracting from real challenges—such as ongoing attacks on trans rights in several countries around the world—and that if it lost the ability to work together, the relatively small trans community, along with its allies, would be hard-pressed to move forward. As an example, they talked about what had happened to me. It upset them because they thought it was not only unfair to me, a spouse and parent to trans people, but also counterproductive for the community as a whole.

To be honest, I wasn't sure how I felt at all just then. I was in a full PTSD spiral—even if I didn't fully understand it as one yet— with no end in sight, while also trying to work through grief. I hadn't yet attempted to take to heart any constructive criticism from the onslaught. Did I belong in that advocacy space? I didn't know. But I listened intently as my name came up again and again in a positive light, and I felt temporarily reassured to know I wasn't universally despised.

This feeling of being ostracized had brought back memories of when I was younger, and how, when I was the target of malicious attacks, no one ever stood up for me. It seemed like the children who weren't actively participating in my torment would try to ignore what was happening to the little kid with the blonde pigtails. But this podcast was taking the opposite approach. These were two trans women I had never met—or to my knowledge, interacted with in any way—taking a firm stand in support of me. It was comforting at a time when comfort was especially needed. Sure, it was primarily being done to make a larger point, but it was still nice to hear it. It didn't make all the pain go away, but it felt a little bit like a hug from far away.

I reached out to the hosts by way of a private message on the show's Facebook page and thanked them for their support. In response, I received warm words of encouragement and a friend request from Maya, who was based out of western Canada.

Later that week, I posted to my personal Facebook page about my near suicide. The post was intense and vulnerable, and it would end up being too much for a handful of people I knew. But I wanted to be honest about where I was at emotionally. Being visible in struggle has always been something I do in the hopes of helping others, and I wanted this time to be no different. And frankly, I really needed to hear from those who cared about me. It was a stark announcement, but at that point, I felt like things couldn't get any worse, so I might as well be honest. I said I was getting good support at home, as well as from my close friends and extended family. I explained that the doctor and I both felt this was some kind of PTSD, and that I was grateful to be on a waiting list to see a psychiatrist for a full diagnosis, even if it might take a while. In the meantime, I asked, did anyone have a recommendation for a good trauma therapist?

A note popped up in Facebook Messenger minutes later. It was from Maya. In it, she told me she was sorry things had become so

challenging for me. She also let me know she was, serendipi-
tously, a trauma therapist.

"I'd like to offer you my help," she said. "I know it can be a
long wait to see a psychiatrist, and I think you need some immediate support. You've given much to our community. Let me give
you something back. No charge."

I read the message, utterly bewildered. We were in the middle
of the first wave of a global pandemic. Therapists were swamped
with distressed clients and drowning in long wait lists. In the
days leading up to my hospital visit, I had tried to call and email
a few local practices, with no success. While I would be able to
access a psychiatrist through the hospital quickly, every specialist
I could work with long-term had stated I would need to wait three
to six months for an initial consult. I wasn't sure if I could wait
that long, given how unstable I was. To have a trauma specialist
reach out to me at the time when I needed it most felt like a gift
from the gods had just landed on my lap. What were the odds?

I didn't know anything about Maya. But then, do most people
know much about their therapists before they meet for the first
time? In looking for a therapist, we might do an online search for
credentials or get the anecdotal rundown from friends who've
worked with them, but connection and trust are two big compo-
nents of a successful therapist-client relationship, and that can
take time to figure out.

Like many therapy-seekers, I had experienced the pitfalls
of unsuccessful therapeutic relationships. Finding out you just
don't "click" with your therapist can be expensive, both finan-
cially and emotionally. Sometimes your personalities don't mesh,

or you can't seem to get to the point where you fully trust them. You often don't realize it until you've completed a handful of sessions, then you find yourself back at square one: trying to find a new therapist, but this time with less money or insurance coverage.

There were a few fundamentally important things I had picked up about Maya simply by listening to her talk on the podcast: she was strong and smart, and had a level of confidence I only dreamed of; she wasn't afraid to speak her mind; and she believed that working together was critical to create change. Also, the podcast episode told me that she had my back. And because she was trans herself, I knew I wouldn't have to spend time educating her on gender identity or have to explain half a dozen times that my family members' transitions had nothing to do with my current struggles. (This is a frustrating issue that trans people and their family members sometimes run into with cisgender therapists who are not well versed in trans issues; gender tends to become the focus when it often isn't the issue at all.)

Most importantly, Maya seemed to want to help me. I just needed to swallow my pride and say yes. And to be honest, I didn't exactly have a lot of pride to swallow at the time. I was triggered, anxious, severely depressed and still suicidal. I had run away from a social media platform with my tail between my legs and was pretty sure my advocacy career had just gone up in flames. What on earth did I have to be prideful about?

But asking for or even accepting the help that was offered was as hard for me as it is for many others, especially as a caregiver. As someone who had largely focused on other people in both my personal and my professional lives, I was used to helping, not being helped. I was the rock in my family and often within my friendship circles—the one who ensured that everyone else was okay and had everything they needed. Falling apart can feel shameful when others depend on you, as if you're not just letting yourself down. I hesitated to accept the helping hand being offered. But ultimately, what did I have to lose? I had not only hit my emotional bottom but also cracked open the floor beneath me, creating a whole new level to fall to.

The way I was headed would inevitably kill me—if not this time, then the next. I would eventually end up taking my own life. I could feel it, and it scared me. I wasn't going to make it without support. This realization made my decision much simpler. Before I could talk myself out of it, I replied to Maya and said I would gratefully accept her help.

"I'm happy to hear it," she wrote back. "I have a spot open tomorrow. Should we get started?"

This woman wasn't playing around.

"Can you put on a record or something?" I asked Zoë. "No offence, but I need some privacy."

First World Pandemic Problem #63: Your whole family can hear when you video-call your therapist.

Zoë looked at me funny but decided not to question it. She smiled, got up from her makeshift office in the dining room, walked over to the record player and put on the *Pretty in Pink* soundtrack. Good choice. I was almost sad I'd be missing it.

"Thanks," I said, happy she was being understanding.

"No problem, babe," she replied, and leaned in for a quick kiss. "Have a good session."

I smiled weakly and walked upstairs, too jittery to be drinking the fresh cup of coffee in my hand.

I sat on the bed and tried to make myself comfortable—an impossible task. My body was worn out from the stress of the week. I ached from my clenched jaw to my constantly tight hips; my hips were the place on my body that always seemed to carry my stress. Maybe down the road, Maya and I would get into why I had this particular physical manifestation. But for now, I just needed to meet my new therapist.

As tired as the parent of a newborn, and yet filled with nervous energy, I clicked on the Zoom link Maya had sent me and had a good look at myself via my webcam for the first time that day. A zombie stared back. My skin was pale, nearly ashen. My hazel eyes were sunk deep into my skull and enveloped in dark bags; they appeared almost lifeless. In normal times, I would have fixed my hair or even dressed up a little. But these weren't normal times. I had only decided I wanted to live two days ago, so the fact that I'd even bothered to put on something other than pyjamas was impressive.

It's strange to think about *deciding* to live. Most of the time, living isn't a choice; it's a given until that choice is taken away by something beyond our control. Yes, clinical depression can be very much beyond our control, and that can lead to suicide. But in most cases, it's something else that gets us in the end: abnormal cell growth can take over our bodies, an oncoming car can hit us on the street or our hearts can give out in our sleep. We don't usually get to control the narrative of our own demise.

But feeling suicidal and not going through with it meant I had decided to live—at least for now. I was actively making that choice today, just like I had actively made the choice the day before, and the day before that. I had to make it every day, and I had to follow through. Sometimes it was practically an hourly decision. I viewed it as a commitment to myself and my family, but it wasn't an easy one. I was hanging on, although I wished I didn't have to. The idea of letting go, and the peace I imagined would come with that, still quietly beckoned me.

"Hi there," a familiar podcasting voice said, and my mind snapped back into focus on the screen. Maya had long wavy hair, several tattoos and a taste for dramatic makeup. She smiled warmly. I liked her already. I genuinely appreciate people with a unique flair about them.

"Hello," I said back, mustering as much positivity as I could.

"Well, look at that: there's a smile on your face," she said. "That's impressive a couple of days out of the hospital."

"My best just for you," I joked feebly. "I usually smile a lot, just not these days. But I hope that comes back."

"We're going help that come back, Amanda," she said. She had a confident look that told me she meant every word.

Maya was not only a therapist with trauma specialization, she explained, but also a master life coach and consultant. Part of her work was with patients who'd been admitted to one of the local hospitals in her city for either suicidal thoughts or a recent attempt. Her plan was to use tools from every field in which she was an expert to help me get better. A few years earlier, I might have been skeptical of this fresh approach. Blending therapy with coaching? And what did she mean by "consulting"? But by this point, I had done all kinds of therapy, including countless private sessions, several group sessions, and two rounds of cognitive behaviour therapy (CBT)—a standard treatment for anxiety or depression that involves recognizing and changing thought patterns. I had been in therapy, on and off, since I was a teenager, tackling everything from addiction to self-harm. While each therapist and group therapy treatment had helped me to some extent, most had not had a long-lasting impact. I could see the benefits of the tools the therapists had provided, but I couldn't incorporate much of what they taught me, no matter how hard I tried. My anxiety would always come roaring back, as would my feelings of inadequacy.

When Maya asked me to go through what I had previously done in therapy, I embarrassingly told her about my long list of unsuccessful treatments and workshops. "I always got stuck," I explained. "And this just made me feel like I was doing it wrong. I could see how the things they were recommending— like examining my thoughts, practising mindfulness and making gratitude lists—could be helpful, but I couldn't make it work for me."

"That's not a failure on your part," Maya explained. "That's a failure in the treatment. You weren't given the right type. If you have a trauma disorder, you're going to need to deal with the trauma first before you can move forward. The other kinds of therapy often don't work well without that as a first step. We'll wait for your diagnosis from the psychiatrist, of course, but that's my guess."

Later, this sentiment would be echoed by other professionals. But at the time, this was the first I'd heard of trauma being a roadblock to other types of recovery. Could it be that I would need to take different or even extra steps to wellness? Were trauma survivors that distinct in our needs? Given my track record, I had to admit that was likely true in my case.

"Here's the thing, Amanda," Maya continued, making eye contact with me through the camera lens—a gesture that would become less weird to me in time. "My methods are going to challenge you. It's not going to be easy sometimes, and I'll need you to give one hundred and ten percent during this process. This will be a little different than other styles of therapy you've had, and it won't work if you're a passive participant."

Well, that wasn't intimidating at all.

Although I wasn't sure exactly what Maya had in mind, I agreed immediately and wholeheartedly. This decision to stick around and find my way out of this mess had not come easily, and I was ready to do the work. What other choice did I have? Also, my professional speaking engagements had largely dried up thanks to the pandemic, which gave me the rare gift of time to focus on myself and hopefully emerge a stronger, healthier Amanda. I had no idea what that person might look like, but I knew I was dedicated to finding out.

Once again, hope was tethering me to this world.

While I might seem like an open book much of the time (including in my actual books), there are a lot of things I don't share publicly. I do this for my own protection and for the protection of those I care about. The world doesn't need to know everything about me—but my therapist does. Therapy is weird because we get emotionally intimate with folks who are just shy of being complete strangers. Other than late nights at a seedy bar with too much tequila, where else does this happen? When we're in therapy, we often start by giving the person sitting across from us (or across the country on a video call) an overview of our lives. Over time, as the trust builds, we dive into the details of some of our most scarring experiences, getting painfully vulnerable and opening up old wounds.

I was already feeling mighty vulnerable these days, so opening up to Maya was particularly tough. Our early sessions wore me out with how emotionally intense they got, and how she constantly probed me to dig even deeper. Why did I care so much about what others thought of me? Why did I feel compelled to read every awful Twitter comment? What was I looking for in my desperate need for control? I had to think on my feet and analyze parts of my life and psyche in ways I never had before. We met on Monday afternoons, and I quickly learned that nothing productive would happen after that. Monday evenings were for pre-made freezer lasagna or pizza delivery. They were for naps on the couch. They were for mindless television with my wife or a good cry in the bath. It was all rest, reflection and recuperation.

That's because Maya could pull emotions out of me so quickly that it left me spinning. She asked great questions, which is a big part of being an effective therapist or coach. One minute I'd be fine, and the next I would say something accidentally profound in response to one of those questions and the tears would start flowing. I have a hard time crying in front of others—another by-product of my childhood. I had spilled tears in a therapist's office a handful of times in the past, but crying over video chat was a new one for me. I would leave the sessions with Maya convinced that she was secretly judging me for something I had said. I imagined her wondering what she had got herself into when she reached out to me. Was she disappointed at getting to know the entirety of me and not just what she knew of me from my public presence? Did she have any idea how broken I really was, and what a project I would become? Eventually, I would realize these thoughts were actually my own judgments toward myself. I didn't like the parts of me I was bringing to the table every week. I didn't like staring at my own imperfections under glaring lights. So in my mind, neither did she.

I was weak in those early days, knocked down by life in a way I'd never expected I would be. My family's emotional rock had cracked in half. I was Humpty Dumpty and couldn't put myself back together again. Maybe I would never get well. Maybe this would become my new normal—although I would find it much harder to adapt to it than I had to other unpleasant things as a child. I had come undone, and at times, the indignity of it almost took my breath away.

While I waited for therapy to work, I needed something—anything—to make me feel useful and whole again.

"I'm going to stain the fence," I told Zoë the day after my first session.

She looked at me quizzically. We had talked about staining the fence every year since we had moved into our house. Dozens of conversations. Seven summers. Eight springs. No stain. There was always something else to do, and besides, it wasn't exactly an exciting job. But if there was ever a time for me to get the brushes out, this was it. What else was I doing, anyway? A person can only take so many naps.

On day one, I discovered the therapeutic benefits of power washing. There is something immensely satisfying about tearing dirt off a surface with water so strong it could take your skin off along with it. The power washer became a metaphor for my life: I was stripping away the top layers to access the raw materials beneath. And then, I hoped, improve upon them. I got a little, shall we say, *into it*. Not only did the fence get cleaned, but I power-washed the house siding, the windows, the shed, the deck and the SUV. The kids eventually confiscated the power washer with a gentle "I think you've had enough, Mom" and rolled it back into the garage.

Next it was time for the stain. This turned out to be the mindfulness exercise I didn't know I needed. It gave me purpose at a time when I felt largely useless. I could no longer stay in bed all day, feeling sorry for myself, eating chips and watching trashy reality shows. I had a job to finish! Having a reason to leave the bedroom was a lifeline—a push to keep going.

That week, we were in the midst of some unseasonably hot days. Every morning I would head outside with a coffee, a water bottle, some sunscreen and my brushes, the sun greeting us all fiercely. I spent time listening to podcasts where guests discussed how they'd battled thoughts of suicide or how public shaming had harmed them in ways they were still trying to unpack. I avoided most phone calls, texts and emails. I stayed off social media and on task as much as possible. This was where I needed to be: here, in this moment, with the fence, the brush, the podcasts, the water bottle, the coffee and the sweet scent of sunscreen on my skin. We were a mighty team. When the waves of anxiety hit, I would pour myself into the job even more, focusing on finishing one board at a time, breathing through the rushes of panic until the storm inside eventually settled. Simply *existing* at that time was painful in a way; there were still many moments when I didn't want to exist at all. But I recommitted over and over to the idea of living, and slowly got better at the practice of choosing life.

One afternoon, though, everything unexpectedly shifted. I was working on a section of the fence beneath a white birch at the back of our yard. A cool breeze gently touched my arms and face. Our two big dogs, Sam and Blue, were chasing each other around, and in between their playful scuffles, I could hear nothing but birdsong.

The tears came out of nowhere. I had to put down my brush and steady myself against the tree. I was crying, I realized, because it was such a perfect day and I had almost not been around to see it. The agony of that realization was a punch to the gut. I felt pure sorrow, through and through, over what I had nearly done. How could I have come so close to taking these beautiful experiences away from myself? My time would come, as everyone's does, but why would I want it to happen now? Look at everything I would be missing out on.

This was my tipping point. It was the moment I knew for certain that I wanted to live, that there was far too much to stay here for. It's funny what led me to that realization—that it was a nice day with a paintbrush in my hand instead of, say, a meaningful conversation or something profound I'd read in a book. But it was more the day itself than the specifics of it. Life can be hard, but it is also filled with beauty. On this sunny afternoon, I was a witness to that beauty.

On the final day of staining the fence, I stopped and watched as wasps buzzed around the last unfinished planks, chewing up little pieces of wood pulp. They would then fly away to their nests and come back again for more. When they found a plank unusable because it was coated in fresh stain, they would simply move on to another, seemingly unbothered by this development. I was still wary of wasps after my trail incident, but they didn't even care I was there, so I tried not to care either. We worked side by side until there was nothing left for them to chew, and at that point, I lost my co-workers to new opportunities.

It was late afternoon by the time I wrapped up. As I stood on the deck and looked over the rich colour I had just bordered our backyard with, I felt a deep sense of accomplishment about what I had achieved over the past few days.

And it wasn't just staining the fence.

Occasionally, the mental health system moves surprisingly fast. I'd expected the psychiatric referral I had received at the hospital to take a few weeks. Thankfully, the wait was short; I had my first appointment with the psychiatrist less than two weeks after I left the emergency department. I was only two sessions in with Maya at the time. The psychiatrist—we'll call her Dr. Brain because

I'm running out of pseudonyms for people—explained that her work with me would be short term and strictly over the phone, since we were still in lockdown. In our finite amount of time together, Dr. Brain would try to find out what was going on inside my head, provide me with a diagnosis and give me treatment recommendations.

She listened attentively as I explained what had happened in the days leading up to what I could only describe as a breakdown. Her empathy was palpable, which I appreciated. Psychiatry can be fairly clinical, and I wasn't sure how warm these sessions would be. Everything that had happened to me was still fresh, and I needed that kind ear on the other end of the line—someone who was a clinician but not clinical. Dr. Brain fitted the bill perfectly.

We went through my past, unpacking the times when similar acts of bullying had happened and how they made me feel. We talked about my early childhood, with its dissociative episodes and panic attacks. I told her about the bullying I'd dealt with nearly every day at school and described the countless times in my adult life when I'd worried about judgment or assumed people were thinking the worst of me. I told her how I'd feared that would eventually become my undoing—which it had, in a very painful and public way.

"I just want to know what's wrong with me," I said. "What's *really* wrong with me. I've been diagnosed with an anxiety disorder and depression before, but I know there's something more going on. I've done everything anyone has asked of me to get better, and I never really get better. I never do." Even I could hear the desperation in my voice. I craved answers.

I wanted an accurate diagnosis, *needed* one, but Dr. Brain explained that she required a bit more time with me to give me something definitive. After we wrapped up our first session, she complimented me on being a self-aware and resilient person. I laughed.

"Thanks for that. But two weeks ago, I was in the hospital begging them to help keep me alive," I said. "That doesn't feel resilient to me. It doesn't feel self-aware not to have known that I needed help until it was almost too late." My voice faltered a little. The fresh emotional injury throbbed again with this retelling of events. Would it ever feel okay to talk about this? Would it ever not hurt? I hoped so.

Her reply was calm and compassionate. "Amanda, you drove yourself to the hospital, didn't you? Not everyone could have made that decision. Do you recognize how much strength it took to do that, given what you were going through?"

To be honest, I hadn't recognized that. I felt that choice was made on autopilot. I was only partially aware of what I was doing, seemingly driven by instinct—pun intended—more than anything. The will to survive is strong. Stronger than any will to die, I assumed, and I had merely given in to that.

"It took resiliency to make it through what you did," Dr. Brain insisted. "And it takes a lot of self-awareness to understand that this is a deeper issue instead of just one thing that happened on the internet recently. Don't shortchange yourself. You have a great deal of strength inside of you."

The thing about strength is that we often don't recognize it in ourselves. Strong people—and I include everyone in this, as we're all strong in our own ways—just do what needs to be done. I had always assumed that being a strong person meant I wouldn't fall; I hadn't yet recognized that it meant falling down and being able to get back up again, which my track record showed I was good at.

I decided not to argue with her. We had another session booked the following week, and I didn't want to get labelled a difficult patient. Besides, maybe Dr. Brain had a point. Maybe I should consider what she was telling me, since whatever I was thinking about myself was clearly being generated by a mind that had thought some rather dark things recently.

After our session the following week, Dr. Brain was ready to tell me what she thought. I took a big breath and waited.

"You have anxiety disorder and mood disorder based in trauma."

Oh. I see.

"Yes, you have an anxiety disorder," she continued. "That diagnosis is correct. And you also have a mood disorder that shifts your mood from stable to depressed in short intervals. But both those problems are a result of complex childhood trauma. Given what I know about you so far, I'm confident that if you receive good trauma therapy, you're going to see those secondary issues get a lot better."

Maya was right. The ER doctor was right. My gut feeling was right too. I felt relieved by these words. There was the diagnosis I needed. This was the revelation I knew would be a game changer.

For the first time in an exceedingly long while, I felt something about my mental health that excited me. After years of struggling, of not knowing how to make things better, I had a path forward.

—

So what is trauma, anyway?

Before we go any further, we need to talk about what psychological trauma is. Everyone has heard the term, but most of us have only a vague idea of its meaning. We might define trauma as "a bad thing that happened to someone, and that person is still haunted by it." When PTSD is mentioned, many of us will think of war films we've seen or veterans we've known who were afflicted by demons and tried to cope with them in dysfunctional ways. Or in terms of civilian life, we might think of an aunt who is afraid to get behind the wheel of a car years after a bad accident or a friend who just hasn't been the same since leaving an abusive relationship. But even if we know someone who's suffering, our understanding of how that suffering impacts a person can be limited. We don't understand *why* they suffer the way they do. Why can't they move on from what happened years ago? Why are they stuck on the side of the proverbial road with smoke pouring from under the hood? And why do others go through similar experiences and seem to get on with their lives more easily?

Bad things happen to everyone, but not everyone who experiences bad things develops a trauma disorder. Researchers are still working out why two people who live through the same frightening experience—such as siblings who grew up in an abusive household or two strangers who faced the same hostage situation—recover in different ways. One might work through the painful experience quickly and go on with their life mostly unaffected, while the other could be impacted by it for years.

Being stuck in past trauma can shape our perception of present events, making the world seem more frightening and our lives less enjoyable.

Studies have shown that the amount of support made available to a victim just after they experience a horrifying event will play a significant role in whether they become traumatized.[1] The more support they have, the more fully they are likely to recover. But that's not the whole story; there is still much to figure out about why brains do what they do. Unfortunately, for whatever reason, some of us end up with wounded, traumatized brains.

Symptoms of trauma can vary by person and type of trauma disorder. Two common forms are PTSD and complex PTSD, or CPTSD. PTSD is most strongly associated with soldiers and victims of war, violent crimes, natural disasters or accidents. Symptoms of PTSD include an increased sense of danger, flashbacks and nightmares, avoidance, difficulty concentrating, irritability, bouts of anger, negative thoughts, memory issues, panic attacks, excessive guilt or worry and a lack of emotion.

CPTSD is complex in more ways than one. While widely recognized by most experts as a form of complex interpersonal trauma, it isn't officially in the diagnostic handbooks yet. Instead, Dr. Brain diagnosed me with a complex trauma disorder that was based in childhood; it's different words to describe the same thing.

CPTSD forms from repeated events, generally interpersonal in nature, happening over months or years. For example, children who grow up abused or neglected can develop CPTSD, as can those who have suffered years of severe bullying or ostracization. Adult victims of abuse can also develop this disorder. CPTSD carries many of the same symptoms as PTSD, but it also includes others, such as a lack of emotional regulation, negative self-perception, trouble forming and keeping healthy relationships and a detachment from self or even out-of-body experiences—also known as dissociation.

Dissociation happens when we're triggered by an external event or a flashback, which can come in the form of a sound, smell, visual cue, memory or situation similar to whatever caused the original trauma. Suddenly, we are thrown back into the nightmare of what we once lived through. A big problem with trauma is that it is stored as a rough and broken kind of memory with no sense of time. So the mind doesn't know it's now safely in the past, and it can feel like we're still living it. The emotions we feel when triggered—when we are suddenly reminded of what we lived through—can therefore be as strong as they were when the original events occurred. When trauma victims react to those flashbacks, we are reliving the nightmare in full colour, as if it's happening right now.

An important thing to know about trauma disorders is that they carry a neurological component. Our brain structure and nervous system play a significant role. To understand trauma disorders, we must, to a limited extent anyway, understand the brain. As I've mentioned, brains are complicated and I'm definitely no neuroscientist, so I won't go into impressive detail. But for us non-neuroscientists, let's break down the brain's anatomy into three simple systems:

» *The hindbrain.* Our most primitive part of the brain sits at the base of the skull, where it attaches to the spine. It does the basic functions we don't have to think about, like sleeping, breathing, regulating heart rate and body temperature, and sensing hunger and fullness. Thanks to the hindbrain, we don't have to remember to breathe all the time. We sometimes call this part of our grey matter the "reptilian brain," and it's the first section to fully form as we're developing in utero.

» *The midbrain.* Among other things, this small part of the brain controls eye movements, visual and auditory processing, voluntary movements and some reflexes. It sits atop the hindbrain and has a lot to do with how we react to the world around us.

» *The forebrain.* This large system does our most advanced work as humans by helping us feel empathy, have a sense of time, stay focused on tasks, make plans, use language, anticipate events, feel inhibition and engage in a host of other functions that make up who we are and how we navigate the world. It allows us to perceive and think in ways most other animals cannot. This complex part of the brain takes up to twenty-five years to fully develop in an average human, and even more time in traumatized ones. Trauma in childhood can physically alter the forebrain, causing problems with emotional regulation, cognitive ability and other areas of function. Research has also shown that both PTSD and emotional trauma cause physical changes to the brain and may result in brain injury over time.[2]

When we experience a traumatic event, the brain begins shutting down everything but essential functions such as breathing, blood circulation and an awareness of danger. It instinctively knows that what is happening in the moment is too much to take in, so it pushes our consciousness out of the experience as much as possible. Some survivors report having out-of-body experiences, where they see what is happening to them from up above or at a distance, detaching them from the event to some extent. Some report remaining very much in their bodies but feeling numb to what's happening, or perhaps hyper focusing on something else in the room (for example, focusing on music videos during a sexual assault). Some victims don't remember the experience at all; the brain blacks it out or creates a new story around the situation that is made up of more palatable half-truths (for example, an abuse victim might remember some of what their abuser did, but not the worst of it, making the abuse appear less severe than it was).

Like a worried mother pulling her child into a hug to shield the little one's eyes and ears from a violent event or accident, our brain takes the hit for us. In some ways, we have a lot to be grateful for when this happens. For many of us, it would be too much to take in every aspect of a horrific event.

But this protection comes at a cost. Traumatized brains learn that this is the way to do things whenever they think we're in danger—and they begin to believe we're in imminent danger at times when we're not. Our minds stay on high alert, waiting for the sky to fall. If the average person operates at an anxiety level of three out of ten on a typical day, those with trauma can operate at an eight or a nine. Like a guard dog, we're always waiting for an intruder at the door. This means we're always that much closer to being flooded with adrenaline.

When we get triggered, the brain flies into panic mode along those same pathways it built to cope during the initial trauma. Trying to keep us alive, it turns off or turns down anything that isn't key to our immediate survival. This means much of the fore-brain goes dark. Our ability to reason, to communicate and to focus on non-critical things becomes compromised. Our bodies go cold (or hot) as we're filled with adrenaline in the same way we would be if confronted by a pride of hungry lions. Our focus narrows on the perceived threat—generally not lions these days—and our extremities can go numb or weak as blood is redirected to the heart and other vital organs. The heart itself races as we get ready to run, fight, freeze or fawn (a lesser-known reaction in which the person tries to calm a tense situation by people pleasing). The body becomes a survival machine and nothing else. We can't think clearly, can't parse new information properly, and are largely unable to regulate our emotions. We can feel as if we are detached from our identity or reality. This is dissociation.

And yet, to the untrained eye, someone going through this might appear nearly normal. Many trauma survivors say they continue to function in a way that doesn't draw attention to them but that feels entirely robotic. This "don't be noticed" behaviour could be a type of survival mechanism in itself. That's exactly what happens to me. As a parent, I learned I couldn't simply shut down when I dissociated (although I didn't know that was what it was called at the time). I had to keep going, keep getting my kids where

they needed to be and keep helping them when they required a
parent. I did this during the Twitter pile-on too, trying my best
to appear as normal as possible to those around me. But I did it
all on autopilot and was unable to focus on much of what anyone
was saying or hold any real conversation outside of a few brief
words. My language and attention centres did not function well,
and I was emotionally numb, which led me to feel like an anima-
tronic version of their mom.

My one giveaway to those around me—especially my children—
was how irritable I would become. My normally cheery disposi-
tion was replaced with a quieter, more distracted and quicker to
anger one. Noise easily overwhelmed me, as would a constant
stream of requests—"When is dinner going to be ready?" "What
are we having?" "Can you drive me somewhere?" "Can I have
some money?" (This is an issue when you have four kids because
you can get asked the same thing *four separate times*.) I've been
known to blow my top, storm off or lie quietly in my bedroom until
my heart stopped palpitating. It was not my kids' fault, and I've
done my fair share of apologizing when I calmed down. I wouldn't
say I was a monster during these times, but I was definitely not the
life of the party. I waffled between irritability, anxiety, and numbness. I could fake a smile or a laugh when needed, but none of it
was really me. I was pretending.

People manage the fallout of a trauma reaction in different
ways, but it all comes down to the same thing: when parts of your
brain are offline, life gets harder to manage. Brain chemistry
varies widely, as do our reactions to trauma. The initial dissociation can last a few hours, but climbing out of it as the brain

systems "reboot" can take a couple of days. Before trauma-focused therapies, I would usually spiral for six to eight hours when triggered, then take up to three days to fully recover. After the adrenaline was depleted, my body and mind were also drained, and regret would set in for things I said or did during a dissociation episode. Shame became a cumbersome blanket, weighing me down and compounding how awful I felt. "Great job not handling life again," I've been known to tell myself sarcastically while I try to put the pieces back together. I would inevitably end up with a stress headache or a sore jaw, tensed-up shoulders and a stomach in knots. As I said before, the body carries the burden of trauma as much as the brain does.

Having my nervous system go offline was not something I could control. I had no ability to "logic" my way out of it. Standard therapy methods for other types of mental illnesses and disorders can help only so much, as does medication. Neurological issues require neurological support. We need for the switch *not* to flip whenever there's a trigger, and this can require specific interventions performed by or taught to us by a trained professional. There are also things we can do to turn the switch back off if we do get triggered and begin to "come online" faster.

Here's the important thing: *none of this is your fault*. If you have tried various methods of support for other types of mental health issues and they came up short, it is not a failure on your part and you are not beyond help. While trauma has been recognized for well over a hundred years by psychiatry, it remains a mystery to many people. It's often not the first thing considered when someone presents with symptoms.

I spent several weeks studying the damage trauma causes and learning how the brain reacts to it. I read books and watched videos from experts, determined to understand what had happened to me and how I could start to overcome it. I learned about the limbic system and how to help soothe it after a triggering event. When I discovered the science of neuroplasticity—how a brain can rewire itself, even well into adulthood—I felt hopeful.

There is life beyond trauma, even when it doesn't feel that way and even if we've been experiencing it for years or, for some of us, most of a lifetime. We can start to feel better, but it takes work. And after my own diagnosis, I knew I was ready to get down to the business of getting well.

victimized, not a victim

DR. BRAIN AND I HAD ONLY two sessions together. She had planned to see me for all six if required, to support me while I found a trauma-informed therapist. Thankfully, I told her I was already seeing one. She was happy to hear this and commended my proactive approach. I laughed, saying that anybody who has been in and out of therapy for most of their life knows a few things by their forties. In my case, I knew what therapies I had already tried and had not seen success with, which made me eager to find something that might actually work. Even the hope that a trauma therapist could help was enough to send me looking for recommendations.

The other thing a psychiatrist does is help with any medication needed to treat a mental illness or disorder. Since I had been on the same medication for a couple of years—an SSRI used to treat my generalized anxiety disorder—she decided to leave it alone.

"We don't tend to make medication changes when you've recently been in crisis unless we absolutely need to," Dr. Brain explained. "It can be risky. So we'll leave this in place for now. But if you find it's not doing its job down the road, you can call me, and we'll switch things up."

With that, Dr. Brain left me in Maya's hands, and we ended our sessions.

Worried little butterflies danced around my insides as soon as I hung up the call. I had made a series of difficult decisions about my wellbeing and had no idea if I had chosen correctly. Leaving the hospital on that sunny Saturday instead of asking to be admitted to the mental health ward had been a difficult decision. The hospital would probably have kept me safe from acting on my dark thoughts while inside those walls, whereas being at home, even with a caring family around, left me ample opportunity to succumb to them. Agreeing to end my sessions early with the psychiatrist was another tough call. I had needed specialized help for years before I finally received it or even understood that I required it. Now I had these supports at my disposal, and they were safety nets I could have clung to a little longer—some extra security at the hospital or some extra psychiatry sessions back home.

It can take months or even years to access care under the public health system in Ontario. As is the case in many places around the world, mental health care is woefully underfunded here and wait lists are long. I got lucky—I had compassionate staff at the ER and was able to move up the wait list to see a specialist very quickly. It almost seemed foolish to give up these supports so soon.

I knew all about the importance of good safety nets. The treatment centre I'd attended as a teen was an intensive live-in program. For six months, we ate, slept and breathed recovery daily. I learned a lot about myself and grew by leaps and bounds while I was there. As my graduation from the facility approached, I felt a great deal of apprehension about returning to my previous life, with all its temptations and dangers. I wasn't sure I could trust myself not to fall back into old habits. The staff had worked with my parents to slowly reintroduce me to the outside world with a few weekends back home, followed by an entire week shortly before graduation. I did well each time but looked forward to returning to my safe place. There was no alcohol inside those walls. There were no drugs, no bullies. There was no Nathan or Dan or someone else's slighted lover with a gun at this treatment centre. There were no people I had wronged or old friends who wouldn't talk to me. There were no teachers who knew my bad reputation. There were only those who had my best interests at heart. I didn't want to leave that. Why would anyone want to leave that? For the first time in years, I felt contented and safe.

At one point during my last couple of months in treatment, someone who had graduated before me returned to the house, having relapsed once back home. He had come back for a few weeks of refresher—an option the centre offered former residents who had not been successful maintaining their sobriety. When we were in the program together before he graduated, I'd looked up to this person a great deal. He was smart and insightful, and he helped me and other newcomers work through some of our tougher moments. I couldn't believe he had struggled so much upon leaving.

"It's hard out there," he told me. "You're going to have to do the work if you want to make it. I let a lot of that slide, honestly. That's why I started using again. It doesn't take long to find you if you're not careful."

It doesn't take long to find you if you're not careful. That advice stuck with me. I silently pledged to stay on top of my recovery. Upon graduation, I diligently attended my one-on-one and group therapy sessions. Staying sober as a teen was a choice I made daily, decision by careful decision: choosing not to go to a party where there would be drinking, avoiding much of the old crowd I used to get in trouble with, hanging out with other sober people and keeping an eye on my mental health for any signs of trouble. These were ways I prioritized my recovery. It worked. Life without a big safety net is harder, but I had developed a skill set to use; I just had to remember to use it. It was a smaller safety net, but still sturdy.

The situation was similar as I faced my current mental health challenges. I had what I needed to be successful: a therapist, a strong support network, medication and a willingness to do whatever I needed to do. I was fortunate to have all this support at my doorstep; not everyone does. I could do this. But it would involve changing something important and more than a little tricky for many of us: my mindset.

A mindset is a person's beliefs about the world and how they interact with it. We tell ourselves stories about how life works and, often without realizing it, create a framework within which we live. The two most commonly discussed mindsets in business and self-help circles are the fixed mindset and growth mindset. Someone with a fixed mindset believes they have a limit to their capabilities and can operate only within them. Meanwhile, someone with a growth mindset believes they are always capable of pushing the boundaries of what they currently know or do. "I don't have a brain for math" would be an example of someone with a fixed mindset. The person set on growth would say, "I can learn new math skills if I work at it." A growth mindset allows you to push outside of your comfort zone ("This obstacle is a learning opportunity"), while a fixed mindset keeps you squarely in it ("I already know I can't move beyond this"). Just about any parameter we use to navigate life can be seen as a mindset. Some people are driven largely by a greed or fear mindset. Others adopt a goal-driven mindset or one of curiosity. We don't often name them, but we all have them.

Most of us don't stick to a single mindset. We might be driven by a fear mindset surrounding health-related issues but have a courage mindset around business ventures. We might have a growth mindset around art but a fixed mindset when it comes to fitness.

I am fortunate in that I naturally operate with growth in mind; I love to learn and push myself well beyond my boundaries. Whenever I find out a problem lies with me, I get weirdly hopeful because the one thing I know I can change is myself. I largely attribute this to what I learned in rehab as a teenager. I was shown that while I can change some circumstances, others are beyond my control. For the situations I can't change, I have to learn new skills to help me live better within them. Acceptance is a key component to living with an unchangeable situation, as is finding gratitude within it. Believing I can do hard things has huge benefits. It has generally helped me feel emboldened and allowed me to move forward in my life no matter what obstacles I'm facing. But like most people, I've also had a few holes in that growth mindset over the years that needed pointing out—sometimes in very unusual ways.

I didn't figure out I was depressed until my firstborn was eighteen months old. Something had felt "off" since his birth, but I had attributed it to postpartum hormones and recovering from a traumatic birth experience as a twenty-year-old. My wife and I didn't get married until our son was nine months old, and the fact that we were young and unwed feels forever woven into his birth story in an unfortunate way. My ob-gyn, who had been nothing but incredible, had to go out of town on an urgent matter on the same weekend I was being induced for sudden onset pre-eclampsia—a serious and potentially fatal condition he had picked up on during a routine appointment. I was a week shy of my due date at this point, so helping my body go into labour was a far safer option for both me and my unborn child than waiting for it to begin naturally. My blood pressure and other markers were so high that the nurses wouldn't even let me leave the hospital following the appointment; one of them escorted me from the doctor's office directly to the labour and delivery ward.

I was admitted as my doctor left for Toronto, which began a forty-eight-hour hell ride of failed induction attempts, a slow onset of labour, painful medication-enhancing contractions, a ten-pound baby turned the wrong way, several emergency medical interventions, maternal hemorrhaging, a blood transfusion and a newborn who struggled to breathe and was separated from me for several hours once he was born.

If all that wasn't traumatic enough, the way we were treated while in the hospital was dreadful. Without the support of my doctor, I felt judged and barely tolerated by most of the staff. I was talked down to and scolded, and one doctor even performed an internal exam in the middle of the night, while I was asleep, without waking me first to ask for my consent. As a rape survivor, I woke up gasping and terrified as I found the doctor's fingers inside me.

"Oh, relax," she said, taking off her gloves. "You're fine. I was just checking to see how dilated you are. You're over two centimetres now, which means you're finally in labour. Congratulations." She left the room as I tried to make sense of what had just happened.

At one point, when I was screaming in pain during the futile pushing phase, a nurse snapped at me for making other patients on the ward uncomfortable with my "dramatics." Hours later, once she was told how large my baby was, she retracted her statement and apologized. "We didn't realize he was so big," she said, as if that somehow excused her words.

When my doctor returned from Toronto on Monday and read my chart, he came to see me in the postpartum ward, visibly upset. He was furious about what had transpired and apologized profusely. I could tell he meant it. He promised he would work to ensure this did not happen to another young mother.

His apology meant a lot, although the damage had been done. Yes, my baby and I were ultimately okay, but I had been traumatized by the experience.

I don't know if I would have had postpartum depression without that incident. But I certainly think it contributed to it. Eighteen months later, I started to realize that the love I had for my toddler was the only thing keeping me going every day. I was only alive for him. Perhaps this feeling wasn't healthy. The joy many new parents experience had for me been shrouded in a mist of melancholy, and it was time to change that. I wanted to *feel* my son's beautiful smile, not just see it. I wanted to *feel* the delight in his laughter, not just hear it.

On a recommendation from a friend, I made an appointment to see Dr. Shore, a local family practitioner. I was told he was compassionate but blunt. "He'll tell you exactly what he thinks," my friend warned, "and you need to be ready for it."

Dr. Shore was an MD with some therapy training (I think), and he provided what might—but probably should not—be called "psychiatry lite." During our first appointment, he diagnosed me with depression and prescribed some antidepressants to help lift my mood. He also made sure I agreed to attend weekly therapy sessions with him, as he didn't believe drugs alone would solve the issue.

Dr. Shore was a little sketchy in the way he operated. In fact, years later I would read an article about him having his medical licence temporarily suspended for doing something well outside of his training. After our time together, this did not surprise me. I had never met an MD who also provided hour-long therapy sessions for patients, nor did I know for certain if he had any professional training as a counsellor or therapist. But I was twenty-one years old and didn't think to question it. What did I know about being a doctor, anyway? Besides, therapy was expensive, and my family was poor. Because he was a medical doctor, the province footed the bill, which meant we could still afford to eat. As far as I was concerned, this was probably the best I was going to get, and I needed the help.

In our first session the following week, Dr. Shore met me at the reception desk with a warm, friendly smile. He ushered me into an office beyond the exam room I had met him in the first time. He was short and solid, with a ring of dark hair around his balding head. He reminded me a little of Danny DeVito. We sat opposite each other in comfortable chairs. He pulled a single piece of paper out of a side table drawer next to him and placed it on his clipboard.

"Let's begin with some background," he asked. "Give me an overview of your life so far."

I laughed, and he looked at me inquisitively.

"You're going to need more than one page," I said, raising my eyebrows. "My past is a doozy."

"No problem," Dr. Shore replied. He grabbed a few more pieces of paper to place over the original. "I'm ready. Go for it."

I went for it. I told Dr. Shore everything terrible that had ever happened to me. By then, I was adept at this storytelling. I had been doing it since I entered rehab, where I was encouraged to pull all that festering pain out of the darkness and into the sunlight to presumably meet its end. As I narrated my life, Dr. Shore listened attentively, nodding at appropriate times, taking plenty of notes and interrupting me only for the odd clarification. I felt heard, which is always a good sign when working with a therapist or family doctor. Or in this case, therapist-doctor, maybe. I still don't know.

At the end of it all, he sat silent for a few moments, looking over the pages of notes that represented all my major life challenges leading up to that moment.

"Well, Amanda," he said with a sigh, still looking down at the pages and shaking his head, "you've been through a lot."

As I often did after opening up to someone about my emotional baggage, I felt vindicated by his acknowledgment of my struggles and accompanying pain. Like many people before him, Dr. Shore recognized why I had felt down for so much of my life. Sure, this time my depression was likely due to hormones, a difficult birth and some challenging postpartum circumstances, but it had been a recurring staple of my existence for years. How could it not be? I had had a hard life, so of course I would struggle. I was glad he could see it.

I was just about to say something to that effect when Dr. Shore suddenly tore the pages of notes free from the clip, crumpled them up into a ball and dramatically threw them over his shoulder. The paper ball that represented my entire history hit the floor. My jaw followed.

"Yes, I'm sure all of that was hard," he said, looking up at my shocked face. "But it's all in the past too, you see. I understand you had challenges. There's no denying that. But do you know what your biggest issue is, Amanda?"

Right now, I thought, *my biggest issue is not knowing what the fuck is going on.*

"You're a perpetual victim," he continued. "You're stuck in victimhood. You have a victim mentality. It's become a part of your personality. You don't know how to extricate yourself from the things that hurt you. You have *become* those things."

Ouch.

"But you are not your backstory," he continued, carefully emphasizing each word. "You are the person in front of me. You are the person you will become. You are not"—he glanced behind him at the crumpled notes on the floor—"*that*."

Well, then. This was going well. If I hadn't been in shock, I would have walked out the door. How could someone speak to me like that?

"Here's what I want you to do," he said. "I want you to go home after our session, get a notebook and write out 'I am not a victim' a thousand times. Bring it back to me next week. This is not a suggestion but a requirement. We're not moving forward until you figure out you are more than your sad story."

I was as floored as the wadded-up notes of my life. I took a deep breath, coolly and calmly collecting myself before nodding. A few brief words were exchanged in the reception area, and I even scheduled a time for my appointment the following week (while silently promising myself I would cancel it as soon as I got home). Although I tried not to show it, I was sure Dr. Shore could tell how upset I was; he was a maybe-therapist, after all. I held back tears in the building's elevator and as I waited for the bus. I stewed all the way home, livid and humiliated. How dare he? How dare he dismiss my experiences like that? How dare he tell me how to feel or not feel about something he hadn't lived through? What an asshole.

I hated Dr. Shore on a deep level all week. But on the other hand, I also wanted to get better, and one of the things I had learned throughout my few years of recovery was that if nothing else is working, sometimes you have to try something you don't believe will. I didn't agree with Dr. Shore's perception of me or his weird method to resolve my issues. But blending one part determination and two parts pure spite, I committed myself to the process. I looked forward to proving him wrong, to telling him that his useless approach hadn't produced any useful results. I grabbed a spare notebook, and in my limited free time as a parent to a busy toddler and a tech support worker at a large internet service provider, I wrote "I am not a victim," line by painful line, filling many pages over many short stints. I felt like Bart Simpson doing penance in detention, except I was scrawling something far less witty than his iconic chalkboard lines.

At first, the work filled me with resentment. Every time I wrote "I am not a victim," I would seethe inside because *of course I was a victim*! I felt like I was betraying myself with each line I finished. I thought of all the frightening moments I'd had as a young child. I thought of all the kids at school who'd hounded me relentlessly, beating me up and telling me to go kill myself. I thought of the creeps in my teen years who had used me. I thought of how many people had treated me like a small adult rather than the child I was, and I thought of the damage this had caused. I thought of the hospital staff and their borderline cruelty, of how they had robbed me of the special moment of becoming a parent.

How could I *not* feel like a victim? I was the victim in all that had transpired. None of that was my fault.

But as my cramping hand wrapped up into a painful little ball after line five hundred or so, new knowledge began unwrapping inside my brain. Yes, awful things had happened that were beyond my control. These things had harmed me, that was certain. But I was paying the price every day by making those awful things my whole story.

There is a difference between being victimized and living as a victim. One is something that happened to you, while the other is how you see yourself.

We can acknowledge things that happened to us without making them our entire story. My identity was built upon all the unfair situations I'd been subjected to, rather than who I was in spite of them. I had always seen myself as a victim, and that did me no good. It affected my sense of self, the way I navigated the world and the choices I made every day. A victim mindset isn't empowering, nor is it an acknowledgment of injustices done. Those injustices can be acknowledged without making them your entire narrative. By internalizing my victimhood, I had shifted from someone who had no control over situations in the past to someone who allowed those past situations to still control me in the present. Seeing myself as a victim in life only caused me further harm. Instead of living in the now, I was stuck in childhood, doing the work of those who had bullied me and hurt me in many unspeakable ways. I had become their unwitting accomplice, carrying on their legacy. I was wasting my days feeling sorry for myself, and that needed to end.

When I saw Dr. Shore the following week, I brought my note-book filled with lines and handed it to him. He looked it over, seemingly impressed.

"Did you get to one thousand?" he asked me.

"No," I admitted. "I got to nine hundred and change. I ran out of time."

"Did you learn anything?"

"I did," I replied, with appreciation replacing the resentment from last week. "I learned that I'm not a victim. I'm not made of those things that happened to me. My past is more than that, and I am more than that."

"Then you got what you needed out of the exercise," he said, smiling knowingly. "That's what matters. Sometimes we have to tell ourselves something over and over in order to start believing it. That's why I had you write it down so much."

Dr. Shore was a quirky man with some fairly unconventional approaches to depression recovery. I can't condone his methods or even vouch for his ability to legally provide therapy. I also don't know if what he did with me would work for someone else or just backfire completely. But as weird as that whole situation was, I can say it helped me fundamentally shift how I saw myself. We went on to have counselling sessions for several more weeks, many of them more traditional than our first. I don't recall most of what we talked about, but the big takeaway from week one stayed with me: I was victimized, not a victim.

And to this day I don't identify as a victim.

—

Another important lesson I learned from my work with Dr. Shore is how well I can respond to some more unusual therapeutic methods. Years later, this became relevant again when I started working with Maya, who prided herself on unconventional approaches to therapy. She explained to me that she tailored her technique to each client to best meet that person's needs. I suppose that is true of all therapists to some extent, but Maya was quite purposeful in this approach. She incorporated plenty of coaching elements into her work, like asking me a lot of questions and helping me set weekly goals, which I responded to well. Maya would often tell me that she used coaching methods about 80 percent of the time when we worked together.

There is nothing wrong with standard therapeutic treatments for most people. They've been developed over long periods of time and have proven successful. The problem for me was that I had tried standard therapeutic approaches like cognitive behavioural therapy on many occasions, both with and without the support of medication, and they had mostly not helped with my underlying CPTSD. Trying to reframe my current stressors, for example, without addressing the trauma that fuelled many of them wasn't helpful. These techniques always felt like putting a bandage over a gaping wound that actually needed stitches to heal.

You see, when we don't fix the real issues at the root of a mental health crisis, it's only a matter of time before we bleed through the bandage. In all my years of receiving therapy, no one had identified trauma as the key component to my struggles—or if they had, they hadn't told me about it. No wonder I wasn't getting better. No wonder I kept cycling back into dark places. I was repeatedly triggered by events that still haunted me from childhood, except I didn't know that what I was experiencing was a trigger, or how to deal with it; I only knew how I felt, which was anxious, frightened, overwhelmed and, eventually, completely shut down. That part of me had never matured or healed. It was locked in stasis, awaiting the next hit. This caused my depression and anxiety to continually bubble to the surface, where they would then be bandaged up, leaving the festering wound unaddressed. The trauma itself and its triggers had to be dealt with head-on.

Right now, the trigger was the cruelty being directed at me online. A lot of people were saying heartbreaking things about my intentions and character, which caused that old childhood wound to open back up again. Everything in me wanted to stop that from happening, even if it meant taking my own life. I've learned that trauma doesn't reason. It doesn't think. It doesn't know logic. It reacts in pure, primal fear to try to keep us safe, and that fear can be all-encompassing.

How I had arrived at a dangerous level of suicidal thoughts was the most frightening thing of all. Not since my teen years had trauma taken over to the point where I became actively suicidal. This public bullying had awoken a slumbering beast I thought I had defeated. I was sure I had conquered my past and was now moving forward. Victimized, not a victim, remember? I had grown up, raised a family and built a life I was proud of. I was a full-grown adult, responsible and logical in so many ways. So why was I suddenly thirteen years old again?

Trauma can lay dormant for a long time, until something rouses it. What that something is might not even make sense in relation to the original event, but it makes it no less real, powerful or potentially dangerous. In my case, I wondered why this incident, out of many others throughout my life, was the one that nearly killed me. I had lost friendships before—real friendships with real people I loved and trusted—but I hadn't felt suicidal as a result. I had been attacked online countless times by massive numbers of transphobic, homophobic and misogynistic trolls, but I had never been so upset about it that I wanted to end my life. Why was this time so different? I hoped I would get to the root of it all because what I needed more than anything was to heal and move forward. I wanted to get well, and I needed to clearly see a path for my future beyond what had just happened.

I had been victimized, but I was not going to live as a victim any longer. I was ready to prove myself a fighter and battle for my life.

A lot of what I remember of the first two or three weeks after my breakdown is fuzzy. To get a full picture, I interviewed those around me to hear what I was like at the time. This mental fuzziness isn't uncommon when you're having a major mental health crisis. The brain is injured in a way, and like any other part of the body, it doesn't function as well as it heals. When I was writing my first book, I slipped on a patch of ice in the driveway and ended up with a concussion. For a few weeks afterward, writing was a challenge that required frequent breaks. I operated in a fatigued haze, my mind forgetful and erratic at times. This breakdown felt similar, except it came with a generous serving of sadness and anxiety too.

I do remember spending a lot of time on the couch, just lying there. It's a nice couch: blue and velvety. I had bought it a few months earlier, when I redecorated the living room—an unlikely choice for someone who usually prefers neutral furniture and adds pops of colour with accent decor. But I haven't regretted that purchase at all; the couch is one of my favourite things. We always have it stacked with colourful throw cushions, which I used in the breakdown days to prop myself up to varying degrees. I didn't have the energy to interact with people much, so I would just lie there, napping, staring at the walls or out the window or skimming magazines I couldn't read for more than a paragraph at a time. My family members would sometimes sit beside me or bring me something hot to drink. We didn't chat much, but the company was nice. Nobody really knew what to do for me, which is likely because there was little that could be done in those early days. I didn't know it at the time, but once my brain had gone largely offline like that, I just needed to ride it out until I could function better. My family's presence was a constant comfort, though, and I count myself fortunate.

Since I don't remember much outside of lying on the frou-frou sofa like an early twentieth-century therapy patient, I asked Zoë to tell me what she saw from the outside. She described me as "despondent and broken."

"You cried a lot back then," she recalled. "You were so fragile and not able to deal with anything. The world was just too much for you. You spent a lot of time alone, sleeping or watching TV."

She seemed heartbroken just thinking about it. "But then," she continued, "you threw yourself into getting better. You knew what you needed to do, and that's what you focused on. Everything was about your mental health for a while, almost obsessively so."

Having an ADHD brain means I sometimes hyperfocus on things. This can often be put to use finishing a true crime series on HBO, so it's nice that I can set my mind on important stuff like wellness too.

I also asked Maya what she recalled from those early days.

"Where do I start?" she said, keenly aware that I was suddenly the person asking the questions in this relationship.

"How about you give me a list of strengths you saw in me?" I suggested. "We can go from there."

She took a long time to come up with exactly two things. "You knew to reach out for help," she finally said. Then she paused again for what felt like two hundred years, searching for another positive trait. "Oh! And you were willing to put the work in."

"That's . . . that's it?" I prompted, trying to sound journalist-y and not offended-y.

"Um," she said, "I could probably come up with more if I think on it for a bit."

"Okay, point taken," I laughed. "Let's move on. We both know I'm glorious anyway."

I winked at the camera on my computer screen. She rolled her eyes at me.

"What about my weaknesses?" I asked, getting ready to be met with another long pause as she struggled to come up with an answer.

"Oh, that one's easy," she said, delivering a swift kick to my ego and firing off a stream of them so quickly I had to ask her to repeat them more slowly.

In her defence, she is trained to seek out areas for clients to improve upon, and it's not like my areas in need of improvement were few and far between back then. After all, a person doesn't fall apart as badly as I had without needing some serious psychological renovations.

"The worst part is how you had absolutely no self-worth back then," Maya explained. "The person in front of me could not see their own value. You let how other people see you dictate how *you* saw you."

Maya wasn't wrong. My low self-esteem had always been there, worming its way into every facet of my life, eating slowly at my insides and leaving me hollow and defenceless. Then, when something significantly painful happened that hit all my sorest spots, I shattered completely. To prevent this from happening again, we agreed that our first task was to detach my feelings about myself from what others thought of me. This would also be the hardest task we faced. It was time to tackle my archnemesis: people pleasing.

the toxicity of people pleasing

KNOCK, KNOCK, KNOCK.

Hello? Hello in there?

Are you going to let me in? It's me, the People Pleaser! I know it's late, but I'm sure there is *something* I can do for you, right? I mean, I wouldn't want to disappoint you. What would you think of me then? How could I live with your negative opinion of me?

And while I'm on my feet, can I rustle up a little cheese tray or something? I'm pretty hungry. Are you hungry? Oh, no bother at all! You can always count on me to go above and beyond.

Did any of that sound uncomfortably familiar? If so, you've come to the right chapter, my fellow social contortionist. Welcome to "Everything I Wish I'd Never Had to Learn About People Pleasing but Am Glad I Did." As I've discovered and now teach both my kids and my clients, it's entirely possible *not* to people-please while also not feeling like a constant disappointment.

I regularly describe myself as a recovering people pleaser. It hasn't been a smooth ride. After years of knowing only one way of being, I now must actively choose to do something radically different every day: put my own needs first. It's gotten much easier over time, but I can still slip back into old habits—like always trying to guess what other people want to hear from me—if I'm not careful. Behaviours we're familiar with are often more comfortable than what's new and unfamiliar, even if those behaviours are not good for us. Maya called this "the default state." But figuring out how the default state was harming me and my most important relationships has helped me to mostly move beyond it.

Trauma might have been running the show for most of my life, but pleasing others at the expense of my own wellbeing was the symptom that nearly killed me. If I had not cared so deeply about what others thought of me, I never would have contemplated ending it all simply because of what happened on social media, nor would I have been as burned out trying to meet everyone's expectations as I had been up until that point. This is a pattern I wish I had been more aware of sooner. Because if I could pinpoint the single issue that has caused me the most grief, it's been my lifelong drive to make everyone around me happy.

Like many people and for many reasons, I grew up a people pleaser. When my elementary school friend Jasmine wanted to stop hanging out with me because my lack of popularity was limiting her social options, I should have told her to get lost, knowing I deserved better. Instead, I made her a card (more than once), wrote her a pleading note about how much she meant to me and taped coins to the inside of it in a desperate attempt to get her to change her mind. If I wasn't good enough for her, maybe money was. I didn't know how my days would be without her, and I didn't want to find out. I suspected I would feel quite alone and be open to even more bullying than I already was. As long as she valued me, I had value because she believed I did. If Mara were to end the friendship, which she eventually did (she was the girl who encouraged her new group of friends to throw their skirts up and yell, "Lesbian!" at me), I would lose my worth.

My reaction to kids who chronically bullied me wasn't to stay as far away from them as possible, but rather to try to earn their friendship. I would bring the other ten-year-olds little gifts—such as trading cards and rare marbles—and watch as they laughed at how pathetic I must have seemed to them. Sometimes, they would *almost* appear to be reconsidering their view of me. They would chat about hanging out with me next recess or hint that maybe I could go to the party they were throwing that half the class was invited to. Those were exciting times when I clung to hope like a well-loved baby blanket. I imagined my life would change for the better with their acceptance. I would be safer, and school would be a place I no longer dreaded. Unfortunately, my hopes were always dashed; those invitations to recess hangouts and parties never came. No matter what I did, the kids who were mean to me continued to be mean.

I never thought that the other kids were the problem—that their meanness and pettiness were issues that had nothing to do with me. I was convinced *I* was the issue. *I* wasn't trying hard enough. *I* wasn't good enough at figuring out what they needed.

I had to do more to earn their acceptance. Because I wasn't innately likeable, I mused, *I* had to be extra generous until they gave me a chance and discovered I wasn't so bad after all. I not only gave them little trinkets but also laughed at their bad jokes, let them believe they had all the answers (even when I knew they were wrong) and allowed them to jump ahead of me in line when-ever the teacher wasn't looking. They took full advantage. Why wouldn't they? I was a doormat who readily gave them somewhere to wipe their feet.

I would dream about the day when the kids at school would finally figure out how wrong they had been about me this entire time and would accept me as one of them. Or at the very least, view me as someone worthy of marginal respect and not a punch in the face.

That day never came.

Grade school was a time when I effectively paid someone to be my friend and gave stuff to kids who were horrendous to me. Every day, I handed a piece of myself to people who didn't deserve it. I longed for acceptance so much that I was willing to do just about anything for it. If there were an award for people pleasing, I would have won it—and no doubt promptly given it to someone else.

My people-pleasing behaviour had been solidified in my early years, made part of the foundation of who I was, and I would spend the next thirty-five years or so playing the same game and expecting less terrible prizes. I was the mother in the PTA meeting who took on the secretary position—the one job that ultimately required far more organization than my disorganized brain could handle and more time than my life with three young kids could manage. I did it not because I wanted to do it, but because I had been asked and felt I couldn't say no.

I was the mom at playgroup who would try to strike up conversations with other moms who were cold toward me. Sure, I hung out with the ones I had a great rapport with too, but there was no chase in those relationships—and yes, I wanted the chase. I had my eye on the prize: approval from the women who only politely smiled at me and would otherwise pretend I wasn't there. Somewhere deep in my mind, I saw them as a threat, as the new bullies who were judging me. Winning them over, my subconscious told me, would ensure my wellbeing. I worked at it tirelessly, giving energy to people who didn't return it. The chase was what I knew, and the idea of it finally paying off enticed me.

When we bought our first house, it officially made me a young mother, a newlywed and a homeowner by the age of twenty-two. These felt like giant shoes to fill for someone so young. Every other adult in our new development had at least five years on me, and I felt like I had to prove we belonged there. I was grateful to get on the property ladder at such a young age, but that gratitude was tied to feeling like an imposter on my own street, playing a role that didn't fit me. Just six years earlier, I was living in a shelter. Only two years earlier, nurses and doctors had treated me like a second-class citizen while I was in labour with a potentially life-threatening medical condition. Now, rather quickly, I had moved from poverty to middle class, from homeless to homeowner. I felt like I was pretending to be something I wasn't, living a life I didn't belong in, and everyone would soon figure it out—if they hadn't already.

I tried to be society's ideal version of mom, partner, friend, neighbour, playgroup-goer and preschool volunteer. I spent an exorbitant amount of energy trying to prove my worth when there was no need to. I had value, but I couldn't see it. I had wrapped it up in what everyone else thought of me, just as I always had.

Because without their approval, I surmised, I was nothing.

Admittedly, I was on the extreme end of the people-pleaser spectrum, but that doesn't mean there aren't a lot of individuals with similar feelings and behaviours. You can find us every-where. We're the ones who everybody seems to recognize can't say no. We're working all hours of the day and night trying to make the lives of those around us better, often making our own lives worse in the process. We forget to take care of ourselves, or we *don't* forget but decide not to because we're convinced doing so would be selfish. Selfishness is the biggest sin imaginable to a social contortionist. Putting ourselves first in any situation creates a heap of guilt because we often don't believe we're as important as other people. We will bend and fold and stretch for everyone but ourselves.

But what happens when we do all that bending and folding and stretching, and people still aren't happy with us?

Well, as I learned the hard way, we get sick. And sometimes it nearly kills us.

—

The internet is a dangerous place for a people pleaser.

Back in the Dark Times, aka before social media, we had smaller social circles that changed over time. We lost touch with some people and had conflicts with others; we might never reconnect with them again. Social media has changed all that by growing and blending our circles in ways the human brain hasn't adapted to. I don't think we are meant to maintain the level of everyday connections we now have online, which can result in some unwanted consequences and added stress. High school band acquaintances and current adult friends occupy the same digital space, as does your mom, your dog groomer, your co-worker, your next-door neighbour and the guy who found you a good mortgage rate three years ago.

What this means is our social circles are now much wider, and the people in them usually know different sides of us in our day-to-day lives. My mindfulness instructor sees me at my most relaxed and my business coach sees me when I'm stressing over all the updates needed on my chronically out-of-date website. But they both see the same content from me online: what I ate for dinner last weekend, that sassy political post I made at election time and all my obnoxious couple selfies with my wife. How that feels to them—along with my current friends, former high school bandmates, mom, dog groomer and mortgage broker—is going to vary and shouldn't really matter to me. It's not my business what other people think, right?

But as a people pleaser, I made it my business. That's my specialty.

Cast that net even wider. I have a following on Twitter that is currently over a hundred thousand. Each person follows my work as a writer, speaker and advocate for their own reasons and reacts to me with their own views of the world as a back-drop. As such, every one of them is going to feel differently about what I say and do. What one finds interesting, another might find uninteresting or even offensive. Of those who find what I say uninteresting or offensive, some will choose to simply ignore it, while others will unfollow or block me for it. And some may even take me to task for it.

For years, I tried to keep everyone who followed my social media feeds happy. Every. Single. Person.

I didn't identify it to myself that way, of course—and if some-one had suggested this is what I was doing, I would have scoffed at the idea and called it impossible—because it is. I knew it was an impossible task, but that's exactly what I was attempting. I put enormous thought into what I was doing, trying to anticipate every possible reaction from every possible kind of person to every single post or tweet I made. Could this be taken the wrong way by anyone at all? Was I going to upset anyone? What would the people looking for flaws think? Olympic-level mental gym-nastics were performed every time I posted online.

Social media became my new schoolyard. I was a lot older and a little bit wiser, so I knew there would be some people who absolutely hated what I did, and I was okay with that. If their worldview involved intolerance, anti-LGBTQ sentiment or alt-right conspiracy theories about the "trans agenda," I wasn't going to be their cup of tea. That was a compliment, really.

But there was another group that I worked hard to impress without even realizing it: other left-leaning activists, particularly the ones who worked in the same LGBTQ circles as me. I followed and looked up to many of them. But not all of them felt the same way about me, especially after my book was published, and they became my focus. The more obvious and public the critics made their dislike for me, the harder I tried to change their minds. The louder they voiced opposition to my advocacy work, the more I subconsciously wanted to win them over. I would attempt to figure out what they didn't like about me and contort myself in all kinds of ways to change it. I tried to anticipate any disapproval before it even happened, any rumblings of disdain before they became louder. I would visit their social media feeds to see what they were saying, and sometimes lie awake at night wondering how I could turn the tide and get them to accept me.

It was a battle I lost—terribly, I might add—because this was a ridiculous and impossible task.

I wish I'd known better. Holding a mirror up to my attempts to please my critics would have revealed the futility of it and the harm it was causing me. But a lifelong pattern of insecurity had made this process my default; as always, I was people pleasing on autopilot. In this case, it all surrounded my activism and what I believed others expected of me. I was told to share more of this, less of that. Speak up about this, not about that. Except the expectations often contradicted each other. One person scolded me for not sharing the words of others enough, while another said I wasn't providing enough original content. Some said I should speak up about trans issues because the community needed allies to be louder, while others argued that when I spoke up, I was drowning out trans voices and hurting the cause. I was chastised for posting selfies and also told they were empowering. I was thanked for speaking about my family in transition but also told I was taking space away from others to tell their own stories. With so many conflicting opinions, how could I possibly do the right thing?

Spoiler alert: I could not to the "right thing" because the "right thing" meant something different to each person. I was burning myself out trying to guess at and meet the expectations of . . . well, everyone. And what had all these people done to earn that work from me?

That's a trick question. As a recovering people pleaser, I now recognize that no one deserves that effort, regardless of how they might feel about me. We should never exhaust ourselves trying to make others happy.

When the online pile-on ensued in May 2020, I had already been playing the people-pleasing game for most of my life. And what did all that time and energy spent trying to make everyone happy get me? At the end of the day, many people I had attempted to earn acceptance from disliked me so much that they spoke out loudly against me, which got the attention of their followers, and their followers' followers, and a bunch of random trolls who hang around the internet just waiting for the next pile-on so they can jump in and have fun. And I was unceremoniously torn to shreds.

The end result of all that people pleasing: I suffered a breakdown and almost died, most of these people still didn't like me and now a bunch of folks who had never heard of me before didn't like me either. By people-pleasing standards, it was the most epic of disasters.

As far as I was concerned at the time, this monsoon of criticism was everything I had ever feared knocking on my door on a Monday morning. I had dreaded this day for years, certain it would eventually come. Sure, the specifics of what would happen had taken on different looks over time, but the worry was always the same: *One day, everyone will figure out you're not worthy of love or respect, just like they did when you were younger, and they will leave you like your father did or hurt you like so many others did. You will be all alone, and life will no longer be worth living.*

It took six days of criticism, some pretty wild accusations ("you're exploiting your trans child for fame"), outright lies ("Amanda gets rich off this grift") and a fair amount of harassment for me to become suicidal. In retrospect, I'm surprised it took as long as it did. Because my perception of self was based on everything good that had been said about me over the years, I quickly became everything bad they were now saying about me and sank into a shame spiral. That is the terrible truth about relying on outside merit—you're only worth what others think you are.

Here's the good news: As awful as this all felt at the time, it was one of the best things that ever happened to me. The experience forced me to stop making proverbial cheese trays for every random knock at the door. Today, I am *done* trying to please everyone else. I owe this realization, in part, to Maya, who is not known to mince words.

—

It was our second video call. Maya had spent the first session learning about me, as most therapist types do. Now it was time to get to work. "One of your biggest issues I can see is people pleasing," she said to me. "You seem to seek out validation from everyone around you."

"I know," I admitted with a sigh, lowering my eyes reflexively. "I guess I never realized how big of a problem it is until now."

That might seem ridiculous now that you've seen the highlight reel of my life. But this pattern was all I had ever known. Over many decades, it had become indistinguishable from my personality. I was always taught that kind people were good to others, and that being good to others meant shelving your own needs. I believed this behaviour was who I *was*, not what I *did*. I couldn't separate the two. If I wanted to avoid more soul-crushing experiences like the one I'd just lived through, however, I needed to break a lifelong habit, and I had no idea where to start.

Who was the person beneath the drive to please? Did I even know?

If we've spent years focusing on other people, we tend to mostly ignore ourselves. My opinion of myself doesn't matter if I allow your opinion of me to take priority. Who I am is irrelevant as long as Instagram, my next-door neighbour and my dog groomer are happy with me, right?

Of course, people pleasers don't tell ourselves this. Just like everyone else, we think we have well-formed ideas of who we are. But that's not generally true. A social contortionist lives to serve, and not in that admirable way nurses on the frontlines do. Our purpose is to mine a sense of self from the approval of those around us: our family, friends, neighbours, managers, fellow parishioners and even strangers on the internet. We give to everyone until we're depleted. We think we're being altruistic in these acts of kindness, but they are anything but selfless.

Here's an unfortunate truth that once kept me up half the night: those of us most afraid of seeming selfish are, without realizing it, using and manipulating the people around us to feel better about ourselves. When I first realized this, I felt terrible. But I couldn't deny the truth in that statement. If I'm doing things to make other people happy so that they approve of me, then aren't I really doing those things for me? I'm not talking about doing a good deed every now and then—I do those to help others, even if it does make me feel good in the process. But if the bulk of my life choices are made only so that others will like me, and therefore, I can like myself, that's pretty selfish.

Again, part of being human is helping out our fellow humans. But there's a difference between giving a little time when we have it and chronically making big sacrifices to do so. When we do things to ensure others aren't disappointed in us, we're creating a false persona; we're not letting those around us see who we really are because we're afraid they won't like us. If we say no, we worry they'll think less of us or will see us as selfish. (The dreaded S-word!) Friends might give us the cold shoulder. Followers might unfollow us. People might form opinions of us we don't want them to have and share them with others, who might adopt those same opinions. They might reject us completely, and that would hurt. So we give them what we think they want. We give them a version of us.

That's subversive manipulation, which is not what healthy relationships are built on.

Ouch. Figuring this out as I unpacked my behaviours over a lifetime was a significant blow to my already wounded ego. How could I reconcile being both selfish and manipulative when I worked so hard at being neither?

I wasn't trying to be selfish or manipulative. I was trying to survive in a world that had taught me this was the only way to behave. Making people happy meant survival. How could I be mad at the little kid inside me who was just trying to make it through another day?

This was not the time to beat myself up; goodness knows I've done enough of that in my life. Now that I knew why I did what I did, I needed to forgive myself and move forward. No part of people pleasing is malicious—it's done with the best of intentions. The behaviour is unhealthy, but that doesn't make us bad people.

Maya and I outlined what I needed to do to break free of people pleasing. It was a nice short list:

1. Set firm boundaries.
2. Cultivate a better sense of who I am.

Great! I love short to-do lists. I could knock those off in no time at all, right?

Right?

boundaries for days

JUST TODAY, I WAS MINDING my own business when a journalist notorious for his transphobia tried to get my attention on social media. This wasn't the first time. Over the years, he has taunted me on several occasions and seemed to enjoy getting his transphobic followers to swarm my feeds. He even mocked me in an op-ed piece during my breakdown.

But I did something different today: I didn't take the bait. I chose not to respond in any way. I didn't give his attention-seeking behaviour any oxygen, which meant he couldn't reply in kind, and no escalation could take place. Because of this, I cut off whatever attempt he was making at the knees, and he quickly went silent. I'll be curious to see if he bothers putting in the effort again. If he does, he will be met with the same response because I am not the same person today as I used to be.

This behaviour is the lovechild of two new tools in my toolbox: mindfulness and boundaries. Mindfulness, which I will be discussing a bit later, allowed me to pause and reflect on what this man was doing rather than be reflexive and reactive about it. I took a step back and remembered what matters to me. (Spoiler alert: Not him.) My boundaries, which I've worked a great deal on over the last while, are firmly in place most days, and I simply decided not to cross them or let him do so.

But I wasn't always this aware or purposeful. In fact, I used to be the complete opposite, as Maya gladly reminded me whenever she had the opportunity.

"You had no idea how to set boundaries," she lamented on repeat. "You just let life walk all over you."

"I *thought* I had boundaries, though," I replied earnestly. "I really believed I had that shit under control."

The fact is, I did have some semblance of boundaries, but they were fairly flimsy things. It was easy to step right over them. It was obvious to anyone looking in that I didn't have a handle on what I allowed into my life and what I didn't. I ended up at the hospital in large part because of my glaring lack of personal limits. People pleasing is an exercise in weak to non-existent boundary setting, and as we know, I was practically an Olympian in that sport. Maya spotted this boundary issue in me almost immediately, but I was completely unaware of how bad things actually were.

You can know a lot about something and not implement it well in your own life. For me, that was the concept of setting boundaries. When I entered rehab as a teenager, one of the first things they taught me was the importance of setting firm limits with myself and those around me. Boundaries keep you safe. Boundaries keep you on track. Given that my life was largely off track before I got sober, this was an important lesson.

As a teenager, I hadn't a clue how to say no to anyone, and this is what got me in trouble most of the time. When a friend called to invite me to a party, I would go, even though I knew I shouldn't because I would struggle to control my alcohol intake. When boys (and men) hit on me and it made me uncomfortable, as it always did, I usually lacked the confidence to let them down or tell them to stop. I knew that if my parents set a curfew but my friends wanted me to stay out later, I would choose to break the rules because I didn't want my peers to think less of me. When someone picked on me at school, I worried that if I stood up for myself, I would get an even worse reputation than I already had.

Boundaries were not a part of my life as a young person, and it showed. We worked on setting them in group and individual therapy at the rehab centre, with the counsellors hammering away at why we needed to stay strong in our commitment to sober living. "People, places and things are what will get you into trouble," they would say to us. "You have to surround yourself with the right ones and keep the wrong ones out." I learned safe boundaries and tried to live by them. I got better at drawing a clear line between what was dangerous and what was not. It was simple and straightforward: if I wanted to make sure my life progressed in a healthy way and I didn't end up in another dangerous situation, like that time in Macie's apartment, I had to follow the rules.

What I didn't realize for a long while was that those rules I set for my safety are merely rudimentary boundaries. Important, yes, but something I could have built upon in the rest of my life had I known how. There were plenty of areas I had yet to work on. I still didn't know how to confidently tell guys to keep their hands off me. I still occasionally ignored my gut and put myself in situations that could have jeopardized my sobriety, then desperately tried to excuse my way out of there rather than just say, "This isn't a good place for me to be right now." I said yes to make others happy far more than I said no to make myself happy.

Never once did I stop to think that I could do it differently—that I could take the "people, places and things" model and branch it out to fit every aspect of my life. I believed that regularly meeting the expectations of others at the expense of myself was how everyone lived. That yes, I was uncomfortable, exhausted and resentful sometimes, but there was no other choice if I wanted to be a good person.

When we have a warped sense of personal limits as young people, we carry that into adulthood with us. I dragged my feeble boundaries through the decades, unaware of how this was affecting me or setting me up for the catastrophe that awaited me in my forties. Because many of those boundaries were set during a period of trauma, they didn't mature as I did. As a helpful kind of person, I wanted to be accessible, approachable and friendly. I didn't realize I could—and *should*—be all of those things with firm limits in place as safeguards. It wasn't until everything fell apart that I recognized how long I had been lying to myself. I wasn't being accessible—I was a complete pushover. I wasn't being approachable—I was a doormat with a face. And I wasn't being friendly—I was being what I thought others wanted me to be at the expense of what I *needed* me to be.

According to the *Cambridge Advanced Learner's Dictionary*, a boundary is "a real or imagined line that marks the edge or limit of something."

When it comes to personal boundaries, that "something" is our wellbeing. In the name of our mental and physical health, we place limits on how far we will extend ourselves and how much we will tolerate from others.

What's inside the boundary? Only what we allow in.

What's outside of it? Everything else.

There are plenty of stressors we have little to no control over in our daily lives, such as unexpected injury, job loss, climate change or, as we've learned once again, pandemics. To be human is to experience anxiety and worry to some degree. But if we can remove stressors we *do* have control over, that can only improve our lives. Setting boundaries helps tremendously with this and allows us to save our limited energy for the times when life throws us those curveballs. Of course, it can be stressful in itself to start setting those boundaries, but over time, the rewards of doing so really pay off.

When I started working with Maya, she had me grab a notebook and draw a layer of bricks at the bottom of a page. Each time I felt I had made significant progress in my growth, I would add another layer of brick. I added the first layer in honour of the day I drove myself to the hospital, and another for learning to meditate and doing it consistently. Over time, that wall grew quite tall, and most of the layers represented a new boundary I'd set in my personal or professional life. Layer by layer, I was building up healthy protections. Little by little, I was learning what healthy boundaries were, and how to make them. Today, I teach boundaries as part of my work as a life coach, speaker and mentor. Without them, we can't build a solid foundation.

Maya and I talked often about why I needed boundaries, and I did a lot of research outside of our sessions on how to set some that would work for me. Today, I don't know how I ever lived life without them. I suppose, if I'm being honest, not very well.

So how do we do it? How do we start laying that base layer of brick in the first place?

In order to set boundaries, we first have to admit that we don't have them, or that the ones we have simply aren't working. That's an awkward conversation to have with yourself. It involves some serious introspection and probably a side dish of disappointment as the reality sets in.

I only ever knew one way of belonging to society: the way that pushed my own needs into the background at every opportunity. It was my normal, my baseline. And like other unhealthy behaviours, it served a purpose: not only did I gain self-worth from others but I felt like a good person because I was "nice," "generous" and "easygoing." This is how I justified all the unpleasant consequences of not having boundaries. It made me a decent person, so it was fine.

Realizing how damaging this behaviour was made me wince. How could I have been so unaware? It felt like the shame that realization caused could have swallowed me whole at this point. But shame had no place here, and I had to let it go. It's not only an unhelpful emotion in building new thought processes but also grossly misplaced. While guilt is an emotion we feel when we believe we've done something wrong, shame is what we feel when we believe *we* are fundamentally wrong. It's the difference between "I did a bad thing" and "I am a bad person." Guilt can help us recognize mistakes and make changes, but shame keeps us stuck. I wasn't a bad person for doing things in a way that didn't serve me well—I just didn't know any better.

When we know better, we do better. Self-awareness is a powerful tool. Human beings make errors. In an ideal situation, we make a mistake, realize that mistake, own up to it and grow from it. Unfortunately, shame impedes growth because we become too hung up in negative thoughts about ourselves to make the required changes. Because shame is so uncomfortable, we can also get defensive at the slightest hint of it. So if we're really committed to growing, we need to let that shame go. Throw it out the window; it doesn't serve you.

Next, we need to overcome a people pleaser's biggest fear: saying no.

This is a tricky one, as it often leads to feelings of selfishness. But I need you to stay with me here, because this is something we can and absolutely must work through—it just requires a mindset shift. Yes, centring ourselves can feel wrong at first, especially to people pleasers, codependents and those of us with childhood trauma who have historically contorted our lives around everybody else. But is being selfish always a bad thing?

Selfishness gets a bad rap. Sure, there's a negative kind of self-ish, an extreme kind that never takes the needs or wants of others into consideration. We can't have a society where everyone is only concerned with themselves because things would break down quickly. Being there for one another is a fundamental part of humanity. There will always be times when we have to shelve our own needs in favour of the needs of others, such as when we're parenting young children or supporting aging relatives, and there will be times when putting aside our needs to help others is good, like helping your little brother move into his first place or shovelling out your elderly neighbour's driveway after a big snowstorm.

But we must always consider our own limitations when doing for others. We can't take on everything, and we shouldn't expect ourselves to. It's not a bad kind of selfish to preserve our well-being. That old saying that you can't pour from an empty cup holds true. If we get burned out or seriously ill, how will we be able to help anyone else?

Here's the first mindset shift: **Self-preservation is kindness in a way that exhausting ourselves for others is not**. It is kind to make sure we're well taken care of because this helps us take better care of everyone we love, including ourselves.

Even when we overcome the "selfish" aspect of saying no, we must still tackle our fears of what people will think of us. This is the people-pleasing trap many of us are stuck in for years. Thankfully, there's another mindset shift that can help with that.

As I've discussed, people pleasing is an inauthentic way of presenting ourselves to the world. We are trying to stay safe from hurt and rejection, so we show those around us a version of ourselves that we think they want to see. Eschewing healthy boundaries in the name of keeping others happy means we're presenting a false sense of self. The person we are showing others says yes when they want to say no.

Envision a life in which you are surrounded by people who not only like you but also respect who you are and what you need. In a later chapter, we'll talk about the company we keep on the road to mental wellness. But for now, let me just say that if you have a friend who would rather you blow your money on her bachelorette getaway than fix your broken car, that is not a friend who has your best interests at heart. If you have parents who insist you hide that you're gay so they can save face with their homophobic friends, they're not respecting you. And isn't it better to let someone know you don't want a second date than to tell them the truth on the tenth one?

I have a rule on my personal Facebook page: we treat each other respectfully. Because the internet can be a cruel place, I use that space as a reprieve for both myself and my friends, many of whom are marginalized and face a lot of hatred elsewhere. Recently, I had to ask someone I've known for years to stop attacking others over a disagreement that broke out in the comment section of one of my posts. I explained that while I welcome discourse, I draw the line at name-calling. When the person became angry and made it clear he had no intention of stopping what he was doing, I blocked him. This boundary, put there for everyone's benefit, is non-negotiable.

When a person gets upset over a boundary we set, it's not about the boundary or even about us at all—it's about them. Their expectations of us and the world in general will guide their feelings. Our responsibility is to let them know what our limits are, and their responsibility is to deal with their feelings surrounding those limits. Initially, people might push back a little (or a lot), especially if they're not used to having these new limits in place. But if a relationship is strong and healthy, it will survive healthy boundaries and grow even stronger. If it's an unhealthy relationship, good boundaries could spell the end of it.

Is that really a bad thing? Not all relationships are meant to last a lifetime. If someone's measure of our value is how much we're willing to sacrifice our own welfare for them, that is probably not a relationship worth keeping.

With that in mind, here is the second mindset shift: **We deserve to be surrounded by people who care about us and respect us as much as we care about and respect them.**

Boundaries are something we develop and work on over time.

I'm an exercise fanatic and do high-intensity cardio and resistance training. But I didn't start out that way. I started with gentle walking and Pilates, using my own body as resistance in lieu of weights. Gradually, over a long period of time, I worked my way into several heart-pounding cardio and boxing sessions each week.

If you had asked me at the beginning of my fitness journey if I could see myself doing the workouts I do today, I would have laughed and emphatically stated: "I'm not a cardio person, and I hate weights." After a lifetime of mostly sedentary living, I would have viewed what I do now as impossible. As it turns out, it wasn't.

I just needed to train myself into it. Now, in my forties, I would describe myself as a cardio person who likes to lift weights. Progress takes time.

Boundaries are like exercise. When we're new to them, sometimes it's best to start small so it doesn't get overwhelming. The last thing we want to do is go too big too fast and decide we're "not a boundary person," so to speak. If we confront our parents, tell our boss we're not staying late on a Friday and skip our friend's bachelorette getaway all in the same week, it can create a rodeo at the chaos ranch that we might not know how to wrangle.

I suggest you choose exactly one boundary to get your feet wet. I'll use an unfortunate example from my own life. Not long ago, my wife and I had an extended relative who made it known they would never accept our relationship and was quite hurtful in the delivery of this news. This crossed a safety boundary for me. I can't tell people what opinions they should have, but I will also not purposely spend time with someone who is homophobic or transphobic, no matter our history. Zoë and I are also fiercely protective of our kids, and for their wellbeing and our own, we knew we would need to limit our interactions with this family member going forward.

Some boundaries are particularly tough to set, and this was one of them. In order to make it stick, I took the following steps:

1. I wrote down how to set the boundary. What does limiting our interactions look like? In this case, it meant not spending time with this family member except when absolutely necessary, such as at a large family gathering. We would not see

them in person otherwise, nor would we respond to emails, phone calls or social media posts.

2. I made a list of possible reactions to the setting of that boundary. I was exhaustive in my thought process. How would this family member react to us taking a step back? How might other family members react? (After all, our decision would affect them too.) There might be some challenging conversations. There was always a possibility that someone would push back against the decision or say we were overreacting.

3. I came up with responses to any potential reaction. Having a plan helps mitigate our anxiety around setting new boundaries. Zoë and I had made our decision, and we were sticking to it. If anyone started pushing back, I had a response ready. In this case, it looked like this: "I understand you feel this way, and I respect what you're saying. But I want you to know we didn't come to this decision lightly. Sometimes we have to make choices about what's best for our wellbeing, and this is one of those times." I had to remember I couldn't control how anyone else would feel or react. I could only control my own reactions.

4. I listed reasons why keeping this boundary was important. This list, made for my eyes only, was my emotional backup if things got hard and I started second-guessing myself. One obvious reason on the list was that nobody deserves bigotry in their lives, no matter who's dishing it out. But there were less obvious reasons as well. What about starting to value myself? What about teaching myself I could do this, and therefore making it easier to do in other areas of my life?

What about knowing I want my relatives to treat me and my wife the same way we would treat them if the roles were reversed? What about making sure my children see an example of how to stick up for themselves? A boundary like this not only helps to mitigate harm but can be the start of a better life.

5. I wrote down obstacles that could make it challenging to uphold the boundary. If I'm being honest, the biggest obstacle was me. If this boundary made things harder for other people when it came to planning family get-togethers, that might make me feel bad and reconsider my position. The people pleaser inside of me would undoubtedly come out to play at some point.

6. I made a game plan to tackle these obstacles. This involved jotting down a list of reminders to look at, like how the person at fault was not me but the one who'd said horrible things about my relationship and wouldn't back down. My wife and I were merely reacting to a lack of tolerance we didn't ask for, and we were well within our rights to do so. Reminders like these are helpful when we're forming new habits and pathways in the brain. This rewiring process is tiring, so it's good to jog the memory with reasons why we're putting in the work. Today, I have a list of revolving sticky notes in my office, reminding me of why I've made certain recent decisions.

7. I decided what the consequences would be if this boundary was not respected by others. Despite our best efforts, sometimes those around us will still not honour our needs. What

happens then? In this situation, we might have to avoid all family gatherings, or cast an even wider net that includes more relatives who refuse to accept this decision. In other situations, it could mean the end of a personal relationship, a complaint to human resources about one's boss or the end of Sunday dinners with your parents. These are hard decisions, and we need to weigh them carefully against many factors. But ultimately, if this is an important boundary, we need to protect it.

8. I found ways to hold myself accountable. I told a couple of friends I trusted about what I was doing and asked for their support. They helped by listening to my early guilty feelings about keeping this boundary and reminded me of why I'd set it in the first place. Ultimately, however, I ended up being my own best advocate for accountability, putting in the effort and reminding myself that our lives would be better for doing this. But having backup never hurts. Sometimes when things are hard, we just need to hear that we're doing the right thing from someone we know has our best interests at heart.

Good news: our extended family members were very support-ive and understood the boundary we were setting, which didn't surprise me. But following these steps helped me feel more confident in what we were doing. Thankfully, we don't have to make a list every time we set a new boundary for the rest of our lives. But it can be useful while we're learning how and when we're navigating a particularly tricky situation. I speak from experience when I say this all gets easier over time. Once I started reaping the benefits of imposing and upholding these borders, it became second nature. I no longer have to think twice about what I allow and don't allow in my life. I have expectations of myself and the people around me that I believe are reasonable and respectful. Despite my initial fears, it hasn't made me more "difficult," nor has it made anyone I truly care about run for the hills. I'm getting better at communicating my own needs, and it's made it easier for the people in my life to know they can do the same with me. Our relationships are getting healthier and stronger.

I group the types of boundaries I've established into four categories: personal, interpersonal, professional and online.

Personal boundaries are ones I set for myself: I will say no to a social gathering if I'm tired and would rather stay home. I don't allow screens (TVs, computers, phones) after 11 p.m. to ensure I get enough sleep.

Interpersonal boundaries are ones I set with others: I will not attend family gatherings with the homophobic relative. I will not be friends with someone who gossips about me instead of talking to me when they have an issue.

Professional boundaries are centred around work: I insist on twenty-four hours' notice for all missed appointments unless it's an emergency. I will not work past dinnertime.

Online boundaries are how I interact with other people via social media: I don't read hate mail. I don't respond to transphobic media personalities trying to bait me.

As someone who can easily get overwhelmed, I find that categorizing the limits I set makes it simpler to assess and uphold each one. As I grow as a person and the situations in my life change, I adjust my boundaries accordingly. I've become dynamic in ways I never expected.

Once I started working on boundaries, I felt like a brand-new person, no longer in denial of how I was living, no longer dragged down by shame and fear, and no longer tied to unhealthy societal and personal expectations. For the first time, I was free. This work fundamentally changed my life. Taking a stand on what we need isn't always easy, but it's far less effort than being a people pleaser—with better results.

But this begged the question: If I spent four decades letting fear drive me, setting flimsy boundaries and contorting myself into whatever I thought others wanted, who the hell was I underneath all that? What was Amanda really made of?

I had no idea. But it was time to find out.

the most important

relationship

"DO YOU KNOW WHAT CORE VALUES ARE?" Maya asked me one day. We were a handful of sessions into our work together now, and the acute distress I had initially felt was starting to subside.

"I think so," I replied. "Core values are the things that make me *me*, right?"

"Exactly," she said. "They're a set of beliefs and principles that guide your life. Do you know what yours are?"

"Not offhand," I admitted. "I haven't really given it a lot of thought."

"Well, that's your homework this week. I want you to think about what makes you tick and come back to me with a list of what Amanda is made of. If you're going to grow and heal as a person, you need to know the person you're growing and healing for."

Challenge accepted. This sounded like a good exercise. I had only a vague idea of what I was all about and had never considered writing it down—and I'm a writer, go figure. Given that I was also now in my forties, I thought it might be a good idea to figure this basic stuff out. I had tied a lot of my identity to the parts of my life that resided outside of me, such as family and work, rather than get to know the person who made these particular life decisions. Why had family always been important to me? Why was having children such a priority? Why did the career path I had taken feel so meaningful? What had been the driving force behind it all?

We all have core values. These consequential little descriptors make up our *why*. They're the reason we choose certain paths and have no interest in others. Someone who values equity might be passionate about human rights or volunteer with an organization helping marginalized or disadvantaged people. A person passionate about education might be a lifelong learner or take up teaching as a profession. Someone who strongly values honesty will likely take greater offence when lied to. "Loyalty" as an individual's core value could mean betrayal is a deal-breaker for them in any relationship. Whether we realize it or not, core values are powerful, and naming them is in itself a powerful act. It's an acknowledgment of the biggest pieces of ourselves.

Thankfully, it didn't take me long to figure out my own core values. All I had to do was look at my life over the past few years and consider what was most important to me, dig down to figure out why, then assign a word to it. Within a few minutes, I had refined my list to the following:

» love

» authenticity

» compassion

» empathy

» connection

» education

» honesty

Love is in everything I do. Authenticity is key to a joyful life. How can I be happy if I can't live as myself? Empathy allows me to see the world through perspectives other than my own. Compassion calls me to help when others are hurting. Connection helps ensure the people around me feel less alone. Education creates change for the better. Honesty forges strong relationships because they are built on what's real. All these values are pieces of me. Core values are what we believe in, and they're also what we might strive to foster more of within ourselves. I'm certainly not perfect in the representation of any of my own values—I don't know anyone who is—but I work at them.

Maya listened as I read them off to her at the following week's session and explained how each one factored into my life.

"Great work," she said.

I smiled entirely too much like a third-grader who just got a sticker on her math test.

"Now that you know what your values are," she continued, "I want you to start consciously making them the focus of your life. Everything you do, from your relationships to your career to the boundaries you set, will be based on these values."

This made good sense. We figure out who we are and then create a life in line with that. But most of us don't consciously think to create a life based on our values, and that's because society rarely provides opportunities to discover and honour them. We're taught from a young age what society's values are—such as power, wealth, beauty and materialism—and we're also taught any specific cultural or religious values we may be aligned with. Much of the time, the expectation is that we will adopt these values as our own and live happily according to them. Of course, living in a society means accepting a certain amount of conformity, but the individual still matters. And when the individual is never allowed to discover and honour who they are—and who they grow into over time—it can create a whole host of problems not only for them but also for those around them. A lack of personal fulfilment often leads to a whole lot of unhappiness.

Intentionally leading with my core values has made my life a lot easier. Whenever I make a decision, I ask myself, Is this in line with who I am? If it isn't, I don't do it. I ask myself this about everything, from what I'm about to say to someone to whether I will accept a new business contract. If what I plan to say or do doesn't line up with the person I know myself to be, I will rethink it. I know who I am and what I'm about, and I want my life to reflect this.

This is now one of the first exercises I do with my own coaching clients. Knowing ourselves well means we can create lives that best reflect our needs. Core values can change over time, so having the opportunity to discover and rediscover them is healthy.

—

The first two months of therapy whizzed by. It was challenging, but I could see the progress that Maya and I were making. Talk therapy—which in this case meant having a safe place to talk about my feelings—was part of the process, but much of the work was done outside of our weekly sessions. Maya gave me home- work at the end of nearly every meeting, and I would complete it and even expand on it as time allowed. I had started to tackle my big people-pleasing problem, was learning how to set healthier boundaries and was figuring out what made me tick. We were even diving into the trenches of my lifelong companion, impos- ter syndrome, which until then I had firmly believed I would never be rid of.

"Some things are here to stay," I'd said to Maya at one point. "And this is probably one of them. I think it's just a part of my personality now."

Simply put, imposter syndrome is the inability to internalize a sense of deserving your accomplishments. You constantly doubt your own abilities and don't see your own worth. You feel like a fraud—an imposter—in your own life. Many people who have imposter syndrome are high achievers, with years of experience and a list of impressive accomplishments. But none of this mat- ters because, deep down, they feel incompetent and on the cusp of being outed as a fake.

I had never known a moment in my life where I felt I deserved anything good. As a young mother, I had received enough judg- mental looks and comments from older mothers early on that I concluded I would never be seen as an equal by other parents. As someone who didn't acquire a high school diploma until my late thirties, I felt uneducated in groups where everyone around me had at least one university degree. As an advocate and author, I felt out of place in a field made up largely of academics and other highly educated people who were supposedly my peers.

One day, as we were wrapping up a session about my overall lack of confidence, I told Maya that the career recognitions I had collected over the past few years were sitting in a box on the basement floor. Plaques, certificates and even a trophy for my journalism and advocacy work were all stashed away. "It's fine, though. I don't need to see them," I said. "They're just things. We make too much of a big deal out of stuff like that."

She gave me that stern look I had learned to be afraid of.

"What's your reason for not displaying them somewhere?" she asked. "Is it really that you don't care about them? Or is it something else?"

"Okay, fine. The truth is I can't look at them right now," I admitted. "I can't even take the most recent one out of its little box. Every time I see it, all I think about are the people who told me I didn't deserve it. That one hurts the most."

That was the real reason behind the "they're just things we place too much value on" line. These "things" reminded me of my breakdown and everything that led up to it. They reminded me of how I felt about myself if I looked too closely, which wasn't good.

I can't blame my feelings on anyone who thought I didn't deserve recognition for my work. Everyone has the right to their opinion, and as a general rule, someone else's opinion of me shouldn't dictate what I do with my life. These opinions are not the reason why those awards were sitting in a box. The reason was my own imposter syndrome, my own inability to internalize or believe I deserved success. Imposter syndrome loves outside criticism—it feasts upon it. When I started hearing that criticism on the internet, it only confirmed what I already believed about myself: I was a sad, woefully uneducated fraudster who had somehow convinced others I deserved to be taken seriously. For those online comments to have any impact, a part of me had to believe them. Unfortunately, I did, and that's why they replayed in my mind every time I thought about what should have been great memories: crossing the stage to collect an award at a gala, seeing my name in a magazine commending my work or watching my book climb to the top of the bestseller list. These were accomplishments I had never imagined possible—dreams that had come true. I should have been proud of myself, but I was too busy being ashamed. Once again, I had taken the messages I had internalized when I was younger and made my whole life about them. What had happened online after the release of my book had only made it worse. I had never felt more like a fraud than I did at that moment.

Maya wasn't having it. "Yeah, we're not going to let your awards gather dust in a corner, okay? You worked too hard for them." She leaned into the camera, her long hair falling over her shoulders. "This week, you're going to go out and buy a shelf, you're going to pull everything out of the box and put it on there, you're going to send me a picture as proof, and you're going to look at that shelf every day until you start to feel good about what's on it. How does that sound?"

This is the same kind of mom energy I've used with my own kids when they've needed a push. Sometimes I need one too.

That night, Zoë and I went to IKEA, bought a shelf and put it up. (Okay, Zoë put it up after I loudly complained too much about not being able to find the studs in the wall, but I'll have you know I micromanaged the installation very well.) I then stared at the neglected box on the floor, and it stared back at me defiantly. The thought of going through it made me feel physically ill. I had associated that box with some deeply negative experiences, and my body didn't like it.

You really don't want to open it, the voice in my head said. *Just leave it alone. We can do it tomorrow or something.*

"No, we can't do it tomorrow," I said to myself. "We're going to do it now. And yes, it's going to be uncomfortable. But it will be just as uncomfortable if we do it tomorrow or next week or next year. So we might as well get it over with."

Noooooooo! The voice in my head responded like a cartoon villain who had just been defeated.

I pulled the box toward me and started fishing things out. I felt sick knowing what lay at the bottom. "One thing at a time," I told myself quietly. "Just do one thing.

I placed my first *Globe and Mail* article, which I had carefully framed in a shadow box, on the right side of the shelf. Next, I took out the commendation from our local MP, who had thanked me for my service in helping LGBTQ families, and placed it on the left. Between them, I put my 2019 *Chatelaine* Woman of the Year blurb, which Zoë had had professionally framed for me the previous Christmas. As I kept pulling things out, I kept getting more anxious. I knew what was coming.

Finally, I reached the bottom, where sat a small dark-blue box. My heart pounded. I closed my eyes as the words hit me.

"You don't deserve that."

"Who do you think you are?"

"Just fuck right off with this."

"You're not trying to help people. You're a selfish, exploitative narcissist who wants to be in the spotlight."

The memories of these online attacks left fresh cuts as they replayed in my head. I didn't believe every word—I knew that I wasn't a narcissist, for example, and that my work was driven by anything but fame—but I didn't have to believe it all; I only had to believe enough for it to confirm my own view that I wasn't worthy of good things. That particular award had been given to me only a few weeks before I left Twitter, and some people made it loudly known that they didn't believe I should be getting it. It hit all the most vulnerable spots at a time when I already wasn't doing well emotionally, embedding that hurt into the part of my psyche where trauma resides.

Just before the pandemic, I had been selected as one of the 2020 Top 25 Women of Influence and was invited to Toronto to receive my award at the annual event. I took my eldest son with me. Having got pregnant with him at nineteen, I wanted him to see that life doesn't always go the way you intend, but you can still do great things. I had gone back to high school in my thirties and graduated with honours at thirty-eight. But I had never received a university degree or college diploma, which had always been a dream of mine. Still, I had built a career I was passionate about, and this award was recognition of the work I had done so far. As I stood on stage holding my award, all I could see was my son smiling proudly from our table. That was the best part of the ceremony for me.

But once back at home, I put the award in its box and largely pretended it didn't exist. I tried to take it out once or twice, but the only emotions I felt were bad ones, so I hid it away again. Just before my breakdown, I decided I never wanted to look at any awards or accomplishments again, and that's when the Box of Uncomfortable Things was created. There it sat, sad and forgotten—until my stern-mom-look therapist made me build a shelf and pull it back out again.

But that shelf alone would not cure a deep-seated lack of belief in myself. Imposter syndrome is about the person experiencing it; it has nothing to do with success or recognition, but rather an inability to internalize our own worth. Our value as human beings has to come from within. I had a significant amount of external validation in my life at that time—every reason in the world to be proud of the person I was. But the part of me that didn't think I deserved the life I had was born well before any personal or professional success. It came to be when I was a child who felt largely unlovable, and I had carried it like a heavy stone on my back into adulthood. I needed to find a way to set that stone on the ground and walk away from it, finally unencumbered.

The first thing I had to do was fully internalize that imposter syndrome is not synonymous with being humble. Humbleness is a good thing; it reminds us that we're the same as everyone else, no matter how much success we may achieve. But it's not a virtue to feel *less than* the people around you. Imposter syndrome is not the opposite of arrogance but the other side of the same coin. Both extremes can be caused by many things, including child-hood trauma that left us feeling small and vulnerable. One wounded person might latch on to success tightly and lord it over others with grandiosity, while another pushes away the very notion that they deserve what they have. In both cases, a lack of confidence is the driving force.

Therefore, confidence is the only real cure—true confidence, not arrogance. We sometimes confuse the two, but they are markedly different. Arrogance is a game of comparison: to be arrogant, we have to look at others and decide we're better than they are. Comparison is also needed for imposter syndrome: to think we're frauds in this game of life, we must point out the people who are "better" than us to justify it.

Confidence, on the other hand, does not rely on outside sources; it's an innate feeling of belonging in this world. We all know confident people when we see them. They're genuine and relaxed. They move through spaces with ease but without an air of superiority. Confidence is sexy because it exemplifies true strength. You have nothing to prove to anyone, and no effort goes into trying to do so. That frees up a lot of energy to spend on better things. (I would give examples of what those might be, but pretty much anything we do with that energy is better than not believing in ourselves.)

After decades of looking for my value on the outside, I needed to start looking for it from the inside. The "award shelf"—possibly the worst name for it, but I didn't know what else to call it—was nice to have, but it would not breed confidence. Awards and other types of career or civic recognitions are not, in themselves, good for this, as they fit squarely into the "outside validation" category. Other people decided you deserved them. If those same people suddenly decided you no longer deserved them, would you lose your value? But any kind of recognition can serve as a reminder of all the work we do that feeds our core values and passions. If that work exemplifies who we are on the inside, the reminder can help build true confidence. Like any tool, it's all about how you use it.

Eventually, after a few deep breaths, I reached down and grabbed the little blue box I had tried so hard to forget existed. It was heavier than I remembered. I opened it up, carefully took out my Women of Influence award, made of both clear and red glass, and placed it squarely in the middle of the shelf. There it was, waiting to greet me every morning when I arrived at my desk with a coffee. It was time to write a new story about my life, the type of story where I would begin to feel like I deserved good things.

I want to say this was easy, but it took a long time. Every day, as I entered my office, I would stop and look at the shelf for a minute. For a while, especially on the harder days, I would hear echoes of those harsh words again, reminding me of how a part of me still felt about myself. But slowly, over time, I started to feel good about what I was looking at—even proud. And that was a far cry better than the Box of Uncomfortable Things, hidden away in a corner of the basement.

Progress, not perfection. May that always be my goal in all that I do.

—

I was totally rocking this healing thing! My mood kept moving in the right direction—the happier one—and I fully expected to continue down this road . . . well, forever. After all, I was doing all the right things. I never missed a session with Maya, and along with taking excellent care of myself between our appointments—exercising, meditating, eating well and getting enough sleep—I did everything she asked me to do as homework and more. I was fully invested in getting better. Between COVID-19 lockdowns and some careful scheduling on my part, my workload had remained light for a few weeks, which allowed me to focus a lot of time on figuring out what could help me move forward. There are many stressful things about living through a pandemic, as we've all learned, but I was trying to use this time as an opportunity to figure myself out. I fully expected to emerge a stronger, wiser and more joyous person once it was all over. I was done with this trauma business. And with all my efforts, why wouldn't I be? I was a freaking powerhouse. What could go wrong?

A lot, actually.

One day, as I was sitting on my trusty blue couch, diligently reading through a chapter of a trauma recovery book like the responsible healing human I was, I began feeling extremely nauseous. The room wobbled. My vision went blurry. My body went cold. My breath came in shallow gasps. I knew I was still on the couch, but I was also somewhere else—somewhere scarier. I was in a corner of my mind I had not visited for a long time and barely recognized.

Danger. A voice warned me.

The inside of a car door. Padded armrest. Stitching in the leather. Window crank, an old-fashioned manual one.

Danger. The voice was mine. It was getting louder.

Everything on a slant, like I'm lying down. Why am I lying down? Where am I? Whose car is this?

You need to get out. You need to get out now!

Treetops. A bird flies overhead. My view is shaking a little as I watch it, and my eyes have to recalibrate to keep track. Back and forth, back and forth, back and forth.

Run, Amanda. Run!

But I can't run. I can't even move. There's something heavy on top of me. Heavy and warm. I don't want to look at it. I don't want to look at him.

Him.

He is someone I had almost forgotten. He is someone I had written a different story about. Him: the one whose name I can't remember. The one who took something from me.

Trauma. It can find you even when you try to run from it.

I was twelve or maybe thirteen. I don't remember exactly how old because up until now, nothing about this event was important to me; it was just one of those strange things that had happened, a funny little story that probably could have turned out worse but hadn't, thank the stars.

I was angry about something at the time. I think that anger was directed at my parents, but probably also at the whole world, given my general attitude back then. I was walking along a quiet road between the edge of our neighbourhood and a wooded area.

We used to call it Racetrack Road because it led to—you guessed it—the local racetrack. It was a hippodrome, to be exact. A couple of neighbourhood friends and I used to go to pet the horses as they grazed in the pasture between the edge of the woods and the track, and at one point, we had made a fort beneath the tree canopy that served as a place for sharing secrets and telling ghost stories.

By this point, I was a couple of years too old for that, and Racetrack Road now served as a place to walk and gather my thoughts when I wanted to be away from people. Because it was the back way into the track's parking lot, only the odd car would go by, which gave me plenty of time to stew in my tween angst. This is what I was doing that day, walking slowly up the road. I likely sported my usual attire: a pair of jeans, a light jacket and hair that had an abundance of hairspray in it (per the requirements of the late-eighties era). Lost in my own head, I heard the sedan coming up behind me but was surprised when it slowed down next to me.

A man in his fifties or sixties reached over and rolled down the passenger-side window. He was white and balding, with a fringe of silver hair. He had a warm smile and a bit of a belly. He looked like somebody's friendly grandpa, or maybe someone's fun-loving uncle. Our neighbourhood was filled with men just like him, and I had grown up with many as part of my everyday life. This was a stranger, however, and his sudden approach left me a bit uneasy.

"Hi," he said. "Are you going up to the track?"

"Uh, no," I replied, taking a couple of steps toward the passenger side door. "I'm just walking."

"You don't go to the races?" he asked, in a way that implied everyone goes to the races.

"No, I'm not old enough."

"But you could go with an adult," he explained. "You've never been?"

I wasn't so sure it was true that kids could go watch the races with adults, but I figured he must know the rules better than I did. "No, never," I said. "I sometimes watch from the field over there, though. It's fun."

"Oh, you should definitely go," he said. "It's a great experience from the seats. I go all the time. You could come with me if you want. I mean if you're not doing anything."

"Uh . . ." I began. "I don't—"

"Hey! No pressure, okay? I'm not trying to be creepy or anything, I swear." He laughed. "It's just an offer. I'm Rick, by the way. What's your name?"

"Amanda."

"Well, Amanda, if you have some time, you can be my guest today. I'd love to take you. It won't cost you a thing."

There are few decisions I regret in life, but I will forever regret getting into Rick's car. Rick, of course, was not this man's name, but I can't remember what he was called. Again, up until I was sitting on a couch reading a book thirty years later, I thought this was some small, innocuous story in which I had done something foolish in my youth and, thankfully, had avoided any serious consequences. I knew it as another one of those "dodged a bullet" situations, which my young life had seen plenty of. I was wrong.

This is the story I told myself for roughly three decades: I got into Rick's car because he seemed friendly and trustworthy. We drove up the road to the racetrack. We went inside. Rick knew some of the people who worked there, and they let me in with him after he introduced me as his niece. He bought me a soft drink, then introduced me to a male friend who was also a regular. Rick seemed popular there, and I could understand why. He was so nice. Everybody liked him. I liked him too. He let me decide which horses to bet on, and we watched some races. He bought me another drink. At some point, I left the track and walked home, safe and sound.

Except I never remembered leaving. That's the funny part. When my mind would occasionally recall this story throughout the years, I couldn't remember saying goodbye, exiting the building or getting home with any sort of clarity.

But I did vividly remember noticing how sore and red I was in a very delicate area later that night. Probably an infection starting, I figured; I had had a couple of them before. If it stayed that way, I would have to tell my mom and see the doctor. But after a day or two, the discomfort and redness went away, and I felt fine. I never thought anything more of it.

Except now, on the couch, I knew. *I knew.* He had raped me. He had taken me back to his car after we visited the track. Rick had violated me well before Nathan came over on New Year's Eve. How did that happen without me remembering it for so long? Had he put something in my drink? Had I somehow agreed? I couldn't see myself agreeing to sleep with an old man, and regardless, I certainly wasn't of age to give legal consent.

No, I hadn't let him. Something had happened. I knew it, felt it, beyond a doubt.

Flashes of the assault were alive in my mind as I fought back the urge to vomit. The fragments of memory hit me like exploding glass. The car door. The window. The treetops. The bird. The man. No face. Don't look at his face. He's not there. Look outside. The car door. The window. The treetops. The bird. Just stare at the window crank. Look at the stitching in the fabric. Don't look him in the eyes. Don't take in more of this than you have to. Don't remember.

Please don't remember.

Except now I did remember. And I was suddenly, overwhelmingly heartbroken for my younger self.

Trauma can stack. Did you know that? This means that after peeling back one layer, you can find another layer, and then another. What had happened to me was, in a way, almost classic. Healing had created more safety in my life, more ability to process incidents from my past. This may have allowed my brain to unlock something it had kept hidden away in order to protect me. As I have previously mentioned, the way our bodies deal with trauma is designed to keep us safe. While often imperfect, this is the intent. I'm grateful for it too. Who knows what would have happened to me if I had not blocked out such a disgusting and violent event? I already had enough to deal with at the time, and my brain likely knew something of that magnitude would destroy me.

But now I had to figure out what to do and how to feel about it all. The first thing I did was make my way upstairs to the bedroom so my children wouldn't see the panicked look on my face as I tried to absorb these new recollections. I was spiralling downward, and I knew I needed immediate support. I texted Zoë, who was working in the other room: "Can you come see me in the bedroom? I really need you." She was there in a heartbeat and sat beside me on the bed.

"What's wrong?" she asked. I was as white as a ghost.

"I just remembered something," I said, my voice shaking. "Something really, really bad. I don't know if it's real, but it feels real."

When traumatic memories explode to the surface and we get triggered, we can often slip back to the age we were when the event took place. I felt like a young, frightened child, emotionally frozen in time. I needed a tether to my adult life, and my wife was it.

Zoë listened as I told her what I had just recalled. Each word took effort to say, each sentence wanted to remain stuck in my throat. But I knew that telling her about it would allow me to share the burden with someone who could help me through it. Zoë is my person, the one I can tell anything to and know I'll be loved all the same. Only a few short years ago, she had confided in me that she was trans, which took every ounce of strength she had in her. Now it was my turn to tell her something I had buried deep. Compassion was all over her face as I recounted what I'd remembered about Rick.

"Are you sure he was the only one who did that to you?" she asked at one point. "You said he introduced you to friends."

"No. I'm not sure," I said. "I don't remember. I only have flashes right now, and this awful feeling in my stomach. I'm so freaked out about all this. I keep wanting to believe I'm making it up in my head or something. I don't know why I would do that, but if I'm imagining it, that would be so much better than it being true."

"This is awful," she said. "I'm sorry, babe. I'm really sorry."

"It's okay," I said, for me as much as for her. "Whatever this is was a long time ago. I know that. I just need to figure out what to do with it now. Guess I'm texting Maya off-hours."

When I messaged Maya, I told her it wasn't exactly an emergency, but that if she had room before our next scheduled session, that would be helpful. She made an appointment with me for the next morning.

I slept horribly that night. My mind was going in all different directions, and I felt haunted by my resurrected past and angry about it too. Was this a real memory, or something I had just made up? If it was real, why couldn't it have stayed buried? What good would knowing this possibly do? I wanted to be free of trauma for the first time in my life, and this felt like a giant roadblock to that achievement. One step forward, two massive leaps back. I hated it with everything I had.

The next day, I told Maya what had surfaced as I was reading. The words were nearly as difficult to get out as they had been the day before. She listened quietly, as she always did, taking in what I was saying to her.

"I'm not surprised," she said. "You've done a lot of work on yourself, and sometimes we remember details of things when we're ready."

"I keep telling myself this can't be real. My mind could be making it up, right?" I asked earnestly. I had heard about false memories before, and how they can feel just as authentic as real ones to the person experiencing them. I needed Maya to tell me I was imagining it. This wasn't the sexual history I wanted to carry with me. Not that my night with Nathan was much better, but at least I knew who he was and had an unquestionable recollection of what had transpired. Rick was a stranger I could barely recall, and older than my father had been at the time. The idea of him—and heaven forbid, maybe someone else—violating me was repulsive.

"It's always a possibility it isn't real," she said. "But this sounds like you're not pulling it out of thin air. You've always known about this event; now it seems like you're filling in some missing pieces. You've always remembered going to the track with that man up until a certain point. The rest has been hazy, and that could be by design. You also remember how your body felt afterward. Blocking out the actual assault makes sense here. It might also be explained if he put something in your drink, as you were saying."

She was right. Recalled memories are not always reliable, but there was something to this one that rang true. There was no reason for me to suddenly make up a new chapter to an old event I hadn't thought about in years. I had heard stories from friends who had been sexually abused and only recalled some of the details years later, but I never thought I would experience that first-hand. It was discombobulating to feel that violence, in many ways, for the first time long after it happened. It was also hard to add to the story of my life a painful chapter I never knew existed before. There is a peace that often comes with time and distance from a horrific incident; we know we're moving away from it, leaving it far behind. We might still carry scars but they're faded.

Recovered traumatic recollections are fresh, which means we have to process them as current while also recognizing they are part of the past. And because they happened a long time ago and often with just memories to go on now, there is less chance for recourse, should we want it. Even if I knew who he was, Rick was likely dead now, or well on his way. I'd missed any opportunity to seek justice or stop him from doing it again. How many more young people had he harmed besides me? I would never know.

I always try to look for the good in bad situations. Even with this agonizing piece of the past surfacing, I thought there was something I could pull from the wreckage. In this atom bomb– sized crater, the gift was the ability to see what happened from the eyes of an adult rather than the child I was at the time. I could handle this far better now than I could have years earlier. If I could just keep reminding myself throughout the process that I was currently safe in my grown-up life, with more love and support than I had ever thought possible, I would be able to guide my younger wounded self out of the pain more easily.

I could also see, from a distance, how this event had shaped me, both figuratively and literally, which helped me make sense of some confusing behaviours I had when I was growing up. I could see that having been assaulted by an older man at such a young age set the scene for others to take advantage of me afterward in various ways. Whenever a man hit on me, I would freeze, losing all my assertiveness and becoming very passive. Part of this could be chalked up to my attraction to women and femme queer people, but it never explained it entirely. When women I'm not attracted to flirt with me, I don't get that same uncomfortable feeling. Now that I knew this kind of attention from men in my younger years had resulted in violence on more than one occasion, I could see how I would immediately view it as something to be wary of. It was a protective measure.

Just when I thought I had moved beyond the most painful parts of my past, there was more to unpack and to heal from. In some ways, it felt like a giant setback, but I tried to reframe it as a sign of healing, like an infection that has to be cleaned out if we want to get better. I had been carrying the weight of this assault around for decades, and now it was finally time to set it down.

loving my whole self

MY ADDICTION ISSUES DID NOT begin with drugs and alcohol; they began with food. Even before my chronic substance use became a problem, I tried to alleviate my pain with what could be found in the cupboards or bought with my allowance at the corner store. Food was my friend, my confidant and, as I hoped each time I went to it, my healer.

I started binge eating at around the age of twelve or thirteen—the same age I was when I met Rick. This was also around the time when bullying at school and other issues in my life had escalated to intolerable levels. With the added stress, it's not surprising I was struggling to find ways to cope with the fear and helplessness I was feeling. I had always loved food, and like many of us do, I occasionally used it as a source of comfort. Who doesn't want their grandma's stew or dad's chili after a hard day? But I found myself eating to the point of sickness as a way to medicate my increasing depression and anxiety. Food was my constant companion, always available in abundance when I still lived at home. We were a family of six, and my parents kept the pantry stocked for us. I never went hungry, which is something to be thankful for. But my relationship with food also hurt me.

There was a deep emotional satisfaction when I ate—a euphoric feeling I only experienced when I was alone with food. This snack was for *me*. I could have as much of it as I wanted. There were no eyes around to judge me, no one to tell me to stop. Every day, I looked forward to the time when it was just me, something I enjoyed on TV and whatever I was going to eat. Food became synonymous with safety and control. But those feelings never lasted long. I would inevitably eat far too much, ignoring any signs of fullness. My stomach would scream angrily after I stuffed it full of things like chips, chocolate and cheese. One night while watching a movie, I ate an entire tray of Oreos and most of a large bag of salt and vinegar chips, and woke up intermittently through the night with stomach cramps and the urge to throw up. I felt nothing but regret, which remained well into the morning.

Shame would inevitably find me the next day as I stood in front of the mirror examining my expanding waistline and growing hips. Some of it was the onset of puberty coupled with genetics, but the rest was likely due to extra calories and chronic stress over time. "Look at you," I would say to myself. "You're disgusting. You're a pig. Why do you eat like that?" I would promise myself that to make up for my gluttony, not a single crumb would pass through my lips for a day or more. I could be disciplined. I could be strong. I could fix what I had done. But by evening, hunger would usually find me again—both the physical and emotional kind. I needed to feed my sadness, even if I didn't know that's what I was doing.

This relationship with food and my body would periodically morph into something different over the decades, but no matter what form it took, the only way to describe that relationship would be to call it unhealthy. If I wasn't binging food, I was heavily restricting it. If I wasn't restricting it, I was punishing myself with copious amounts of exercise to try to compensate for what I was putting in my mouth. I didn't know moderation—it was all or nothing, feast or famine. For a long time, food was the only thing I felt I could control in my life, which is why I used it to literally feed that need. I controlled in extremes.

Trauma and food issues often go hand in hand, and I am, once again, a classic example of this. (I'm starting to feel like I should get an award for being so exemplary. I could put it on my shelf.) Beneath all this bingeing and its accompanying behaviours was an instinctive desire to protect my body. I wanted to stay safe, and subconsciously tried to create a physical barrier around myself to do so. This logically makes sense: not only do physical barriers protect us from harm—think of the walls and roof of a house, for example—but bigger people walk through the world differently. Our society is extremely fatphobic. A lot of people are repulsed by larger bodies, or at the very least, they ignore them. Many fat people have stories of being judged harshly or feeling completely invisible.

One of the worst experiences I had as a bigger person was try-ing to find a wedding dress for our ceremony in 1997. I was twenty years old and five months postpartum, my body still recovering from pregnancy. My maid of honour, Monique, and I stepped into a bridal shop I had been eyeing for some time. We were greeted by a petite older woman who took me around to view dresses. There were only a handful in my size, and most were quite expensive.

"We're on a tight budget," I admitted. "What do you have that would work?"

"Maybe you could try this one," the salesperson said. She pulled out a mermaid-style dress, which I knew wouldn't look good on me.

"I don't know about that one," I said.

"Well, it's in your price range, dear," she said. "At least try it on."

I did, and immediately knew it wasn't what I wanted. The dress hugged my body all the way down, highlighting parts of me I didn't want it to. It made me feel uncomfortable. I took it off, then handed it back to the salesperson. "It really doesn't work on my body," I explained.

"Well, dear," she said, returning the dress to its hanger, "if you're going to get married, you really should think about losing some weight."

I stood there, shocked at what I had just heard come out of the woman's mouth. Did she really just tell me, a young mother to a baby, that I was too fat to get married? The sting of her words caused tears to well up in my eyes.

Monique, far more assertive than I, threw the woman a look that could kill. "We're going to go somewhere else," she said. "My friend deserves better treatment than this."

Later that week, Monique called the manager to complain, and the woman was subsequently fired. While I appreciated the vindication, it still left a wound that is all too familiar to many fat people. We are treated poorly simply for having bigger bodies. The weight of that reality is the real issue.

My genetics dictate that I am a larger person by nature, and I don't feel terrible about that by any means. Beautiful, strong people come in all shapes and sizes. But for many years, I saw my body as damaged and treated it poorly. I ignored my own fullness cues so many times that I didn't know what they were anymore. I ignored my own early hunger cues as well, to the point of feeling famished by the time I finally ate. At other times, I treated food like the enemy, creating an unrealistic approach to how I ate and calling it "healthy." I tried various fad diets (including everything from eating for my blood type to being limited to only what our ancestors could forage), had an assortment of weight-management books and even hired a trainer who scolded me for eating basically anything but fish and spinach.

In short, I didn't set healthy boundaries around food consumption and chose a chaotic approach governed not by need, joy or health, but by pain. When I was in pain, I ate more. Then the shame of that caused me more pain, and I would punish myself by eating less or working out excessively. I wasn't in control like I thought I was—instead, I was haunted by the trauma caused by Rick, Nathan and many others. Haunted by times when I had no control at all.

I want to say that everything has magically turned around in the food and body image department, and that I am now the poster child for recovering from a lifetime of habits that didn't serve me. But that would be a lie. Unfortunately, I still carry internalized fatphobia that I fight against daily. There are moments when I still categorize my food as "good" or "bad." When I look in the mirror, I don't always appreciate what I see.

My body is shaped by many things, including the genetics of the father who abandoned me, the men who raped me and the classmates who harmed me. Loving my body means doing so in spite of what was done to it, what society thinks about it and what wounds it carries.

But you know what? I'll take that challenge.

Today, I would say I love my body all of the time and like it most of the time. This work started in my teens and has evolved over the years to mean something beyond merely tolerating the shape and size I am. Several years ago, I decided I wouldn't spend another minute hating myself. I came to this decision after growing tired of trying to meet unrealistic expectations and constantly falling short. Why was I doing this to myself? Not only was it a colossal waste of what could be a much happier life, but it also set my children up for their own confidence struggles. One of our children had just come out as trans, and I could see the importance of becoming a better role model of self-love and acceptance; they probably needed that lesson more than most. Whether we realize it or not, the children around us are watching and learning from what we say and how we act. What was I telling my kids when I looked in a mirror and made a disgusted face? What message was I sending by trying to hide my body with oversized clothing? The last thing I wanted to do was perpetuate a harmful cycle. The media does enough damage to a child's self-esteem; I didn't need to help. In fact, I consider it my job to undo as much of that as I can.

So I diligently worked on learning to love my body for what it was. I opted to treat it well, which can mean different things depending on the day. I do high-intensity cardio, but I also allow myself rest so I don't overtrain. I lift weights, but I'm mindful of the shoulder and knee injuries I have and modify accordingly. I eat what pleases me as well as what nourishes me. I challenge fatphobia when I hear it leave the mouths of loved ones—not just for me but for others. There are no more fad diets, no more severe restrictions. There is no more binge eating or exercise used as punishment or as a reward to earn higher-calorie foods. I dress in ways that feel good and don't hide my body anymore.

Not long ago, I wore a bathing suit to the beach for the first time in years. This took a lot of courage on my part. The last time I had done that was when I took our firstborn to the water when he was a baby, more than two decades ago. Two college-aged guys were lying on a towel behind us. When I walked by, one of them nudged his friend and said, "Look at the beached whale," loud enough so I could hear. They laughed noisily. That same month, Zoë and I went on our first date night since becoming parents. We were walking home from a downtown restaurant when a girl leaned out the passenger-side window of a car and yelled, "Fat cow!" as she pointed at me.

The following year, right before I was diagnosed with post-partum depression, I had taken our son out to the local Tim Hortons for lunch. I remember feeling content that day, pleased to be out with my toddler for a little bit. Two men in suits watched us as we sat down at a nearby table with our food. They kept casting glances our way, which I assumed was because they were admiring my baby. Before they left, they walked up to me and put a business card on the table. "Think about it," one of the men said, smiling, before walking away. I looked at the card. "Want to lose weight?" it asked, followed by a number. I walked home, sad and humiliated.

Each time one of these situations happened, it was a blow to my confidence and self-esteem, and it added to the belief I already carried within me: I was somehow less than everyone else because of the way my body looked. Being a bigger person was a moral failing. If I just tried hard enough—and clearly, I had never tried hard enough—I could be thin, which was what healthy people who had it together were.

It took significant effort to challenge these beliefs within me. I still have to challenge them regularly.

Anyway, let's head back to the water: After much work on how I saw myself, I decided I would conquer that fear of judgment and take back rights over my body. To do this, I would go to the place I feared most: the beach. In 2016, my mom gave me the most adorable bathing suit when I was over one day. "Try this on," she said as she threw it me. "It's going to look great on you." It did. She was right. I looked beautiful in it. The tropical pattern of bright green and blue was an eye-catcher, and the cut was absolutely fetching.

I felt like a million bucks. This was what I would wear, and I would own the shore in it.

We had a great day. Zoë and I met up with some friends, beach chairs and a cooler in tow. We swam a bit, but mostly just kicked back in the shade and chatted, cool drinks in hand. Later that night, I put a couple of pictures of the day on my Instagram page and talked about what a big step it was for me to wear a swimsuit in public again.

Not long after, I received a message from a Facebook friend. "I saw your photo on *The Dirty*," he said. "You should report it and make them take it down."

The Dirty? I had never even heard of it. As it turns out, *The Dirty* is one of those gross sites that puts up hateful content as clickbait. Sure enough, they had taken the pictures and written a post titled "Amanda Jetté Knox—Fat Pig." In the post itself, they refer to me as "the fat pig sloot with the freak family" and go on to say a bunch of transphobic nonsense. (Yes, they spelled it "sloot." I'm not fluent in Bigot, so I don't pretend to understand why.)

The transphobia in itself was awful, of course. That made my blood boil. But the fat-shaming and name-calling? Not so much. I practically fell out of my chair laughing. This is who I had been worried about judging me? People who had never matured beyond a fourth-grade level? Their problem with my body was their own issue, and a pathetic one at that.

Again, I ask: What's the good in all this? This time, it was contrast. Not long before, I would have been deeply wounded by words like these. Now I found them laughable. This is the power of reclamation in action. I took my body back. I took my confidence back. I took my life back. I will not allow anyone else to have control over them again.

Don't want to see a fat person at the beach? Then don't go. The beach is for everybody, and if you can't handle that, that's not my issue. Want to make fun of the way I look? All it does is tell people who you are, not who I am. I am completely unbothered by what someone thinks about me, because it has nothing to do with me.

But if you must insult the way I look, at least be creative. There are bonus points for originality.

Core values. Self-discovery. Finding the gift. Building confidence. Reclaiming power.

All these tools helped me move through trauma and to the other side of it. They solidified who I was fighting for and who I was healing for. These realizations were peeling back layers and helping me become the person I was always meant to be, the one buried under the pile of rubble from my childhood.

For years, I'd tried to stuff the pain down with food, and for a time, with alcohol and other drugs. As I began to heal from the trauma, my body released this need to self-medicate. After several weeks of hard work, I was ready to emerge into the world again. But what would that look like, and how would people react to this new person? There was only one way to find out.

THIRTEEN

the company we keep

FRIENDS: THEY'RE THE BEST.

In many ways, I value close friendships as much as I do family relationships, tending to them as best I can in between raising a family and working a job that doesn't follow traditional office hours. As they say, friends are the family we choose, and I am very grateful for the ones I have. I know I'm not alone in my appreciation of good friends, but I'm probably more aware of this appreciation because of my history. With few friends when I was a child, I became dependent on those I did have to keep me afloat when the rest of the world felt unsafe. I would go to school and face my bullies five days a week, but I had my lifelong pal Emmy on weekends. I would get harassed by other students as I walked home, but I had Robert, who went to a different school and didn't seem to care what those kids thought of me, to meet up with at the park. True friends were like islands in a choppy sea, and their shores allowed me a reprieve before I had to start swimming again. Those "island moments" earned these friends a special place in my heart for a lifetime.

When I suffered my breakdown, I felt all alone, but that was far from reality. Yes, a lot of people weren't happy with me on social media, but many who knew me personally defended me courageously by publicly speaking out against some of the accusations being lobbed in my direction. They sprang into action to try to mitigate the damage they knew was being done to my psyche, often at great personal cost. Some of them were attacked and wound up on the receiving end of their own unfounded accusations—and a few even lost friendships of their own in the process.

It became clear pretty early on that no one could stop the tsunami of words on the internet. Nor could my friends take away my pain, and I think they knew this too. But they could do what they seem to do best through every big change or challenge our family has faced: let us know we were not alone. Our friends had been doing this since our child first came out as trans in 2014. Those who stuck around—and that was most of them— showed their support in every way imaginable. They educated themselves so they could use the right language and stood up for our child in their own circles when people would say transphobic things. They brought our tween gifts that affirmed their gender identity and continued to invite us to their gatherings as if nothing had changed (because as far as they were concerned, it hadn't). When Zoë came out the following year, our friends did more of the same, and further tightened their protective ring around us. One of the big reasons my family was able to successfully navigate two transitions was because of the absolute support we received from those around us. We'll never forget it either.

So it should come as no surprise that when my friends started recognizing how unwell I was, they sprang into action. It was clear days before I went to the hospital that I was growing unstable. My posts on Facebook had become raw and rambling. My usual filter that allows me to carefully word what I say had started slipping. These were obvious warning signs I was falling apart.

A couple of days after I left Twitter, my friend Sarah stopped by with an emergency care package that contained comfort foods like ice cream and coffee, along with other items she and our friend Jenn had put together. Our next-door neighbour sent over a chocolate gift basket. "It's either chocolate or booze in these situations," she joked. A fellow mom of a trans kid came by with a bottle of wine. "Wine won't solve all your problems, but it helps," she quipped. A friend who came out as a trans woman after reading about Zoë's experience a couple of years earlier stopped by with a batch of homemade butter tarts—my favourite dessert on the planet.

We were in a pandemic, and nobody could hug me. They couldn't come inside and visit. Those who cared were limited in their ability to show their concern. So they did the only other thing they could think of: they showed their love through gifts. After my hospital visit, several bouquets of flowers were delivered. More care packages and cards arrived from near and far away. This continued for two or three weeks. We started running out of room to put everything, so I made the executive decision to put a lot of it in my mouth (not the flowers).

My extended family was there for me too, as they had been through everything. On a beautifully warm day not long after my trip to the hospital, my sister invited me on a walk with my young niece and nephew. The border between Ontario and Quebec had opened back up for a short while, so we took advantage of it. We walked through the park behind the bungalow where I'd lived when I had my first panic attacks as a child, and I watched the tiny humans I love hop on tree trunks, look for tadpoles and experience some delights of nature for the first time. It occurred to me that I had almost not been around to see these wonderful kids grow up, and it made me sad to think about. I soaked in the time with them, even managing a few laughs, and then stopped by for an outdoor coffee with my mom. She had some wise things to say, as she often does, and I left feeling like I might be able to come back from this after all. Maybe there was something good waiting for me on the other side of this trauma.

It has to be said, however, that nobody in my life, as wonderful as they are, could have prevented my inevitable mental health crisis or near suicide. It had been building for months, slowly pressurizing inside me until that catalyst moment. Mental illness isn't something you can fix with a gift basket. Trauma disorders aren't solved with a trip to the park. I needed professional help, and had I not got it, I likely wouldn't be here today. This is especially important to remember for caregivers of those who are mentally unwell or even suicidal. Their illness is not because you're not doing enough. We can do everything we can for someone, but we can't cure a disease or fix a disorder.

The job of caregiving, however, is still vital to the healing process. As I've mentioned, one known factor in helping to stop a traumatic event from morphing into a trauma disorder is to receive strong support at the time of that event. What my friends and family did for me during that period helped minimize the long-term impact this difficult time would have on me. Human beings are social creatures, and in times of crisis, we need to know we are not alone. This provides a critical element of safety. When I think back to that time now, I still remember the awful parts, but I also remember folks I love showing up. Their actions are intrinsically linked to the situation, which undoubtedly changed how my brain stored that memory. It is less traumatic because of them.

Unfortunately, not everyone reacted in ways that were helpful. One friend stopped talking to me completely and ended up unfollowing me on social media, but not before writing a long post about how people, especially those who have a spotlight on them, shouldn't be discussing their mental health recovery so publicly. It was clearly a post about me without naming me. And unluckily, I saw it.

While I respect her right to that opinion and her agency over what she says on social media, I vehemently disagree that we shouldn't speak openly about mental health, trauma disorders and suicidality. While these topics can be uncomfortable and even triggering for some people, silence only creates more stigma and shame. My openness about my own issues has helped countless others get help for themselves; I know this because they've been writing to me since the week I left the hospital. I won't go as far as to say my transparency is saving lives—I'm not nearly that powerful—but I know my words have helped others find the strength to ask for help and save their own lives.

A few days after I left the hospital, I noticed that another friend—someone even closer to me—had unfriended me on my personal Facebook page. When I looked more closely, I saw that she had unfollowed me on other social media too. She'd been silent since my breakdown, but I had assumed she either had her own issues going on or just didn't know what to say. I texted her when I saw we weren't connected online anymore and asked her what was wrong, then immediately thought better of it. It would be smarter to have a face-to-face discussion, I thought, where we could see each other's reactions and hear each other's voices without having to guess at tone. Maybe we could work things out by taking a walk together rather than sending a flurry of emotional messages back and forth. I sent a follow-up text suggesting that we talk in person about this when she was ready, since I didn't believe I could handle doing this in texts right now.

That was my boundary, and she crossed it. She replied with a long text that began with how triggering she found my content since I went to the hospital—a fair point. Then she spoke about the ways in which I was a bad friend and let loose resentments she had kept for nearly two years. She explained that she believed getting published had gone to my head. It seemed like everything she had always wanted to say to me was unleashed in a long string of angry words. I don't know why she chose that particular moment, when I was at my lowest, but she did. I can't think of a worse time to share that kind of feedback with someone.

I read her text and immediately came undone again. Zoë heard me sobbing at the dining room table and came rushing over. I was inconsolable, crying harder than I had since this all started. The dam had burst, and my emotions were flooding the room. "This work has cost me so fucking much. I hate it. I hate this all so much!" I yelled through the tears. "I should never have written that book! I should have just kept my mouth shut!" The hurt was pouring out of me. Once again, my world felt damaged beyond repair.

The only time I had felt in serious danger of self-harm since leaving the hospital was that evening. Her words hit an open wound that hadn't had time to heal yet. It was one thing to lose people I didn't feel particularly close to, or to have folks I barely knew say negative things about my character, but to lose someone who was a big part of my social group felt like more than I could handle. I considered going to the hospital again and asking them to keep me this time, but instead I decided to sit outside on another friend's deck while I cried some more. I left with a heavy heart, but safe. I would be okay.

The company we keep is not only vital to our wellbeing but also a reflection of how we see ourselves. When we like who we are, we treat ourselves better, and when we treat ourselves better, we make better choices about who to spend time with. Back when I was a self-destructive teen, most of my friendships enabled that self-destructiveness to continue. As a young closeted parent who wanted to hide in the typicalness of suburban family life, I spent a lot of time with other parents who exemplified that existence. As my family members and I started coming out of the closet in our various ways, I began connecting more with members of the queer community, while also insisting that friends who were straight and/or cisgender be supportive of us and willing to learn and grow as needed.

Healthy relationships require strong communication skills, kindness and empathy. All relationships take time and effort, and we have only so much of these to give. Emotional investments should pay off, so I try to invest in relationships that fuel me. I don't care if we have the exact same interests or even similar lives. I don't care if we go long stretches between connecting, as long as we can pick up where we left off.

I've had a lot of time to think about what I look for in a relationship of any kind. I've had some excellent examples in my life to pull from and some not-so-good ones to learn from. Some of the questions I ask myself about my relationships today are:

» Does this person share core values similar to mine?
» Are they there for me in times of crisis?
» Are they accepting of who I am?
» Are they understanding that life gets busy sometimes?
» How do they treat me when I'm at my lowest?
» Do they communicate with me kindly and respectfully?
» Do I usually feel rejuvenated after we spend time together?

And then, because friendship is a two-way street, I ask these same questions of myself.

These inquiries are significant not only to friendships but to other relationships too. My close relationships with my extended family members have a lot to do with the type of people they are. No, we can't choose our family, but we can set boundaries around how we interact with them. It needs to be said, however, that abusive situations, in particular, can be difficult to get away from, as well as dangerous. In this case, simply setting a boundary isn't often enough, and seeking help to leave that relationship is the best course of action. Someone trying to leave a domestic violence situation, for example, will likely need outside support to do so safely.

While getting something good out of our relationships is essential, it's unrealistic to think our closest ones will be equal all the time. The closer we are to someone, the more they will need us when things fall apart, and the more we will have to carry when that happens. They will need to do this for us too. This is part of loving someone. When my friends go through challenging times, I certainly don't expect balance in our relationship. When we speak during those times, the conversations we have are often hard and don't leave me feeling rejuvenated. But my role is to be there for them, and when our situations are reversed, it's to let them be there for me.

I really believe that personal crises should be treated as inevitable. At some point in all our lives, we will face difficult and uncertain times. When that happens, the company we keep will matter more than ever. Taking inventory of how others treat us—and in particular, how we *allow* others to treat us—is best done before these crises happen. We should also examine how much we show up in a relationship, and how. No, we don't want to be rampant people pleasers who exhaust ourselves giving to others, but we can—and should—give back in relationships while preserving our wellbeing.

Yes, a few friends left during my worst time. While that hurt, it ended up being its own gift. Since then, I've grown to know myself better and also have higher expectations of who I give my time and energy to. Having people show themselves out of my life meant I didn't have to put effort into relationships that were not able to meet my expectations anyway. It also afforded me the space to nurture a handful of new friendships with folks better suited to where I'm at today.

As we grow, our lives need to grow with us. But growing isn't always straightforward or painless. It often involves getting hurt and learning from that hurt—sometimes more than once. When a baby tries to stand up and hits its head on the table two or three times, it learns to scan for obstacles first. We do the same thing in different ways throughout our lives. When something isn't working, we need to recognize it and figure out how to change it. Bad relationships of any kind fall into that category; we either repair them or we let them go. When they end, we should take the time to assess what didn't work to help us make better decisions next time. Were there early warning signs before things fell apart? In the case of the two friendships I mentioned, the red flags were there—I just chose to ignore them.

I don't hold any grudges toward these individuals, though. I only have my perspective to go on. In their eyes, I clearly crossed lines and said things that didn't work for them. It's not my job to decide what their boundaries should be. I may not like the way they handled things, but they had every right to make their own choices. I made sure to take the time to reflect on the part I'd played, and I learned a few things about myself that I was able to use going forward.

But more than anything, what the period surrounding my breakdown taught me was how valuable my closest relationships are to me. I have many solid friendships and a family that has never given up on me. I don't know what more I could ask for, really. The company we keep matters, in part, because reflecting our own worth back to ourselves matters. Choose people who remind you of how much you shine. Do the same for them. Love is a powerful mirror.

we're getting better.

now what?

RUBBLE. IN LATE SUMMER OF 2020, I was standing on a proverbial pile of it that represented my old life. But that was okay. I was used to this, having been here a handful of times throughout the years. As I had learned, your foundation can give out occasionally, and that's when you know it won't serve you going forward and it's time to rebuild. This happened when I went to rehab, again when I moved out of my parents' home at sixteen and in the time between my wife's coming out and our realizing we were going to make it as a couple and a family. Each time, it felt like the end. Each time, it was merely the beginning of something better. Once I learned that, I stopped fearing change. I had always worried that I wouldn't be able to handle it, but experience has taught me I have what it takes. I believe we all do.

In the months following my breakdown, I dug through the pile of rubble and pulled out pieces of my old life to examine more closely. What still served me from before went into building my new foundation, while what no longer did was discarded. I kept my compassion for others and desire to be kind. I kept my most important relationships too. Traumatic events from my past had for the most part shifted to unfortunate memories that ached but no longer stung. In place of people pleasing, I now had boundaries. My fear of rejection was traded for the knowledge that I am worthy of love. I threw out imposter syndrome and adopted a healthy sense of recognition of what I had worked hard to achieve.

It felt good to be starting over, even if I wasn't sure exactly where I was going yet. For a good while, I didn't think I would ever dip a toe into LGBTQ-related advocacy again. I was so afraid that what had happened before might happen a second time. Besides, what good was my presence in that space anyway? It was clear a lot of people didn't want me there.

"You'll figure it out, Amanda," Maya said to me. "Just remember that it hasn't been that long yet, and you're still raw. Part of healing is the work we're doing now, and part of it will happen gradually over time."

"Maybe I'm meant to do something else," I replied. "Maybe all of this was a sign that I need to step away and let other people take over."

"Perhaps. Or maybe you're scared of what will happen if you go back?" Maya offered.

It's not that I hadn't been doing advocacy work in the past few weeks. Shortly after I fell apart, a well-known children's author released a long essay on her website stating her views on trans people, which were, shall we say, less than good. Among other things, the author pushed back against the idea of trans women being accepted as women and raised "concerns" about trans teens having access to affirming medical care. Not only were young people in the queer community deeply hurt by their once-favourite author's views, but her words were shared by prominent anti-trans activists and politicians who wanted to create laws limiting trans rights. Given the size of her platform and global influence, I felt compelled to speak out against her comments on Facebook, where I dismantled her arguments with facts in the hopes of mitigating some of the damage. I also wrote a well-received article for *O Magazine* about it from the perspective of a disappointed LGBTQ family whose children grew up on her writing. On top of this, I had a couple of speaking engagements and book club appearances that I had committed to prior to my breakdown. Despite how tired I was healing from this mental health crisis, I found the work oddly energizing. Maybe Maya was onto something. Maybe I really was meant to do this work.

The question was how.

I worked really hard at getting better. Therapy sessions were one day a week, but I spent the other six days learning new coping skills that could carry me well beyond this triage stage of my life. When you fix your engine, you need the right tools. And I was getting ready to drive this car back onto the road.

After three months of therapy, Maya and I wrapped up our weekly sessions together. We both felt it was time to move from the acute stage of healing and into the management stage, which I was prepared to do without her. We would still stay in touch, but our time as therapist and client was officially over. Once again, I had let go of a big piece of my safety net. But growth requires us not to stay stuck in place out of fear. If something is no longer serving us, we have an obligation to ourselves to usher it out of our lives so we can make room for something new. In this case, "new" simply meant that my weekly sessions with Maya transformed into meeting up on Zoom to have coffee instead. And we agreed that I would have to find a new therapist down the road if I needed one.

It was the rest of my life that I had to worry about. And in order to move forward, I first had to decide what to do about social media. If I wanted to keep doing advocacy work, I needed to figure out how to incorporate these platforms in more positive ways.

Say the words "cancel culture" and you'll probably spark a flurry of reactions from those around you—everything from "Cancel culture is destroying lives!" to "Cancel culture doesn't exist! People just don't like being held accountable for their actions. We should be calling it 'accountability culture.'"

But I've come to realize that as with most things, the truth lies somewhere in the middle. Society casts a wide net when it comes to what it considers cancel culture. It can be anything from celebrities and politicians getting chastised online to an everyday person losing their job for a single viral tweet they insist was taken out of context. It's a rapper getting told off for a tone-deaf post about buying an $88,000 handbag while many of her fans were out of work during the pandemic, and it's also anonymous internet users harassing a journalist because they don't like who she interviewed or the publication she works for. And once, for a couple of weeks in May 2020, it involved a writer and advocate who, having been on both sides of what some would call cancel culture, has mixed feelings about how society takes people to task.

There's no denying accountability is important. The #MeToo movement grabbed the media industry by its shoulders and shook fiercely until the bad apples started falling to the ground. This was long-awaited accountability in action, and it allowed victims of sexual harassment and assault who had been cast aside by abusive, powerful men and the industries that propped them up to finally be heard. Another example of this is the Black Lives Matter movement, which shone a bright light on systemic racism and police violence. Often the only way to make things better is to shout until those with privilege and power are forced to listen and make change. Advocates have to use every tool at their disposal, and social media is a powerful tool.

I've had a Twitter account since 2009 and have seen the site grow from a microblogging platform that highlighted what everyone ate for dinner to what it is today—which is hard to sum up. Twitter is a lot of things, from a news-sharing resource to a verbal boxing ring. Some of the best jokes I read are still crafted and shared there, but so are some of the most hateful views I've ever seen. Anonymity undeniably fuels much of that hate by providing safety to those who want to say what's *really* on their minds without facing repercussions. At best, bigots can fly under the radar, seeking out others who share their horrible views and lobbing their finest insults at people they have never met. At worst, their accounts will get reported and maybe permanently suspended—until they can make a new one under a different handle. While some of the major platforms, like Facebook, Instagram and Twitter, have put effort into combatting hate speech, others have become havens for alt-right groups, some of which were implicated in the insurrection attempt on the US Capitol in 2021. On these websites, there is little to no distinction between free speech and hate speech.

As an artist, you can put work out there, but you can't dictate how it will be received. Some people loved my book and others did not. Some loved my advocacy and others did not. Communities are not monoliths, and it's not for me to dismiss that or argue against what people think of me. I have no right to tell anyone from any marginalized community how they should feel about issues personally affecting them. Trans people have a lot to be angry about. Society has a track record of treating them terribly. And while criticism is not a comfortable part of visibility, it's an important one, especially when we work with and alongside marginalized people. We need to always be listening, and I've always tried my best to do that. Regardless, it would have been impossible to ignore this particular tempest of criticism, even if I'd wanted to.

But not everyone felt this way. Many trans people stood up for me, even days and weeks after I deactivated my Twitter account. They maintained I was a good person and didn't deserve what was being said about me. This created more friction. Arguments broke out everywhere, relationships were hurt, people were blocked and an already fractured community was fractured further. Then the people who had been the loudest in their accusations against me started being attacked themselves and even receiving threats—usually from anonymous accounts.

Meanwhile, I began receiving emails from transphobes who attempted to get me to sympathize with their cause. "Do you understand now?" one of them said to me. "Do you see what we've been talking about? All you've done is support them and look what they did to you. I hope you can see now that we're not bad people for questioning their beliefs." It was a distasteful tactic to approach me like this at my most vulnerable. Thankfully, even I could see I was being played.

I still wonder if this criticism turned pile-on did any good for any of us. I'm not in a position to answer that. Only those who felt it was an important conversation to have in that moment can do so.

But ultimately, I can't blame anyone for my own trauma or the breakdown I suffered. These were issues I had been dealing with for decades. The moment produced a perfect storm that brought together grief and every insecurity, hurt and deep-seated fear of mine until I couldn't take it anymore. But it was also the catalyst that helped me get healthier, and as awful as it was, I have a lot to be thankful for today. I'm doing far better and feel equipped to handle just about anything that comes my way in the future.

Not long ago, I met a trans woman who was accused by others within the community of faking her identity because she had used language to describe her experiences that some believed an actual trans person would never have used. It was brought up publicly by someone with a decent Twitter following, and I watched this woman unceremoniously get torn to shreds. Old tweets were pulled up and pulled apart. She was accused of being a secret transphobe or a journalist trying to "infiltrate" trans circles. She denied all the accusations, asked the community for mercy and explained her history of suicidality. We had never spoken before, but I reached out to her at the time out of concern for her safety. She told me she recognized she was in danger and would need to seek help. The next morning, she checked herself into a facility and went offline completely.

That same week, I heard from another young woman who had experienced a similar pile-on on Instagram. She was also accused of lying about who she was. No one had the proof to back up these claims, but it didn't matter. She was torn apart by people who used to do nothing but compliment her. Despite the support of a loving family, she attempted to take her own life. Thankfully, she survived, but this experience has left her feeling cut off from her community and scared to go back online.

By reaching out to people who knew them personally, I was easily able to verify that these women were exactly who they said they were. Why didn't anyone else do that, instead of publicly calling them out? Both women were caught completely off guard by a tsunami of accusations and harassment, which overwhelmed them and exacerbated their pre-existing mental health issues. Both could have died as a result.

A quick online search will reveal many tragic stories of children, teens and adults who faced an angry or mocking online mob and died by suicide not long after. Each time, these people left behind loved ones who will spend the rest of their lives grieving. These are real people, not stories or statistics. Their lives mattered as much as anyone else's. Why didn't those who attacked them think of that when they were hurling insults through a screen?

The science tells us we enjoy attacking people online because it gives us a sense of righteousness—and righteousness comes with a reward.[1] When we stand up for what we feel is just, we get a burst of dopamine, the happy hormone, as a little brain snack. Our brains love these snacks! They're rewards for a job well done. Back in the cave days, it was imperative to our survival as a species that we keep our primal group of humans safe from those who would cause us harm. Ganging up on the intruder kept our caves harmonious and safe. As our communities grew, we had to learn to live around those we didn't necessarily agree with. If we had argued at the inn with the blacksmith one night, we would probably try to smooth things over the next day because this was the guy we had to see whenever we needed a new farming tool. He would offer his own apology, too, because he didn't want a small dispute to turn into a larger feud involving others in the town. It was best for both parties to make amends. We didn't have to like each other, but we at least had to be civil unless a serious wrong was committed.

Yes, things got out of hand in small communities at times (see: Salem witch trials). But generally speaking, there were real-world consequences to having it out with folks in person. That hasn't changed today. We're usually much more careful about picking a fight when we know we'll have to see someone again and may need to rely on them in the future. This keeps that primitive reward system in check. Our brains must weigh the positives and negatives of an all-out assault.

In contrast, for most of us there are few measurable consequences to arguing on social media. This is regrettable because it means we can unleash without restraint more easily. I don't think we were meant to scale how we disagree as human beings to an online world—at least not yet. Our evolution hasn't caught up to technology. Our brains can't process an interaction with a stranger five hundred or five thousand miles away the way they can an interaction with someone at the local park. We can't interpret an online stranger's statements in the same way we can when chatting with another customer in line at the coffee shop down the street.

Why? Because much of our communication is through body language.[2] When we interact with someone through text, we're unable to read the subtleties of their tone or gauge their facial expressions. We don't take in how loud or quiet their voice is. We don't know what their eyes—the windows to emotion—look like when they're speaking or listening to us. How can we get a full picture of personality and intent through a quick online interaction? Through a few Instagram comments? Through a two-hundred-character tweet?

We can't. It's not possible. But because technology has advanced so quickly and brains evolve so slowly, we often react in primal ways to online situations that require something quite different.

—

Since I went public with my own story of trauma and the effect online culture has had on me, I've had countless folks reach out privately to share similar stories where what began as criticism snowballed out of control. They have expressed thoughts of suicide or admitted attempts, and they've told me of lingering depression, anxiety and intense fear. Most are terrified to speak up for worry of it happening again. A few have deleted some or all of their social media accounts for self-preservation. Journalists and activists I respect have left platforms like Twitter because they couldn't handle the abuse they received there anymore. Some friends have left Facebook after getting piled on by strangers one too many times.

To be frank, this is the hardest part of the book for me to write, because the last thing I want to do is dismiss any constructive criticism given to me or others in the past because it happened to lead to a firestorm of unconstructive attacks. Constructive criticism is healthy and needed. We should welcome diverse opinions and recognize that we all make mistakes and have room to grow. I have a long history of apologizing publicly and sincerely when I recognize an error. I'm not perfect, but I always try to do better. That's all any of us can do.

This important conversation should never be about denouncing or avoiding criticism, which is what many people seem to do when they bring up terms like "cancel culture." This is about personal attacks, character assassination and spreading outright lies. This is about the snowball effect of denouncing someone in a very public way. This is about using social media to tear someone down, rather than help them learn and grow. This is about disregarding a person's boundaries, ignoring their distress and thinking our own emotions are more important or valid than anything they might be experiencing. It's about potentially weaponizing our own pain and trauma to cause pain and trauma to someone else. It's about casting aside a person's humanity to feel vindicated, and about not caring what our words and actions are doing to them or the people who love them.

My children saw what happened to me. They read what people were saying. And then, they almost lost their mother. This is not hyperbole—it's fact. And while the internet is not responsible for the trauma I carried into that event, it is responsible for continuing to pile on when I made it clear I had reached my limit. For someone to put making a point over my humanity and safety was cruel and unnecessary. I'm not the first person to have experienced this, and I won't be the last. But unlike many others, I'm still here, and I feel a deep responsibility to help shift how we have online discourse because of it.

If we claim to be people who care about mental health, and a lot of us do, then we need to care about *everyone's* mental health—that includes those we don't necessarily like or agree with. We don't have to coddle them or avoid difficult conversations, but we needn't be petty or vicious. And if someone is clearly demonstrating distress, it's time to back off. If we can't abide by this concept, we have no business declaring ourselves mental health advocates or allies in any context.

There are plenty of ways we can have healthier conversations. Whenever possible, we can begin by asking for clarification on what was said, rather than assume intent. "Is this what you meant by what you said?" is a great starting point. "Can you explain what you mean by that?" is another.

Perhaps, too, we can start these discussions by calling people *in* when we can. Private conversations can avoid a lot of public shaming. Shame is not a good educational tool, and it's what many people feel when they're publicly called out. Yes, there is a time to make a person squirm under the public microscope, and I will not pretend to know that exact moment in every situation. But calling people out without even first trying to reach them in what could be a safer, more productive and more educational way is happening with increasing frequency, and it can often do more harm than good.

We're replacing one-on-one conversations with the digital equivalent of a schoolyard shouting match at recess. We're replacing compassionate growth opportunities with vindication and its accompanying dopamine hit. While it might be the current trend in discourse, I don't believe it to be a sustainable one if we want to preserve meaningful relationships or work for common change. We're fracturing already fractured communities. We're creating new traumas in already traumatized groups and people. There must be a better way than this. I hope we shift to it soon.

This is not just on us as users of social media. Yes, part of this is our personal responsibility, but part of it is on the tech companies that own and manage these platforms. On social media, users are the product, and the goal is to keep our eyes on the screen as often and as long as possible. Algorithms play a large role in what we see on our feeds, and controversy garners a lot of attention. Even if we don't respond to a comment thread in which people are actively arguing, many of us are more likely to read it for the same reason we rubberneck on the highway when there's an accident. When we read these disagreements, social media algorithms show us more of them, cultivating our feeds to bring us what it assumes we find interesting. And before long, we're arguing too, because that's what we're constantly seeing and being fed. It's our new normal—what everyone around us is doing. It's hard to be positive when all you see is negative.

We need to be smarter than the algorithms. It's like that time-less scenario parents throw at their kids: "If all your friends jump off a bridge, are you going to jump too?" We need to actively push back against what we're being fed on social media. Just because the bulk of what we're seeing is argumentative, that doesn't mean everything out there is. Every so often, I ask my followers what accounts bring joy to their scrolling experience, and I'm flooded with suggestions. I follow whatever I find interesting, from an alpaca ranch that provides work and shelter for trans people to a couple of dogs whose human scientist friend teaches us interest-ing facts. Find the joy, follow the joy, engage with the joy, and soon your feeds will be full of it.

I believe we can use social media empathetically and still fos-ter learning and change. While this change needs to happen on a global scale, it begins with small steps made by individuals.

And after a good amount of healing, I was now ready to make that change.

I reactivated my Twitter account several weeks after I left. I was able to do this because my account was verified—meaning it had that little blue checkmark that many brands and public figures have—and that gave me a full year instead of only a month to decide to reactivate before it would be permanently deleted. I surprised a lot of people by returning, including me. I didn't think I would ever go back.

But if life has taught me anything, it's that I'm stubborn as hell. I had left that platform with my tail between my legs, pleading for compassion. The only other time I had ever felt that way was when I got the stuffing kicked out of me as a child and was on the ground, begging for it to stop. I had often dreamed of going back in time to stand up for myself, but I knew I would never get that opportunity. In this situation, however, I could. When your older self can show love to your younger self in some way, it can foster healing.

Returning to Twitter was an exercise in taking my power back. I had no desire to verbally duke it out with anyone or to proclaim myself somehow "victorious." What I wanted to do was come back with my head held high and a promise to myself to treat social media like an extension of my offline life rather than a place with its own unique rules. If I did it right, I could change the game. I would be friendly, thoughtful and kind, but also strong and assertive. I liked the challenge of creating a positive space on a platform known for its toxicity. I believed it could be done, but it was all about setting boundaries.

One day I tore a page out of a notebook and wrote down my guidelines for healthy social media use. They included the following:

» what I will use social media for (working, helping others, learning new things, meeting people)
» what I will not use it for (name-calling, pile-ons, infighting)
» how I will use it (no more than X hours a day, no mindless scrolling of negativity, no logging on when I have nothing to share)
» how I want to feel while I'm there and after I leave (happy, calm, productive)

Then of course, I used a bunch of washi tape and cute little stickers and put them all over the page before affixing it to the wall next to my monitor. Presentation is everything.

As a coach, I like to help my clients discover their own motivations for actions they may not always think about. Using social media is something most of us do regularly. But why do we do it? What is the gain, and is it outweighed by drawbacks we haven't considered? There are usually ways to do something better, but awareness is key. Having these reasons where I could see them was especially helpful in the first days after I reinstalled the Twitter app on my phone.

Within a couple of days of my return, hundreds of people had welcomed me back with open arms. I hadn't realized how much I'd been missed. However, some of my loudest detractors were once again encouraging people to unfollow or block me, and anti-trans accounts were laughing at me and declaring: "Why are you back to lick their boots? Didn't they almost kill you?"

Much to my surprise, none of it mattered at all. I remained largely unfazed—I could see that this was all happening *around* me but it wasn't *about* me. There were thousands of people reacting to my return, and everyone had a different opinion about it. I did this one thing, and it was interpreted in all these different ways. One action created all these outcomes. That was clearly not about me but about the people interpreting that action.

Upon my return, I talked about what had happened to me, careful not to mention anyone involved and clearly stating that it was water under the bridge. I said I'd had a breakdown and was suicidal but was doing much better. I thanked people for their support and explained I was now getting back to doing the work I loved. Finally, I stated what my boundaries were and stressed that they were non-negotiable. I would block abusive people, no matter who they were, and would not be apologizing for that.

I had reached a point in my life where I knew who I was. I knew what I came to social media to do, and I certainly knew what I *wasn't* there to do: try to please everyone. That impossible task was behind me now. I had advocacy work to do, and Twitter was one of the places where I would accomplish that, no matter what anyone else had to say about it. This space allowed me to connect with others doing similar work, engage with a large audience and get breaking news that mattered to the community I served. It was good to be back.

Reinstalling the Twitter app was both a small thing and a big thing, given my history. I had just done something I thought I would never be able to do, and this showed me how strong I had become. I had finally stood up for my younger self. Buried beneath the trauma was a force to be reckoned with.

And I liked it.

layers

YOU KNOW WHAT'S WEIRD about not having an undiag-
nosed and untreated trauma disorder after living with one for
nearly your entire life? Everything.

I'm serious. Everything feels different today because I am
different at my core. Enough layers of childhood trauma have
been peeled back to reveal parts of the person I would have been
had it not taken over all those years ago. It's nice to finally meet
that calmer, happier, more assertive person.

Or maybe that's not the case. Maybe I wouldn't be this person
at all, but someone very different. Would I stand up for injustice
the way I do if I had not been the victim of so much of it in my
past? Would I protect trans children with the ferocity I do if there
had not been times when I didn't feel adequately protected as a
child? Would I be as staunch a feminist without the Nathans and
Dans and Ricks in my life? I might have had similar strengths but

used them in different ways. I might have developed more in some areas and less in others. Who knows for sure?

But I do know one thing: I really like who I have become.

Living without trauma steering me through life is a strange new reality. For one, I feel things more deeply. I'm more likely to cry watching a movie. Recently, I had to stop reading a book because I empathized with the character too much, and he kept getting the shit end of the stick. I was always the person a friend would come to in a crisis because they knew as well as I did that I could handle it. What I didn't understand was that trauma had made me numb in most crisis situations. But now? I feel things. *Big things*. And I've had to learn to manage these feelings so I can continue to be there for those I care about.

I talked to Maya about this during one of our coffee chats, several months after she stopped being my therapist. We were still meeting weekly, but now just to catch up.

"Is this how normal people feel?" I asked. "Because it's annoying. How do they live with all these . . . emotions?"

"Welcome to the other side," she replied with a laugh.

"Hey," I said, "there's one thing I've been worried about. Can you put on your therapist's hat for a minute?"

She took off an imaginary hat, reached down and put on another. "Ready!"

"My one-year anniversary is coming up soon. You know, of the day I drove myself to the hospital?"

Maya nodded.

"I'm just—" I began. "I'm worried."

"What are you worried about?" she asked.

"I think it's going to be hard."

"It probably is," Maya admitted. "You might have dealt with a lot of the trauma from your past, but what happened last year was traumatic in itself. You haven't had a lot of distance from it yet, so I wouldn't be surprised if it challenges you."

"Yeah, that's what I was afraid of," I replied.

"I have an idea for you, though," my ex-therapist with the pretend hat continued. "Treat it like a celebration. You lived, right? Plan something special. Tell your family. Get yourself a cake. Do something good for yourself that day."

This was a genius approach. By treating the day not like a solemn anniversary but like a celebration, I could start to rewire the parts of my brain that associated that date with fear and pain. With a couple of months to go, I had time to start getting excited about it, rather than dread it.

And just like that, all my problems went away!

Just kidding. Something bad happened.

It was early in the morning about a month before the anniversary. I had just driven our daughter to one of her college classes and was heading home on the same road I'd taken to get to and from the hospital. I had driven that road countless times since then without issue. But there was something about the sunshine on this day that must have reminded me of something about the weather on *that* day. That's all it took. My nervous system exploded in fear. My breath was suddenly fast and shallow. My heart pounded. I felt overwhelmed and terrified. Tears filled my eyes, and I started sobbing at the wheel.

"No, no, no, no, no," I said between gasps. "This can't be happening. Stop. Please stop."

I was almost home. Almost there. I tried to focus on my breathing, but it wasn't working like it usually did. I could hardly see the road. I pulled over in a gas station parking lot to wipe my eyes and stayed there until I stopped shaking and could see again. Then, carefully, I travelled the rest of the way home. I parked the car and made a beeline for the bedroom, where I crawled into bed, curled up into the fetal position and eventually sent an SOS text to my wife.

As always, Zoë was working in the office across the hall. She came in, curled up behind me and held me as I shook.

"I don't know what's wrong," I said as I sobbed. "I was fine and now I'm not. I'm really not."

She stayed there for a long time, reminding me I was safe and holding me until my body began to believe it was true. Then she gave me a kiss and went back to work, checking in on me periodically. I cried on and off for hours. And once I finished crying, I slept for hours more.

Sometimes triggers are obvious, and sometimes they're not. The weather was not the kind of trigger I'd anticipated, but the reactions it brought on are not as uncommon as you might think. When trauma memories get stored in the body, all senses can become involved. Smelling the perfume worn by an abusive mother or hearing the song that played during a sexual assault can both trigger the abrupt return of those memories. In my case, I vividly recalled the beautiful weather outside the hospital on the day I nearly died, so it made sense that I would associate that weather with the event. Similar weather continued as I stained the fence and tried to process a lot of what had happened. Warm, sunny spring days were now a reminder of something traumatic.

What I've had to do since that car ride in April is actively create new memories involving similar weather conditions. Rather than avoid the beautiful days, I challenge them. I sit outside in them, watching birds and squirrels. I laugh with friends in them. I plant pretty flowers in boring kidney-shaped suburban gardens in them. I walk forest trails in them.

Again, this is an act of power reclamation. We can take control, but it involves some work, plenty of self-care and a lot of patience. It doesn't tend to happen overnight. We must give our bodies new and happier associations.

The good news is that this trigger would end up being my biggest that year. On the day of my anniversary, one year from the day I chose to stay alive—the day I now call Stay Day—I bought myself some flowers and a little white cake with rainbow sprinkles on it. I posted a photo of me looking strong and happy. It wasn't a lie. I won't say it was the easiest day, but it was a good one. I spent a lot of time reflecting on the year I'd nearly missed out on and being grateful I was still here.

Thank goodness I didn't miss out on that year because there was much more good stuff to come.

A few months after finishing trauma therapy, I made the decision, with the help of professionals, to wean off my anti-anxiety meds. I had been taking twenty milligrams of escitalopram (also known as Cipralex or Lexapro) for a few years. But more recently,

I felt fine and didn't experience enough anxiety for it to qualify as a disorder anymore. Given the amount of work I had done on myself, it made sense to me to try living without the medication. This experiment lasted nearly a year.

But then, I got sick.

In the spring of 2021, I noticed the lymph nodes in my neck were swollen. They had been that way for several weeks. I didn't seem to be fighting anything off and I didn't have any pain, but it warranted a trip to the doctor to get assessed. Lymph nodes don't tend to swell for no reason.

Before I could make an appointment, though, I started getting symptoms of a dental infection. As it turned out, one of my molars with an old filling had cracked, and I had probably been fighting off a mild infection for months. Now it was beginning to abscess. This quickly turned into a medical emergency. It was late July, and my dentist was out of town. My doctor was also unavailable, so I had no choice but to go to the same emergency department as I had that fateful spring day the year before. The doctor I saw put me on antibiotics, and not a minute too soon. Within hours, my neck, cheek, jaw and ear were swollen and painful. By the next day, before the medication kicked in, I felt extremely sick and weak; the infection was making its way into the rest of my body. Thankfully, I had been given a powerful broad-spectrum anti-biotic, which likely stopped my body from becoming septic.

Unfortunately, this would end up being one of the worst and trickiest infections my dentist had seen in his decades-long career. It took about three months, four different antibiotics, an emergency root canal and an almost pulled tooth. I was sick and in severe pain for several weeks. Then, just as I was beginning to heal, I was bitten by a tick and had to be on a fifth antibiotic to prevent Lyme disease. Despite eating Ottawa's entire supply of yogurt and downing probiotics daily, I wound up back in the hospital for a bout of antibiotic-induced colitis. I could barely walk when I arrived, and my insides were swollen and screaming.

Bad things happen in your body when you least expect them to.

This experience triggered an old foe: the return of health anxiety, in which my mind began to compulsively go to dark places surrounding disease and death. While I was physically improving, I was mentally declining. Frightening compulsive thoughts wouldn't leave me alone. I started believing my chest was full of tumours, and if I checked carefully enough, I would certainly find them. The impulse was so strong that to prevent myself from chronically checking, I had to watch TV while hugging a pillow.

I was convinced the shrinking lymph nodes in my neck weren't really shrinking at all, and I was dying of cancer. I checked so often I ended up bruising the side of my neck. And was that a heart attack I was feeling? Or maybe the Lyme disease wasn't killed off by the drugs they gave me? I stopped sleeping well and could hardly eat. Every day was spent trying to convince myself I wasn't dying.

I tried all my usual tricks: meditation, exercise, journaling, visualization, even talk therapy. Nothing worked. By the time I saw a doctor to ask to go back on anti-anxiety medication, I scored twenty out of twenty-one on the standard generalized anxiety disorder test. Thankfully, I was once again met with understand-ing and compassion by a medical professional and didn't have to fight for what I needed. I started on the same medication I had taken before, at half the dose, and it stabilized me. I still recall the day it started working; it felt like my entire body had just exhaled a deep breath it had been holding in forever.

I'm a big proponent of medication used in conjunction with other supports when needed. When I stopped taking mine the previous summer, I had made a promise to myself that I would go back on it without hesitation if required. Well, now it was cer-tainly required. With my medication, I could more easily dismiss the dark and disastrous thoughts, and my brain was able to reason more effectively. Eventually, I was able to stop hugging a pillow while watching *Ted Lasso* too.

Inflammation occurs in the body during illness to fight off infection by releasing inflammatory cells and cytokines that kill bacteria. That inflammatory reaction can happen everywhere, including in the brain. There is evidence to suggest the inflam-mation that comes from chronic infection and autoimmune disorders can lead to an increase in mental illnesses.[1] Given what my body had been through, I'm not surprised how unwell my brain became. Given how out of control I felt, it's not a surprise that health anxiety found me again either.

I made a point of telling others I had started back on medica-tion, and I stressed that this was not a setback but a tool I had used before and was grateful to have access to again. I function better on mental health medication today, and currently have no plans to step off the dose I'm on.

Part of the work I do today as an advocate is being transparent about my healing journey. It's not a straight line, and there may never be a time when I feel completely healed. My brain has been shaped by genetics, experiences and trauma. CPTSD will always be a part of me to some extent, whether I like it or not. But now I know how to manage it better. I fixed the busted engine and got us back on the road. I'm the one driving now, not my trauma.

Sometimes it still picks the playlist, though.

While writing this book, I experienced something incredible. I was working on a particularly emotional chapter when I started to feel the early warnings of being triggered. My body started getting tingly and numb, my breath became shallow and moved from my diaphragm into the top of my chest, and my jaw instinctively clenched. These are some of the telltale signs of my nervous system reacting to what it believes is danger. Historically, I've been unable to stop this completely; by the time I noticed, it was too late. Even if I got my brain to calm down, the effects were already stampeding through my body.

"This is a trigger," I told myself out loud at my desk. "What you're feeling isn't happening now. It happened a long time ago. This is a trauma reaction, that's all."

I then clapped my hands and stomped my feet for a few seconds. I rose from my chair and paced around, whispering, "You're safe, you're safe, you're safe," in a soothing way to myself. As I did so, I also made a point of consciously looking at things around me: a painting, a mirror, a light, a book, the grooves in the floor.

And then, miraculously, it was over. I felt fine. My brain hadn't shut down anything non-essential, and my nervous system was quiet. I could still think clearly and I wasn't anxious. I went back to work on that tricky part of the book, spent time with my family over dinner and attended a virtual book club for an hour later that evening. I slept well that night and woke up refreshed.

What I had done, upon the first signs of a trigger, was employ as many senses as I could to ground myself in the present. These grounding techniques can save trauma survivors hours or days of heartache. By using my auditory, tactile and visual senses, I stopped the memories from taking over by reminding my brain of where it was: not back there in Terrorville, but here, in my rather uneventful suburban existence of today. This was a huge step in my healing, and one I've been able to pull off many times since. Again, the effects of trauma might never leave us completely, but how we manage them can change.

Staying well takes effort and consistency. A lot of the tools I use today have been adopted through trial and error. What works for someone else might not work for me—or it might work only if I do it a certain way. We are all different, which is why I appreciate talking to other trauma survivors about how they get through their days.

I have a list of fourteen things I do (almost) every day to stay mentally well. This list might seem like a lot, but the list was built up over time. I didn't suddenly start doing it all—that would have been overwhelming. Instead, I added to it piece by piece, tool by tool. It does take time out of my day, but so did trauma—often far more of it, far less predictably, and in less positive ways. Given the alternative, I'll choose this.

1. *Meditate.* I mediate for at least ten minutes each morning and try to do another ten before bed. Meditation has been shown to help increase happiness, reduce symptoms of mental illness and improve focus. I have found all of these to be true.

2. *Exercise.* My exercise routine is simple: I do an intense cardio workout one day, usually high-intensity interval training (HIIT), then take a nice walk or do some weights the following day. I take a day or two every week to rest completely. Exercise has been helpful, not only for mood and nervous system regulation but also for allowing me to reclaim agency over a body that hasn't always had it.

3. *Read positive affirmations.* The affirmations I really like I've put up on stickies around my work area. One of my favourites is an anonymous quote that says, "Release yourself from the expectations of others." Positive affirmations help balance all the negativity I see in my day job. If dozens of people are going to call me terrible things on the internet that day, the least I can do is show myself some love, right? That holds far more weight than anything they could say anyway. I also have a book of daily reflections I read every morning after meditating, which gives me something to think on over coffee.

4. *Catch triggers.* This doesn't need to happen every day anymore, but I'm always mindful of what sets me off. Knowledge, as they say, is power. This is a practice that gets better with time, and the payoff is significant.

5. *Practice breath work.* Breathing is an important nervous system regulator. Big deep breaths send signals that we are safe from danger. I try to take purposeful breaths whenever I can, meaning that I stop breathing automatically and begin to breathe intentionally, controlling each step—deep breath in for a count of five, hold for five, release for five. It's part of my meditation practice but can also be done on its own. I often breathe mindfully while driving or making dinner. I'm even doing it now while I write this paragraph.

6. *Monitor and limit time online.* Managing the amount of time I spend online gives my brain some breaks from the onslaught of notifications, queries, bad news and bigotry. The internet is a wonderful tool, but it can be overused. I find this one of the trickiest tasks, as the online world can also be really addictive.

7. *Practice mindfulness.* I could have also called this "checking in with myself regularly" because that's really all mindfulness is to me. I do a body scan for tension, ask myself how I'm feeling and try to remember that thoughts come and go like clouds in the sky. They don't belong to us—they just are. I'm the person experiencing the thoughts, and soon I will be the person experiencing different ones. Being a spectator when my thoughts get overwhelming can help tremendously. These are also good times to purposely relax my shoulders and jaw, which hold a lot of tension.

8. *Take medication and supplements.* I take mental health medication because I need it as part of my toolkit. I have an iron deficiency, so I also take an iron supplement every day. To help my colitis when I was healing from it, I took a probiotic.

When our bodies are low on what they require, like vitamins and minerals, it can sometimes affect our mental health too; it's all tied together.

9. *Set and reinforce boundaries.* This is a daily part of my work, especially online. I have to remind the internet to behave itself and implement Ye Olde Block Button when necessary. Boundaries keep me safe, and feeling safe keeps me healthier.

10. *Schedule downtime.* Between a job, many children, a partner, extended family, friends, pets and volunteering, I will burn out if I don't make sure I rest. Resting was never a big part of my life before my breakdown. In hindsight, I can see that was because taking downtime allowed me too much opportunity to think, which would in turn drive up my anxiety. So I kept busy. In the long run, this only hurt me. Today, I recognize how much rest I need to repair the ways in which life wears me down, and if I'm unable to rest, I ask myself what I'm worried about and do my best to address it.

11. *Prioritize sleep.* I really like streaming TV shows, reading books and articles, and doing other things that can keep me up very late. But I've learned that I'm an emotional disaster ball rolling haphazardly through life if I don't get enough sleep. A lack of sleep makes everything worse, including my mental wellbeing. Nobody needs Messy Amanda (especially Amanda).

12. *Embrace education.* I try to read or watch something about trauma or anxiety whenever I can, whether it's a documentary, a chapter of a book, a YouTube video or someone's Instagram post. Education has helped me understand myself better, and that's empowering. We often think of education

in the formal sense, but a diploma or degree is just the tip of the iceberg. So much of what we learn, and arguably what's most valuable in the long run, happens outside of school.

13. *Practice gratitude.* I make a mental list of five things I'm grateful for each morning and list off five more before sleep. Gratitude has significant positive impacts on outlook and can aid in fighting depression. Also, it's just a nice way to remember the slices of goodness in life. We all have them, even if we have to dig a little deeper sometimes to find them.

14. *Seek out micro-joys.* A micro-joy is what I call anything that makes me smile. I find little bursts of joy every day. I'll watch a funny video, have a quick chat with a friend, joke around with my kids or take the dog outside to play. Whatever I do, I take stock of how good it feels. Joy is a precious commodity these days. Seeking it out never hurts.

Healing is work. But healing is worth it too.

when the wound opens back up

IF THERE IS ONE THING I've learned on this journey to better understanding and dealing with my trauma, it's this: I can't control what happens around me, only how I decide to react and deal with it. This is also true when it comes to confronting the actions those in my life decide to take—especially when those actions are harmful. Unfortunately, I don't always notice the red flags signalling danger until I'm in pretty deep—and then, much of the damage is already done.

In the early 2000s, a good friend of mine was diagnosed with cancer.

Amber was a mom I had met through mutual friends. She was expecting her third child while I was pregnant with my second. We hit if off famously, bonding over our mutual love of coffee and less-than-ideal early lives. I rarely connected with someone as quickly as I had with her, which told me we had something special. Before long, we were spending several days a week together, and we eventually co-created an online support forum for other parents of young kids. This meant that even when we weren't seeing each other in person, we were still seeing each other online every day.

One afternoon about two years into our friendship, I received a frantic phone call. Amber was experiencing excruciating pain on her lower right side. I dropped everything, picked her up in my minivan and drove her to the hospital emergency room. I was ready to park and go in with her, but she waved me away. "I'll be fine," she said, and hobbled through the sliding doors despite my protests.

We were both in our mid-twenties, young and strong. I told myself this over and over as I drove away. As I anxiously returned home and waited for news, I assumed she would be diagnosed with either an ovarian cyst or appendicitis. The next day, I received a teary call from Amber with some frightening news.

"They found something on my ovary," she said. "They've sent it to pathology."

A few days later, Amber told me she had been diagnosed with ovarian cancer—a rare kind that most often strikes the young. Thankfully, the surgeon had caught it early, and with the right treatments, she would be fine. For the next few months, I took turns with family and other friends driving Amber to and from chemotherapy and oncology appointments, babysitting her children, cleaning her apartment and picking up groceries.

Over the next six years, Amber went in and out of remission. Twice, she told loved ones that her cancer had come back and was terminal. We watched as she shaved her head to deal with impending hair loss from chemo treatments. Her eyebrows vanished. She and her fiancé pushed their wedding up with a lot of financial support from family members who wanted to make it special for them.

The first time her diagnosis was grim, but an experimental treatment she never could fully explain saved her life. Unfortunately, the disease came roaring back a couple of years later. As Amber made goodbye videos for her children and posted them online, I spent nights grieving the friend I was going to lose. I cried when she wasn't around and put on a brave face when she was. She needed those of us around her to be strong and make her remaining time as positive as possible.

When my youngest child fell ill with a rare autoimmune disease at the age of two, Amber showed up at the hospital, wearing a matching striped sundress and hat. I was in awe of how beautiful she looked and found it especially touching that she would visit my son when she was so ill herself. She acted a little cold, however, and kept her distance from him by standing awkwardly on the other side of the room. I assumed this was because hospitals and illness made her uncomfortable.

A week later, as our toddler was being discharged from the hospital, someone even closer to Amber than I was let me know that our mutual loved one had never had cancer at all. Some of Amber's family members had discovered she made it all up. This, it was explained to me, was part of a lifelong pattern of pathological lying. When I confronted Amber via Facebook Messenger, she didn't deny it, apologize or seem remorseful whatsoever. She was cold, impersonal and quick to dismiss my feelings. Then she immediately blocked me and disappeared from my life.

I had lost my friend after all, but not to cancer.

After I talked to others close to Amber, I realized the clues that something was amiss were always there. While many of us took turns dropping her off at the hospital (Amber didn't have a driver's licence), no one had ever gone to an oncology appointment or chemo session—not even her parents or husband. Amber had insisted that she do these things alone and not "bother anyone." None of us had ever seen a test result or gone with her to the pharmacy when she was picking up medication. When she was pressed for details about medical procedures, her responses were often vague and confusing. She would never discuss specifics of her treatments or doctor's appointments. Toward the end of our friendship, when I picked up on conflicting details in one of her stories, she became angry with me for asking about it and snapped that I wasn't being supportive.

Some speculated that Amber's initial abdominal pain had likely resulted in an emergency appendectomy, and for whatever reason, she concocted a story of something much more serious. I will never know her reasons for doing this. I do know, however, from those who have been in touch with her over the years, that she remains unapologetic and unremorseful.

It took me a long time to move past what Amber had done and start trusting people again. The betrayal was worse than anything I had ever experienced. How could somebody take countless others on an emotional roller-coaster ride like that? How could she appropriate the very real experiences of cancer patients and

292   ~   AMANDA JETTÉ KNOX

not feel badly about doing so? If one of my best friends could lie about this, who could I possibly trust? Amber moved on with her life as if nothing had happened, remarrying and eventually relocating to another country. Meanwhile, many of us who were once close to her were left with this lingering sense of hurt and confusion.

Over the years, I'd largely made peace with my feelings of betrayal. One of the ways I did this was by promising myself it would never happen again. I would not allow my emotions to be manipulated in this way a second time.

So imagine my shock when it did happen again.

And this time, it was so much worse.

There are people all over the world with big hearts. In May 2020, when I started working with Maya, I was reminded of the kindness of strangers. It was nothing short of serendipitous that she, a trauma-informed therapist, had sent me a friend request on Facebook just before I became dangerously suicidal. It was good fortune, too, that she reached out to offer her services when she saw I was in crisis and had room in her schedule to see me that very week.

Because it's always a good idea to do so, I asked Maya about her credentials before we started our sessions. I was experiencing trauma and still struggling with suicidal thoughts, so I needed someone with a lot of experience and training. She told me she had a master's of psychology but didn't bill as a psychologist because the degree was under her old name—the one she used prior to transition.

"That's too bad. Are you not able to get your name changed on your degree?" I asked. I had known many trans people who had done this successfully. It usually wasn't difficult; proof of a legal name change was often enough to have a degree reissued.

"Unfortunately, no," she explained. "The school I went to is very conservative, and they refuse."

"Have you tried recently?" I suggested. "Laws surrounding these issues are changing very quickly."

"Yes, I have," Maya replied. "The school is in Florida, and they won't budge on this. I've had lawyers look into it. You know what it can be like down there."

Unfortunately, I did. There are several places in North America where being trans is more difficult, and Florida is one of them. This is the same state that would go on to pass what is known as the "Don't Say Gay" bill in 2022, making it illegal for teachers of students under a certain grade level to discuss any LGBTQ issues. I found it easy to believe that a Florida university would refuse to change a trans person's name on their degree.

I didn't question Maya's story. In fact, I didn't question anything for a long time. Why would I? This incredible woman had come into my life when I needed her most, offered her services for free and seemed to expect nothing in return. When we first met, I was in a highly vulnerable state, desperate for support. Maya gave a lot of good advice, even if it was fairly unconventional at times. She used more coaching questions than therapy techniques and challenged me in firmer ways than most therapists would ever dare. As we worked together, she delighted in watching me improve. Over the weeks and months to come,

Maya repeatedly told me how seeing me heal was the best reward of all.

"I offered to do this for you because you help so many people," Maya would tell me. "Helping you is my way of helping others in the trans community."

It was clear to me that this was an altruistic act by someone with a very big heart. Why else would she put so much time aside for me? Why else would she give so much of herself?

In the foggy landscape I navigated after my breakdown, it was hard to spot the red flags. But they were there. When you're spending every day just trying to make it through to the next one, it can be all but impossible to focus on anything except what's directly in front of you. I had tunnel vision. All I cared about was healing. Maya was a part of that healing, so I ignored things about her and our relationship that didn't feel quite right.

I wish I had seen it all sooner.

It was now early 2022. Maya and I had been done with our therapy sessions for well over a year. We were now solidly into friendship territory—a red flag I noticed but dismissed. As a coach, I know it's not advisable to befriend my clients; this is a boundary that protects us both by recognizing the power dynamics at play at the beginning of that relationship. But since I had paid Maya for only one session, and since we had met for a reason other than therapy, our relationship was unorthodox from the beginning. Even though she was a trained therapist who had been treating me, it could also be looked on as one friend helping out another friend, couldn't it?

Several times, Maya told me she had made an exception to her usual rule by becoming friends with me. We had hit it off so well, she explained, that it was a connection worth keeping. Knowing she felt the same way I did was nice. I had noticed our connection, too, and was more than happy to shift to a friendship once our three months of therapy was over.

Over time, however, I started to notice that Maya was forming friendships and even exploring business opportunities with people she told me were clients or the loved ones of clients. I found this strange. What had happened between us didn't seem to be the exception to the rule but more of a pattern.

As I started to get better, Maya became more interested in my writing and speaking work. She was full of ideas for new entrepreneurial endeavours and wondered if there was something we could do together to help people. Maybe, she suggested, I could use my notoriety to introduce the world to what she had to offer, which she believed was very different than what other therapists offered.

"But maybe I won't call myself a therapist," she said. "Someone might ask for my credentials, and I'm not showing them a degree with my old name on it. I don't want to deal with that, but I also don't want to be accused of lying. Maybe I can be a behavioural consultant and coach or something."

Again, I encouraged her to push for a name change at the university or even to get her province's psychology licensing board to change her number to her current name, which I was all but sure they could do. Being a psychologist lent her credibility, I argued. Why wouldn't she want to leverage that if she could?

Again, Maya dismissed these options as impossible. So I let it go.

I kept marching past those red flags. I was so grateful to Maya and so proud of what we had achieved together. In the span of a few weeks, I had gone from suicidal to mostly happy. I was back to doing the job I loved. I had even returned to Twitter—a platform I swore I would never use again—and could now more easily handle the vitriol being thrown at me. Why wouldn't I want to share what Maya had to offer with others?

We talked about starting a podcast. We considered speaking engagements together. I thought about writing this book, and we wondered aloud how much of a role she might have in it. Maybe we could co-write it as a self-help book. Or maybe I could do a third book, Maya suggested, and tell her story this time. If the goal was to help people, she said, what she had to offer would definitely do that. Maya was confident and convincing, and I had put her up on a pedestal. She had, after all, saved my life.

I didn't see what was happening.

The resurgence of my health anxiety disorder in the summer of 2021 was sudden, frightening and all-consuming. It took everything I had to stay emotionally afloat, and some days that didn't happen no matter hard I tried. I would cry in Zoë's arms about how exhausted I was from fighting against the constant intrusive thoughts. Anxiety ruled my world once again. No amount of exercise, meditation, mindfulness, reflection or even fresh therapy sessions with Maya made it better.

Still, each time I brought up the idea of returning to the anti-anxiety medication I had been taking as an additional support,

Maya would remind me of how far I had come and how this was likely only a small setback.

"If you can just get to the root of the problem," she would say, "you won't need medication. It might be a psychological issue. It might be your physical health. But I don't think meds are the solution here."

Over the last few months, Maya's views on the "over-prescribing" of mental health medications had become glaringly obvious. She believed they were largely used by lazy or over-whelmed practitioners who didn't want to do any real work with their patients. Medication was a Band-Aid solution, Maya believed, and if therapists would learn new treatment methods, like the ones she used, they wouldn't need to be prescribed as often. When I was weighing the decision to step off my own medication the year before, she'd encouraged it. When I made the choice, Maya celebrated my success in doing so.

"See?" she had exclaimed. "After all those years, all you needed was the right therapy."

If that was true, then why was I struggling again less than a year later? Was I not trying hard enough? Did I not learn the lessons well enough?

As a mental health advocate, I know medication can be part of a healthy recovery and, for some of us, a lifelong companion in wellness. Some brains simply need extra help—better living through chemistry, if you will—no matter what else is done to support them. This, I had to conclude after a time, was how my brain worked. It had been shaped by early trauma, and nothing I did now would fully fix that.

When I brought this idea up to Maya, she pushed back with a concerned look on her face. "But have you considered the side effects of these medications?" she asked.

I couldn't believe a trained therapist would say this to me, even as a friend. I was hardly sleeping or eating, my nervous system was shot and my body was regularly getting flushed with adrenaline. Maya had seen me in tears more than once recently. I needed support from someone I thought had my back. This felt like a political position on her part more than a conversation about what was in my best interests.

"If we're going to talk side effects," I shot back, "let's talk about the effects of chronic stress on the body when your anxiety is as out of control as mine is."

Maya didn't argue with me, but we ended our call early. I made an appointment with my doctor for the following day. I knew what I needed, even if my former therapist and current friend couldn't see it.

If I were to pinpoint when I started to wake up to the issues in my relationship with Maya, this would be it. As the medication I was prescribed started working, I began to notice inconsistencies in Maya's words and actions that I hadn't picked up on before. Why did she claim not to care about money or prestige, but also talked about her large home, nice cars, designer clothes and expensive dinners? Why did she continually bring up wanting to work with me when she'd repeatedly told me she didn't care what I did for a living and just wanted to be friends? Why did she say she wasn't interested in fame but also talk incessantly about the importance of building her brand on social media and how nice it was to get recognized in public because of it?

Maya said she didn't "see" other people's weight but often equated thinness with beauty, including her own. She would sometimes shame me for the food I ate and talk about how healthy her eating habits were. She once told me I would "be beautiful again" when I lost some of the weight I had gained before my breakdown (and subsequently apologized when I talked to her about how harmful ideas like that are).

I don't expect perfection from my friends. Everyone can be hypocritical at times, and all of us can hold biases we might not even realize. I'm guilty of this too. But my friendship with Amber years before had taught me something valuable: pay attention to your inner voice. My inner voice was now screaming at me that something was wrong here. Who Maya claimed to be and who she actually was seemed to be two different people.

She would contradict herself in stories and tell me about celebrities she had talked to through her "connections." She would sometimes swing wildly from one end of the political spectrum to the other and even startled me one day with a sudden admiration for prominent alt-right figures—including one who regularly takes aim at the trans community.

Who was this person? Did I really know her? The values she claimed to hold were not represented in her daily life, and when I finally saw this, it sent all my alarm bells ringing.

After weeks of growing concern, I did what I had been avoiding out of fear of finding something I didn't want to see: I typed her name into Google. It looked like Maya was using several names. This revelation led me down a rabbit hole, fact-checking everything she had told me about herself.

On different websites, Maya claimed to have received a master's degree in psychology from three separate universities in two different countries. In one instance, her psychology studies overlapped with her studies toward a technology degree from a separate institution. How could she complete two very different degrees in two countries at the same time?

More recently, Maya had begun to publicly claim on social media that she was a registered psychiatric nurse in her province. Based on conversations we'd had, I knew this couldn't be true. I checked with the nursing governing bodies in her province under the various last names she had been using online—I had found four—and she was not registered under any of them.

In my searches, I also came across the name she had used prior to transition. That was never my intention, but it was easily found. I looked for any history of psychology degrees, research papers or a therapy practice under that name anywhere in North America and came up empty. Finally, I looked into degree name changes at all three of the universities she claimed to have attended for psychology. All of them have easy ways for a trans person to be issued a new degree. It might have been difficult at one point, but it certainly hadn't been for a while.

I felt hurt, angry, scared and deeply betrayed by these revelations. Not only had I allowed Maya, someone who didn't seem to have the qualifications she claimed, to tinker inside my head while I was struggling with suicidal thoughts, but I had shared my deepest secrets and traumas with her. If Maya wasn't a registered psychotherapist, did I have any promise of confidentiality? I had also referred other people to her, including some family members and friends who were in crisis. What if something had happened to them because they were working with someone who didn't have the training needed for these life-or-death situations? I was filled with guilt about this, and eventually got in touch with them to suggest they do their own digging.

I can't conclusively prove that Maya lied about her education or about being a registered psychologist or nurse; I can only say I couldn't find any proof that she was. And hours after she was confronted with this news, she deleted all her therapy-related websites and most of her social media accounts, and she removed all references to having a psychology degree in the bios she chose to keep online. I watched in amazement as she quickly rebranded herself with a new last name, shifting her focus entirely to business coaching and technology ventures. We haven't spoken since.

Finding out your therapist does not in fact appear to be a therapist is traumatic on its own. But I had also lost someone I thought of as a friend, which made it worse. A few days later, one of the few people I had shared this revelation with sent me a link to Maya's TikTok account, where she was in the process of releasing a series of videos about how a "friend and former client" had just stabbed her in the back. In the short clips, she produced a fake bloody knife for effect, pulling it out from behind her to illustrate the pain this person had caused.

Maya didn't name me, citing a fear she might be sued, but it was obvious who she was talking about. She said I had betrayed her and tried to ruin her reputation. She repeatedly stated that I had "validation issues" and "narcissistic tendencies." Maya claimed I had ditched her for "fame and fortune" but that she was going to be just fine because she didn't need friends like me. These videos, she said, were to help people learn how she moved past my betrayal within a matter of days; she wanted to share her wisdom with the world. But mostly, they were about what a terrible person I was.

I shouldn't have watched them, but I did. They made me cry. It wasn't that I believed what she was saying about me—it was the sheer cruelty of making these videos at all. This was someone who knew exactly what had sent me spiralling to near suicide less than two years before, and she seemed to now be using that knowledge as a playbook. She spun a negative narrative about me and posted it publicly, likely knowing her followers would slam me in the comments. And slam me they did—even if they didn't know my name—because that's what happens on social media. To them, I was the villain, the scammer, the selfish narcissist.

This felt like a malicious attempt to hurt me, and it was successful. It hit every trauma wound that was just healing up, from betrayal to violation. She had weaponized everything she knew from our so-called therapy sessions against me. I spent a full day curled up on my bed, hardly able to move. My nervous system had shut down from the stress. If history repeated itself, it wouldn't be long before I was planning to end my life.

Except that didn't happen. I never got there. Instead, I did something that took all my strength: I got out of bed and asked for help. I found a new therapist—a real one—and started trauma therapy all over again. I was not going to let this situation undo everything I had done so far.

The first thing Paula did when I entered her office a few days later was show me her degrees and insist I google her. "You just went through something awful," she said, "and you deserve to feel safe with me." I already knew that Paula had a good reputation and I wasn't worried. But I liked how up front she was. That alone told me I had picked the right person to work with.

Paula was around my age, with a friendly smile and a lot of wisdom. Her office was bright and serene, with my favourite colour, teal, accenting the space. I sat in a comfortable chair, hugging a big teal pillow and drinking an herbal tea. I felt small and fragile as I recounted what had happened with Maya.

"It's so confusing," I said at the end of the story. "I don't know how to reconcile it all. Even if she didn't have the training and the credentials, our time together helped me move forward and I can't deny that. But if she's not a real mental health professional, what exactly happened?" The tears started to flow. "Did I fucking heal myself or something?"

"Actually, yes," Paula replied. "That's exactly what you did. You took some good starting points she provided, and you ran with them. You just told me how hard you worked in between your sessions with her—all the reading and research you did. You took the time to understand trauma and develop the skills you needed to get better. Even as an actual psychotherapist, I don't heal any- one either. You healed yourself with a little bit of help."

Well, holy shit.

But I still had the hurt and betrayal from what had happened with Maya, and that told me I had more work to do. Paula and I went back to the beginning, back to my childhood with its painful memories and events, and worked through it all again from the base up. After one particular session a few weeks in, I felt something click in my head, as if some gears that had been slightly out of place, clunkily grinding along for a lifetime, had suddenly shifted. Everything within me felt . . . better. My body relaxed in a way I had never felt before, and I breathed a deep cleansing sigh. I felt right with myself. I was whole. That feeling has yet to leave.

It will likely take a long time for me to move beyond what happened with Maya, just as it did with Amber. I will need to work on trust for a long time to come. But I'll get there. I know it. All I need to do is look at all I've done so far.

We are so much stronger than we give ourselves credit for.

rise

I GOT A PHOENIX TATTOO a few months after leaving the hospital. It's delicately inked in black on my left forearm, its flowing tail feathers as long as its body. These mythical creatures die and are then reborn from their ashes. I found the symbolism fitting. After discovering my new love of this fiery bird, a friend bought me a phoenix necklace, which I wear almost every day. This mythological creature has become a theme for me, and yes, it's totally cheesy. I know it is. But some symbols just resonate, and this is one of them.

The thing about rising from the ashes, however, is that we don't always look the same when we do.

Have I mentioned that trauma has layers? *So many layers.* Sometimes when you peel back those layers, you start to discover a part of yourself you didn't even know was there.

I had a dream one night, a little over a year after my break-down. It was beautiful. In it, I told my wife that I was nonbinary, meaning I was not a woman or a man, but somewhere else on the gender spectrum. She was overjoyed for me and immediately accepting. But most importantly, *I* was overjoyed. In fact, I was the most joyous I had ever been. With the weight of that realization off my shoulders, I could finally be myself. I walked through my dream life with my head held high and a spring in my step. I could see my entire life laid out before me, filled with promise.

And then I woke up.

What a weird dream, I thought to myself. *Imagine me being nonbinary? That would be so funny! I have to tell Zoë about this.*

Except I didn't tell Zoë, and I tell her pretty much everything, including all my strange dreams. But there was something really uncomfortable about saying anything about this to . . . well, anyone. Doing so felt too real, too scary, like I might unleash a realization I wanted to keep reigned in. My brain had created some truly fantastical dreamscapes, but there was something different about this one. Digging too deeply into it, my gut told me, would change something profound about how I saw myself. Besides, our family had been through two lifetimes of changes already. I couldn't possibly contemplate another one.

No, I would just try to forget this dream. It didn't mean any-thing anyway. We imagine all kinds of things when we're asleep, and they usually don't have any significance, right?

A few months earlier, I had toyed with the idea of using gender-neutral pronouns. I didn't know why, but I thought I would explore them a bit. I'm always telling people that it's good to try out different pronouns, and that there's no harm in doing so. However, "they/them" felt a lot better than "she/her," and that realization left me quite unsettled. I was wrestling with feelings about my gender that I wasn't ready to look at. Around the same time, I had started switching up my wardrobe to include more masculine clothes and feeling better and better each time my presentation moved in that direction. Meanwhile, I kept asking my stylist to cut my hair shorter at every appointment. "Is it just me, or do you get more lesbian every time you're here?" she quipped.

But whatever, right? Gender expression can change over time, and plenty of cis people, who identify with the gender they were assigned at birth, think about their pronouns. This didn't mean anything.

Nothing.

Not a thing.

I tried to build a wall around these thoughts to keep them in. I couldn't be nonbinary. I was a cisgender woman. Society had always told me this, and I had existed within that box for over four decades now. Being part of the trans community was for other people. My role was to support them, to fight for them. If I just ignored these thoughts for a while, I was sure they would go away.

So why couldn't I shake that dream and the feelings within it? Why couldn't I tell anyone about it? Why, when I thought about living as an out nonbinary person, did it feel both petrifying and almost euphoric?

Because I was nonbinary, obviously. But I didn't want to admit it to myself or anyone else. We were already pushing boundaries with two trans people in a family of six. There couldn't be three. The transphobic parts of society would have a field day. Also, how could I possibly be trans and not realize it until now, over seven years after my child came out?

Just in case I forgot to mention it before: trauma has layers. And sometimes, when you peel them back far enough, you discover the person you were supposed to be. As much as I tried to ignore this new realization, I found it impossible. One of my favourite sayings is, "You can't put the genie back in the bottle." Yet here I was, desperately trying to stuff that magical guy back in there.

Well, shit.

This was a pickle, indeed. My head swam with thoughts. Maybe I could stay closeted. Maybe I could tell just a handful of people. Maybe I could quietly change my pronouns on social media and in my email signature. I didn't have to make a big deal out of this, right? Was it really that important for people to know this about me?

No. But it was important to *me*. This was the conclusion I came to over time. Authenticity is a core value of mine. If I wanted to live authentically, as I helped others live authentically, I needed to come out. But I still felt sick just thinking about it.

I knew just the person to talk to. I took our nonbinary kid for a drive in the country. We drank Starbucks and listened to good tunes, travelling down winding, tree-lined roads. Then, about thirty minutes in, I ever-so-casually-not-casually said, "So, I'm thinking about adding some pronouns to my life. They/them, specifically."

"Oh, that's cool," they said, completely unfazed.

"Because I'm thinking that I'm kind of, maybe"—I hesitated for a moment—"nonbinary."

"Yeah, I could see that," they said, scrolling through their playlist in the passenger seat.

"You're the first person I've said that to," I admitted.

"Nice," came the reply. "Thanks for telling me."

"That's it?" I asked.

"Yeah, it's great. Good for you. I'm happy you told me. It's really not a big deal, you know. You're going to be fine. Check out this song I found, though. It's awesome."

And that was the end of that. One of the best conversations of my life.

Weirdly enough, I was scared to tell my wife I was nonbinary. You know, my wife, who is trans herself? But of course she was wonderful about it, hugging me tightly and saying she was happy I had figured this out. The rest of our kids were equally support-ive. Everyone in my life felt very much the same, from family to friends. It either wasn't a big deal, or they were happy for me, or both. This, in large part, is because of the company I keep. If you surround yourself with people who share your values—and by now, I certainly had—it makes all the difference in times like this.

Coming out on social media, of course, was a mixed bag. I wrote short posts on Facebook, Instagram and Twitter, telling my followers that I had discovered I wasn't cisgender. Hitting the

Post button made me feel nauseous each time. I knew that once I did it, I couldn't take it back. Most people were supportive, but there were the usual trolls who made a sport out of mockery and insults. The nice thing about coming out after trauma therapy, however, is that none of it fazed me. Yes, there's a vulnerability piece in letting the world know who you are, but for the trolls to get under my skin, I would have to believe what they were saying. I knew myself far too well by this point for that to happen.

One person mockingly asked, "What gender are you today?" and I replied, "The one that's going to piss you off the most." Weirdly enough, I never heard from him again.

I was added to a user's Twitter list entitled "Weirdoes with Pronouns" and promptly turned it into a personalized mug, as I do many of the finest insults flung my way. (Maven of Triggerwarning Kingdom and Loathsome, Gaslit Handmaiden are among my favourites for a morning Americano.)

Stepping into my truth was one of the best presents I ever gave myself. If I thought I felt confident before, this blew that feeling out of the water. Everything about me changed, from my posture to my smile. Being able to finally be who I really am, unleashed from the burden of expectations I had placed upon myself for a lifetime, felt incredible.

"You have swagger now," one friend remarked. "And I love to see it."

Me too, buddy.

A few weeks into my trauma healing, I received some meaningful apologies. Two in particular stood out. They were from a couple of the loudest voices who had spoken out against me on Twitter. To protect their privacy, I won't be sharing any details of their apologies or the reasons they gave me for what they had done. Those stories belong to them.

What I will say is their words meant a lot to me. I didn't expect anyone involved to say they were sorry, nor did I need them to. But these messages were healing, nonetheless. In particular, when they asked me how amends could be made—if there was anything specific I needed from them—it was meaningful. It's one thing to say you're sorry and another to be willing to put the work into righting a wrong. There is power in these forms of reconciliation, and I'm glad these people provided an opportunity for us to move forward.

That being said, we can accept an apology—or provide one—and still hold boundaries. I was happy to accept what they were saying and make peace with kindness, but we didn't become best friends and start braiding each other's hair. We're no longer connected on social media, and we basically ignore each other while travelling in similar advocacy circles. But that's fine. We worked it out, and now we can move on. That's the beauty of conversation.

During the pandemic, I went back to school to become a certified professional coach. After seeing how coaching was largely responsible for moving me forward, I decided this was something that would be a great addition to my advocacy work. In class, which I did online, I learned to listen intently, ask key questions and allow clients to discover their own innate wisdom. We all have it—we just don't know we have it. Graduating from the program with top marks felt incredible. As a fun aside, I now had letters to put after my name for the first time in my life: Amanda Jetté Knox, CPC.

Today, on top of writing and advocacy, I work with clients from all over the world and facilitate workshops on setting boundaries, building resiliency and embracing who we really are. I couldn't have done this work before because I didn't have the tools I needed to help myself, let alone someone else, in these areas.

We help ourselves and then, if we're lucky, we get to help others with what we learn. This is how we lift everyone up. This is how change is made.

At the season opener of the Ottawa REDBLACKS game in August 2021, my wife and I were ushered onto a stage during halftime with a bunch of friendly cheerleaders, a mascot who looked like a lumberjack, the mayor and one of our city councillors. There, with fifteen thousand CFL fans looking on, they presented me with a community service award for my work in mental health and LGBTQ advocacy. It was a very special moment.

Standing on stage, I felt *alive*. Truly, remarkably, completely alive. I recognized that had I died the year before, this would never have happened. My wife would not be standing beside me. My children would not be in the stands cheering. Our family's story would be one of heartbreak, not hope. The people who told me how much my work had helped them would not have found this particular light in the darkness because that light would have been gone.

Gone.

I would have been gone.

But I am not gone. Miraculously, I'm still here, and I have things to do.

Trauma has layers. From beneath them all, I rise.

epilogue

WHILE WRITING THIS BOOK, I took a drive to my home-town to visit some of the places where my worst moments happened. I wanted to see if I would remember anything else I could add to the story, while also taking note of how I would react to these places since undergoing trauma therapy. I went by the arena, Matt's place, Nathan's old apartment and the high school where I was set on fire. None of these caused the strong reactions they used to; they only made me sad for my younger self.

I saved my least-favourite place for last: Macie's duplex.

I had gone by Macie's old place on countless occasions in the past, usually while taking my children to preschool or to the library, and each time I'd experienced a visceral reaction. The building was old and dark, with weather-stained grey stucco covering its walls. Its windows were small, its front unwelcoming. It was a place where bad things had happened, and even its appearance told that tale. My plan this time was not only to go by but also to stop in front. I wanted to stand there for a minute and face it. I expected it would be a meaningful confrontation.

Except when I got there, the building was gone. Demolished. In its place, a large, bright, beautiful new building was being constructed, with giant windows on the ground floor to capture the light. It rose several storeys higher than Macie's old place. I stood outside and closed my eyes, imagining all the families who would move into this building, and their various new beginnings.

A place of pain, fear and violence was gone. I would never have to see it again. That was *my* new beginning.

"Are you seriously still getting your hair done? We have to be at city hall in three hours!"

That was my friend Lil, texting me frantically after I sent her a picture of my hair in the middle of a dye job.

"This is a special night, friend. My hair needs to be absolute fire," I joked. Except I wasn't joking. The hair was important.

A few weeks before, I'd received a call from the Chief of Protocol at Ottawa City Hall. "I'm pleased to tell you that you've been selected to receive the Order of Ottawa," he said.

"The what of what now?" I replied, quite professionally.

He laughed and went on to tell me that the Order of Ottawa is kind of a big deal. Each year, a selection committee at the city chooses fifteen professionals from various areas of expertise to be inducted into the order. A ceremony takes place, with photos and a reception to follow. I was being inducted for my work supporting trans children and families. Behind the scenes, several people had secretly put forth my nomination. And as far as I knew, I would be the first visible nonbinary person to receive this honour.

So yes, Lil, my hair was important, thank you very much. If I was going to represent my community tonight, the pink-and-peach streaks needed to proudly complement my side shave. I had carefully selected a monochrome outfit: black blazer, pants and shoes, with a black-and-white patterned button-up shirt. This was to make my hair the centrepiece. It would end up being the coolest look I've ever worn.

Not wanting to miss out on the fun, feelings of doubt and unworthiness, and a lifetime of imposter syndrome soon had me questioning whether I deserved this recognition. To be honest, I still don't know. I just do work I love every day, and I hope it helps people. But no matter how I might have been feeling at that moment, I wasn't going to let old beliefs ruin a good thing. I made a promise to myself that I would graciously accept this honour and even get excited about it. Hence, the hair.

The night of the ceremony, I stood nervously in an upstairs room at Ottawa City Hall with the other well-dressed recipients. They were doctors, business leaders, scientists, sports team owners and others with impressive resumés. It was hard not to feel out of place with my high school diploma from seven years ago and extremely gay hair. But when I confided my own insecurities about being there, many admitted they didn't think they deserved the recognition either. We were all in the same boat, even if we had climbed aboard from different places.

The group of us lined up behind some ceremonial guards. Bagpipes, flags and a great deal of pomp and circumstance preceded us into chambers. We took our seats with an audience of loved ones, politicians and journalists behind us.

When my name was called, I made my way up to the middle of the room, where the mayor pinned a medal on my lapel. I signed a fancy piece of paper while photos were taken. I was nervous and didn't even look at what I'd signed; I might have agreed to an increase in my property taxes, for all I knew. Then I went back to my seat, trying not to cry off all my makeup at the reality of this moment. I could hear Zoë and Lil cheering behind me.

Somewhere in city hall is a photo of several smiling people. Sitting right next to the mayor is a person grinning so eagerly they look like the excited kid in every class photo. That person had one of the best nights of their life, and it shows. Because not only had they survived but they were now thriving too—with great hair, I might add.

If I had to walk through it all again—all the pain, fear, doubt and hate—to get to where I am today, I would do it. I know that might sound surprising, given what I've been through. But if that was the only way to reach the level of joy, contentment, wisdom and resiliency I have now, I wouldn't hesitate. Because the person I am today is someone worth fighting for. The person I am today deserves to be here.

I am not my trauma; I am the one healing from it.

acknowledgments

I WAS ONCE TOLD THAT IT TAKES A VILLAGE to write a book, and that statement has proven absolutely true. This memoir challenged me in many ways, and it wouldn't be on the shelf today if it weren't for that village.

First and foremost, I want to thank my agent, Samantha Haywood of Transatlantic Agency, for believing in the importance of this story and championing it early on in its creation and beyond.

Thank you to everyone at Penguin Random House Canada for believing I had another story to tell. Diane Turbide was the editor of *Love Lives Here*, and just before her retirement, she helped ensure this second book of mine also found a home. Scott Sellers, who edited *One Sunny Afternoon*, helped shape it into what it is today with enthusiasm, sensitivity and excellent insights. Janice Weaver's excellent eye and sense of humour were deeply appreciated during the final edits.

To my wife and kids, thank you not only for supporting me in writing these pages but also for helping me be here to write them at all. You are the brightest lights in my life. To my extended family—and in particular, my niece and nephews—thanks for bringing me so much joy in dark times. I needed you more than you know.

Ya-Ya was a sounding board during the most challenging parts of writing. Julia and Ben loaned me their peaceful cottage more than once to finish this book. April took good care of an earlier (and still very rough) version of this manuscript with her careful eyes and feedback. Dani jumped at the chance to take my new author photos, which meant a lot to me. To every friend who cheered me on over the past couple of years, you mean the world to me.

Liliane, Jason, Jacob, Liam and sweet little Sophia, you are always in my heart and have been throughout this writing process. The strength of your family gives me strength too.

To the medical team at the Queensway Carleton Hospital in Ottawa, this book is a testament to the care you provided someone in crisis. I would not be here today without you. Thank you for seeing me through one of the scariest times of my life.

All my love to every trauma survivor. We change the world one story at a time. This is mine. If you are able and willing, I hope you will also tell yours to someone who needs to hear it. But mostly, I wish you nothing but peace and happiness moving forward in your life. You deserve that.

suicide prevention resources

No one resource is right for every person who is in the midst of a crisis. If you are in imminent danger, please call 911 or go to your nearest hospital emergency department.

Talk Suicide Canada
In Canada: (833) 456-4566
In Quebec: (866) 277-3553

Kids Help Phone
https://kidshelpphone.ca
In Canada: (800) 668-6868

Trans Lifeline
https://translifeline.org
In Canada: (877) 330-6366
In the US: (877) 565-8860

Canadian Association for Suicide Prevention
https://suicideprevention.ca

Centre for Suicide Prevention
https://www.suicideinfo.ca

Mental Health Commission of Canada
https://mentalhealthcommission.ca/what-we-do/suicide-prevention/

notes

Chapter One: The Adaptive Captive

1. Christopher G. Lucas, Sophie Bridgers, Thomas L. Griffiths and Alsion Gopnik, "When Children Are Better (Or at Least More Open-Minded) Learners Than Adults: Developmental Differences in Learning the Forms of Causal Relationships," *Cognition* 13, no. 2 (May 2014), https://sciencedirect.com/science/article/pii/s0010027713002540.

Chapter Five: Breakdown

1. Heather Stuart, "Violence and Mental Illness: An Overview," *World Psychiatry* 2, no. 2 (2003), https://ncbi.nlm.nih.gov/pmc/articles/pmc1525086.

2. World Health Organization, "Suicide: One Person Dies Every 40 Seconds," September 9, 2019, https://www.who.int/news/item/09-09-2019-suicide-one-person-dies-every-40-seconds.

3. World Health Organization, "Suicide Across the World," 2016, https://www.who.int/health-topics/suicide.

4. Tanya Navaneelan, "Suicide Rates: An Overview," Statistics Canada, June 16, 2017, https://www150.statcan.gc.ca/n1/pub/82-624-x/2012001/article/11696-eng.htm.

5. "Suicide in Canada: Key Statistics," Public Health Agency of Canada, July 18, 2019, https://www.canada.ca/en/public-health/services/publications/healthy-living/suicide-canada-key-statistics-infographic.html.

Chapter Six: On a Fine Spring Day in May

Karen M. Grewen, Bobbi J. Anderson, Susan S. Girdler and Kathleen
C. Light, "Warm Partner Contact Is Related to Lower Cardiovascular
Reactivity," *Behavioral Medicine* 29, no. 3 (Fall 2003), https://ncbi
.nlm.nih.gov/pubmed/15206831.

Chapter Seven: Hope in Diagnosis

1. Krzysztof Kaniasty, "Predicting Social Psychological Well-being
Following Trauma: The Role of Postdisaster Social Support,"
Psychological Trauma: Theory, Research, Practice, and Policy 4, no. 1
(January 2012), https://psycnet.apa.org/record/2011-07447-001.
2. Florian Raabe and Dietmar Spengler, "Epigenetic Risk Factors in
PTSD and Depression," *Frontiers in Psychiatry* 4 (August 2013),
https://www.frontiersin.org/articles/10.3389/fpsyt.2013.00080/full.

Chapter Fourteen: We're Getting Better. Now What?

1. Mount Sinai Hospital/Mount Sinai School of Medicine, "Motivation
to Bully Is Regulated by Brain Reward Circuits," ScienceDaily,
June 29, 2016, https://www.sciencedaily.com/releases/2016
/06/160629135255.htm)
2. "Nonverbal Communication: Speaking Without Words," Rensselaer
Polytechnic Institute, n.d., http://www.rpi.edu/dept/advising/
american_culture/social_skills/nonverbal_communication/reading_
exercise.htm.

Chapter Fifteen: "Rise"

1. Robert Dantzer, Jason C. O'Connor, Gregory G. Freund, Rodney W.
Johnson and Keith W. Kelley, "From Inflammation to Sickness
and Depression: When the Immune System Subjugates the Brain,"
Nature Reviews Neuroscience 9, no. 1 (2008), https://ncbi.nlm
.nih.gov/pmc/articles/pmc2919277.

© Danielle Donders

AMANDA JETTÉ KNOX is an award-winning journalist, writer, certified professional coach, and human rights advocate with a special focus on LGBTQ2+ rights and mental health. *Love Lives Here: A Story of Thriving in a Transgender Family* was a #1 bestseller, an Indigo Best Book of the Year and Staff Pick of the Month, and was chosen for the 2020 Canada Reads Longlist. Their work has been featured on the BBC, CBC, *The Today Show*, *O Magazine*, *The Social*, and *The Marilyn Denis Show*. They are a 2019 *Chatelaine* Woman of the Year, a 2020 Top 25 Women of Influence, and were chosen as one of 2020's Most Influential Parents by *Today's Parent*. Amanda lives in Toronto.